THE BIRTH OF JAPANESE ART

THE BIRTH OF JAPANESE ART

THE BIRTH OF JAPANESE ART

by J. Edward Kidder, Jr.

Photographs by Kenishi Ozawa

FREDERICK A. PRAEGER, *Publishers*

NEW YORK · WASHINGTON

BOOKS THAT MATTER

Published in the United States of America in 1965 by Frederick A. Praeger, Inc., Publishers
111 Fourth Avenue, New York 3, N.Y.

First published in Switzerland in 1965 by Office du Livre, S.A., Fribourg, under the title of
Japon · Naissance d'un Art

Library of Congress Catalog Card Number: 65-16808

Printed in Switzerland

ACKNOWLEDGMENTS

It was only due to the kindness and generosity of archaeologists, curators and collectors that this book came into being. The simple inclusion of their names here hardly conveys my gratitude for their cordial willingness to open their doors to the photographer and share with me their wide knowledge of local archaeology and the history of their collections. There are others who gave permission or who stood time-lessly by. To all I wish to express my sincerest appreciation for their self-effacing help.

I am especially indebted to Mr. Fumio Miki and Mr. Yoshimaro Noguchi of the National Museum in Tokyo, and Dr. Kyōichi Arimitsu and Dr. Takayasu Higuchi of Kyoto University along with Mr. Kōichi Yokoyama, and Professor Hisashi Suzuki and Professor Naotune Watanabe of Tokyo University, and the good offices of Dr. Sugao Yamanouchi. We received unusual services at the Yamato History Museum from Dr. Masao Suenaga and Mr. Teizō Kojima, and personal aid from Mr. Yoshihisa Nishiyama. In Matsumoto city and thereabouts, Professor Makoto Suzuki of Shinshū University and Mr. Sohei Fujisawa did everything in their power to ensure adequate time to photograph in each significant collection, and all this in a way which will long be remembered. At the Osaka City Art Museum Mr. Masahiko Sato and Mr. Mitsuteru Fujiwara furnished most helpful services, as did Mr. Hiroshi Suzuki in the Kyoto National Museum. I wish to include Mr. Eiji Miyasaka and his son of the Togariishi Archaeology Museum, Mr. Masayuki Komatsu of the Nakayama Archaeology Museum, and Mr. Hiroyoshi Kawakami of the Ibaragi Prefectural Art Museum. Mr. Ishichi Ohara and his family of Iizaka deserve special thanks. Mrs. Tetsuko Aikawa allowed us to work in the Aikawa Archaeology Museum under trying circumstances. At Shibayama, Hiraide, Idojiri and the Sakai Remains Museum we were given all possible assistance.

This is the opportunity to call attention to the names of the owners who are indicated in the captions of il-lustrations and catalogue items. These collectors have graciously given permission for their possessions to be photographed. For allowing the use of excavated ob-jects not formally published, or kept in the collection under their jurisdiction, I would like to thank Dr. Sueji Umehara, Mr. Shinji Nishitani and Mr. Hiroshi Kanaseki of Tenri University, Professor Nobuosu Itō of Tōhoku University, and Mr. Fujio Naruse of The Museum Yamato Bunkakan.

The energy of Mr. Ozawa's assistant, Mr. Masakatsu Yamamoto, was a major contributing factor to the success of the photographs, and for his interest in the project an extra word of appreciation is due. Mr. Ozawa's skill speaks for itself, and it was a genuine pleasure to travel and work with him. I have had help at different times from various assistants, Mr. Takashi Sōma, Miss Reiko Abe and Mr. Shūzō Koyama, and the many tasks they performed facilitated the work greatly. Their services are gratefully acknowledged.

By all rights this book should be dedicated to my wife. She has taken an interest amounting to a partner-ship in its production, and I wish to add this final note in appreciation of the time and thought she has devoted to it.

J. EDWARD KIDDER, JR.
I.C.U., May 15, 1964

Plate 1 (Frontispiece) *Haniwa* farmer, from Akabori village, Sawa county, Gumma prefecture. H. 92 cm. Late Tomb Period. National Museum, Tokyo

TABLE OF CONTENTS

Abbreviations:

Pl. I to XII : Color Plates
Fig. I to 100: Black and white illustrations in the text
Cat. I to 99 : Black and white illustrations in the catalogue
*: An asterisk before a number refers to a textual reference in the outer column of the page

I. INTRODUCTION

Prehistoric man in Japan scattered his *débris* deeply and widely, from the coasts to the inland mountains, on large and small islands, in an area with which we will deal, extending from Hokkaidō in the north to Kyūshū in the south. The insular nature of the country, coupled with its own internal geography and topography, were powerful factors in moulding the character of its successive prehistoric cultures.

Despite the shape of the Japanese islands — linked as they are to the continent in the north and south like an arc — it is on the Pacific side where nature's endowments are superior and where man has therefore traditionally chosen to live. Low plains, fresh water sources, relatively mild temperatures, warm inlets, fertile land, constant vegetation and adequate food supplies are all combined on the east coast, and serve to lighten considerably the daily chores required for subsistence. By way of comparison, the often rugged, frequently sheer, colder and windy west side has only small pockets of protected land. Much favored also were the east and south sides of the central mountains. A good example may be seen in the vicinity of Lake Suwa in Nagano prefecture, Japan's highest major lake at the altitude of 738 meters, and the setting for many Neolithic sites. Other parts of the country such as the Yamato Plain, the Inland Sea, and the Ariake, Shimabara and Yatsushiro Bays on the west side of Kyūshū, to mention only several important areas, have their own special reasons for attracting and holding early settlers.

The country of Japan is composed of traditionally recognized regions, the precise outlines of which are not usually a matter of natural limits. The outer islands are self-explanatory in this regard, hence reference to the most northern and the two major southern islands,

Hokkaidō, Shikoku and Kyūshū respectively, presents no ambiguities. For the main island of Honshū, however, some explanation may be useful of the regional terms as I will use them.

The northern quarter of the main island is the Tōhoku region, an area which was for long separated culturally during historic times from the remainder of the island because of its occupation by people the Japanese called Emishi or barbarians. This separation, however, is not a monopoly of the historic period. Northern traits may be observed in the archaeological data of prehistoric times, showing that distinctions got an early start. But later developments strengthened these distinctions which are now most apparent in the dialect and the survival of certain older customs and conservative ways.

The plain in which Tokyo is situated, the Kantō, because of its size and water sources, has always been a pivotal region in Japanese history. This was specifically so in later historic times when the Kamakura military capital of the thirteenth and fourteenth centuries exercised its power, and again when the national capital was transferred to Edo in the late nineteenth century. The confluence of modern train lines, the extensive port facilities and the inevitable convergence of industries has succeeded in stretching the capacity of the region to the point where a resulting interest in decentralization means ever-expanding pressures toward its remote corners.

Agriculturalists of prehistoric ages discovered the advantages of the Kantō Plain as had the bands of hunters and gatherers before them. It is hardly by accident that the Bronze-Iron culture is named after a site in the Tokyo area, the locality of Yayoi, for the occupation of the plain was widespread then and modern research on Japan's prehistory had its beginnings in the institutions of Tokyo. In the following Protohistoric period and certainly after the fifth century A.D., the Kantō supported large groups of people of tribal affiliations under some degree of subservience to the Yamato state.

The Kantō Plain rises on its west side into foothills of prefectures which are primarily mountains. The central mountains occupy an area which may be referred to as the Tōsan. Its highest peaks have been popularly called the Japan Alps. On the far west is the Hokuriku, a coastal strip less inhabited in prehistory just as today, for the warm currents and the year-round moderate climate are lacking. Extending into the central area is the Chūbu, the Middle Section, and more exactly, the broad valley leading toward Matsumoto City is the Shinshū region. The eastern coastal zone is known as the Tōkai, a well travelled route in recent centuries when it served as the connecting link between the earlier and later capitals of Kyoto and Tokyo.

The Kantō marks the east end of the mountains, the Kansai the west end. This latter name is a loose geographic designation for the area dominated by the cities of Kyoto, Nara and Osaka. Traditionally it has been the Go-kinai, the Five Home provinces and has been commonly known as the Kinki district. The Yamato state, the first militarily organized government in Japan, is reported in the ancient literature to have been born here. In so doing it has given its name to the plain. I find the term Kansai the most useful, for it has what seems to me to be more flexibility for prehistoric and historic periods alike, but Kinki is the choice of most Japanese archaeologists.

Moving down the chain of islands in a southwesterly direction, one reaches the body of water separating southern Honshū and the island of Shikoku, a maze of small seas and bays broken by a host of little islands, the Inland Sea. The large island of Shikoku on the south protects the shipping channels from undue roughness. But the limitations on level land in this region put an unusual premium on it and forced settlers into cramped quarters which were, during the Neolithic and at least as late as the early centuries after metals were introduced, concentrated more on Honshū than Shikoku.

The marine resources of the Inland Sea are substantial and would in themselves draw migrants and semi-sedentary people, but it is as a highway in ancient times that the region takes on real significance. Most dramatically, it is witness to the cultural shift from north Kyūshū to the Yamato Plain, first in the movements of rice cultivation and Yayoi pottery, then close on their heels, the conversion from bronze weapons to bronze bells.

Southwest Honshū is referred to as the Chūgoku, the Middle Provinces; the number of sites, rather evenly distributed between the three major prehistoric periods, is evidence of the continuing role the area played in cultural advances achieved in south and west Japan.

The recent rapid reorganization of administrative and post office zones has played havoc with the listing of archaeological sites. Due to the existence of hundreds of thousands of neolithic sites, distinctions between neighboring ones can only be made by pinpointing their positions. While the site name has usually remained constant, in numerous instances postal designations according to village (*mura*), larger zone called a *machi* (resembling a township), and city (*shi*) have been changed in the last few years. The administration of a city has usually been removed from county (*gun*) jurisdiction.

Every effort has been made here to bring these locations up to date, yet despite the annual publication of such new zones by the Post Office Department, accuracy in this respect is at present one of the most frustrating matters facing archaeologists in Japan. It is believed that the redistributions will be settled in a few years and the designations permanently fixed. Until then one manages as best as possible, asks for indulgence, and warns that differences in listing of sites from book to book may well be due to this. Several local attempts on

Plate II Figurine from Satohara, Agatsuma-machi, Agatsuma county, Gumma prefecture. H. 31 cm. Late Jōmon Period. Coll. Mr. Yoshio Yamazaki

the part of archaeologists have been of immeasurable help. The association in the prefecture of Nagano, for instance, has drawn up new designations rather regularly and made them available for wider use. This is not an area, however, where the post office and archaeologists are inclined to cooperate.

The terminology for Japan's prehistoric periods grew up locally, without relation to the traditions of classifying successive stages of human development to which the western world has become accustomed. Whereas the predominant use of stone, bronze and iron follow this order, the proximity of Japan to the continent, where metals had been produced centuries earlier coupled now with upheavals going on there, brought about a situation in which bronze and iron were carried to Japan almost concurrently. There is therefore little correlation between the Jōmon, Yayoi and Tomb periods and the Neolithic, Bronze and Iron Ages. The Bronze-Iron period is separated and divided on the basis of the series of introductions, the earlier of these being continental bronze weapons, rice cultivation, jar and cist burials, the later being the building of large tumuli. The former is the Yayoi, the latter the Tomb period.

The Yayoi period opens in north Kyūshū in the third century B.C. Before the advent of the Christian era, the use of both bronze and iron were well established and moving through the Inland Sea. The cultural centers drifted east as native workshops learned techniques and more land was explored for agricultural needs, until the rulers in the Yamato Plain commanded adequate wealth to adopt the novel method of burying their dead in huge grave mounds. This was a level of affluence reached by the end of the third or the beginning of the fourth century. The practice was widely accepted and greatly patronized in local kingdoms until the arrival of Buddhism in the sixth century. Buddhists turned slowly toward cremation and encouraged the diversion of personal wealth into temple construction. The extravagant habit of depositing belongings with the dead had been a steady drain on the country's economy and was recognized as such in the 646 decree by Emperor Kōtoku. This edict prohibited the making of mounded tombs for ordinary nobles and limited their size for the ranks of ministers and up, forbidding the burying of grave goods and the conducting of human and horse sacrifices. The decree may have been enforceable in the home provinces, but it is generally assumed that outlying districts kept the tumuli practice alive for another century or more.

THE STONE AGE CULTURES

Japan's long chain of islands which extend for more than 1800 kilometers and are at no point much over 400 in width, inevitably include the sort of differences in climate, topography and natural resources which would affect the attitudes of their inhabitants. These attitudes are given material form in the paraphernalia the early people invented to cope with the problems of daily living. The east coast lies along the path of the warm current, a natural advantage which has successfully nurtured fertile breeding grounds of almost inexhaustible supplies of sea foods. Some 2000 shellmounds attest to this abundance. The population was concentrated around especially blessed bays and along the banks of rivers: the Matsushima islands and the long narrow Kitakami Plain in the north; the old fresh water courses of the Kantō, where half of the known shellmounds are estimated to exist; and the Atsumi Bay, somewhat south of the city of Nagoya. The Yamato region itself has poor access to the ocean, although the large Kii Peninsula is not without its share, but farther south, the shell-mounds are rather prevalent in the Inland Sea, clustered in the vicinity of modern Okayama and along the islands, and then again in the west side of Kyūshū, in such regions as the Ariake Bay of Kumamoto. Fewer are to be found in the east of Kyūshū, the prefecture of Ōita being able to claim the most. Only a handful are known on the west coast of Japan, where natural conditions are by and large less conducive to the growth of shellfish.

The remains of the coastal dwellers give only an incomplete view of the Jōmon period. Other peoples, by choice or tradition, resided in the forest fringe areas, along the sheltered slopes of lower mountains or in the upper plains, relying heavily on the ample variety of edible plants and animals for their subsistence. Deer, wild boar and bear were widely hunted by both coastal and inland people, and both supplemented their diet with the meat of smaller creatures like the badger, raccoon-dog and hare. Walnuts and chestnuts were available, and there may have been some dependence on the *imo*, a tuber not unlike a potato.

Agriculture, with the connotations it usually conjures up, has yet to be proved for the Jōmon period. I feel, regardless of this, that the extent of the figurine cult and (at least the way I would interpret) one type of special deposit have a direct bearing on the fertility of the land and would represent the material form of cults surrounding an embryonic form of cultivation, whether of vegetables, fruits or nuts, from the Middle Jōmon period onward.

Nature has richly endowed Japan, through eventual slackening of volcanic activity, a generally mild climate and adequate rainfall. Most areas must have shared these natural benefits in ancient times, although they are best seen today in the lower mountains and upper plains, where human habitation has not so extensively obliterated the natural providence. With the knowledge of no major climatic changes since the end of the Jōmon period, some understanding is to be had of the wealth of resources available to prehistoric man.

The large Middle Jōmon sites, numbering their pit-dwellings by the score, but probably not all in use at any one time, occur in spots which supported groups of people adequately for generation after generation if one may judge from appearances. The inhabitants must have had an intimate acquaintance with the cyclical reproductions of nature. Their unusually large clay containers, overgrown with rich decoration, may have been designed for storage purposes. The profusion of chipped tools in every community site could well have been used for working the ground, and an occasional stone floor speaks for a considerable degree of permanence in the dwellings.

By and large, however, the commonly looked on features of the Neolithic elsewhere, customarily given as the presence of agriculture, the domestication of animals and the grinding and polishing of stone implements, are late in appearing in Japan and are overshadowed in the Jōmon period by less advanced traits. Only very late shell-mounds have yielded bones of the cow — a short horned variety — while hand-worked, smooth stone implements remain proportionally few until the end of the period. The dog became a household pet at an early date, but domestic and wild cat bones cannot be differentiated, and the pig was not introduced into the main islands during prehistoric times. The horse was known but probably not in very wide use. This leaves the evidence for agriculture largely inferential except for the discovery of millet, sesame seed and the hairy podded kidney bean in Latest Jōmon Kantō sites. It has yet to be established what sort of cultivation of these, if any, was carried out.

A pre-pottery culture is now well represented in numerous sites, some of which may be satisfactorily termed Palaeolithic. The chopping tools recently discovered in the Nyū Plateau of Ōita prefecture may even be ultimately demonstrated as belonging to a Lower Palaeolithic type.

In such a stage of antiquity, Japan was joined to the Asian mainland in the shape of a large curve, the Japan Sea resembling an immense lake. The connection in the north lay through what are now the islands of Sakhalin and Hokkaidō and in the south through Kyūshū and Korea. Kyūshū was probably additionally attached to the Ryūkyūs, Taiwan, the Philippines and Indonesia. The lowering of the land to form the islands of Japan itself may not be as old as might at first be thought. A genuine possibility may be within the limits of 40,000 years.

These natural land bridges were open to prehistoric creatures whose wandering took them east and who then found themselves stranded and eventually died out, yet not before certain local characteristics, particularly in size, were able to materialize in some cases. Mammoths never reached Honshū. They were stopped either by the presence of the Tsugaru Strait which separates Honshū from Hokkaidō or by the warmer climate farther to the south. It may be presumed that the majority of human migrations into this region now known as Japan were from the north rather than the south, the Nyū Plateau vestiges notwithstanding, inasmuch as uneven geological transformations accounted for an earlier isolation of the southern islands.

The small bands of Palaeolithic migrants enjoyed a far vaster hunting area than do the teeming millions of today. Fossils of extinct fauna have been fished out of the Inland Sea in the region where the first physical remnants of what are claimed to represent Palaeolithic man were found. Discovered in 1931 near Akashi city but destroyed during the war, the bone is called a part of the hip of a hominid. Further digging at the site has not been productive, leaving this nebulous individual, Nipponanthropus akasiensis as he has been labelled, rather less than an established type. Slightly more acceptable, but still fragmentary and without accompanying stone tools, are parts of skeletons from Ushikawa in Aichi prefecture and an arm bone from Mikkabi in Shizuoka prefecture, both of these from sites lying in the southern Tōkai. They did, however, yield animal fossils in conjunction with the human bones. There is some evidence to the effect that at least one strain of fossil man in Japan was a small individual, perhaps not much larger than a pigmy.

The tracks of these pre-pottery people have been less elusive. Chipped handaxes, blades and points, knives and scrapers, found with the *débris* of fire, are country-wide testimony to their presence. But there is nothing along the order of art and nothing that indicates more than the barest form of existence. Volcanic activity was still considerable in many parts of the country, discouraging the growth of natural vegetation and the animal life which fed on it. Not until close to 8000 B.C. did this activity slacken to the place where vegetation could grow unimpeded, opening the way for the birth of a population which has steadily expanded until hardly a niche in the main islands now remains unoccupied.

The pottery period in Japan goes by the name Jōmon, after the cordmarking on its surface. Jōmon is an old title, in the vocabulary at least since the nineteenth century. The profusion of pottery in Jōmon sites never fails to impress, and it is to the eternal credit of the prudent man who labelled it that he recognized the decoration. Trained archaeologists have not always been so fortunate. Discussion still persists as to the various ways by which the marking was applied, but recent studies have reduced the possibilities greatly.

Being hand-made pottery, the product of a six thousand or more year old tradition, manufactured in plains, valleys, hillsides and along coasts all over the country, by groups in semi- isolation or in migration, it is not hard to understand that variety looms large as a major characteristic. The figurines are caught up in this same current and, because of it, there are compounded the complications in interpreting their use. Where new shapes are produced in the pottery and a broader selection of ritual vessels becomes available, a proportional increase in the number of figurines is almost always a corollary.

Carbon 14 dates for the earliest ceramic types of the Jōmon period have implied an incredibly early time for the invention of pottery. It may be that extremely slow progress was made by the culture—that it remained in almost a suspended state for two to three millenia. In any event, further verification of these dates is necessary before they become fully acceptable. The entire Jōmon period has been subdivided into five stages which, for convenience in English, we may call Earliest, Early, Middle, Late and Latest. They have also been called Early, Early-Middle, Late-Middle and Late, as well as Proto-Jōmon, Early, Middle, Late and Epi-Jōmon. The following chart, simplified to be sure and arranged to read from the earliest, may demand revisions as more dates are forthcoming. At the present, the chief C 14 dates for the island of Honshū suggest each subdivision may be roughly viewed as a span of approximately one thousand years except in the case of the enigmatic Earliest. Some dated sites are given at the right of the following table as a quick guide.

Earliest Jōmon Period
Prior to 4th Millenium Natsushima, Kanagawa pref.
                        7,491 ± 400 B. C.
                        (early phase)
                        Kijima, Okayama pref.
                        6,443 ± 350
                        (middle phase)

Early Jōmon Period
4th Millenium   Kamo, Chiba pref.
                        3,145 ± 400
                        (latter half)

Middle Jōmon Period
    3rd Millenium   I.C.U., Tokyo
                              2,608 ± 150
                              (earlier half)
                              Ubayama, Chiba pref.
                              2,563 ± 300
                              (latter half)

Late Jōmon Period
    2nd Millenium   Kemigawa, Chiba pref.
                              1,122 ± 180
                              (latter half)

Latest Jōmon Period
    1st Millenium to ca. 300 B.C. in south Japan
                              (later in the north)

Since the pottery typology has been subjected to excrutiatingly fine shades of division, these of dubious value in following the general direction taken in cultural advances, only those type names which have a precise bearing on the discussion need be used, and these will be largely limited to the Kantō Plain. The convenience of the five divisions is unquestioned; it allows wieldy terms for manageable time periods when the typology has been overrefined.

The sparseness of artifacts and small size of the sites of the Earliest Jōmon period attest to the migrancy of little groups who could not have lingered long in one spot. The fewer and less adequate stone tools of the time deterred the inhabitants from building more than simple dwellings on the surface of the ground despite a colder climate than today. The pottery vessels in the Kantō have pointed bottoms, simple profiles, and bear a rudimentary kind of cord-marking. The earliest known figurines were the work of one of these small bands. They turned up at the Hanawadai shell-mound in Ibaragi prefecture, dated perhaps very conservatively to the neighborhood of 5,000 B.C. The two complete examples and several fragments are all rather plaque-like, more or less fiddle-shaped, have a slight projection for the head and rounded breasts. Any kind of surface decoration at such an early date and in this region is completely lacking.

*Fig. 2

Cat. 1

Very few of the early types, however, are represented by figurines. The cult was slow to be adopted, and cannot be proved archaeologically to have had any continuity until the Middle Jōmon period. Future investigations and readjustment of the typology may fill some gaps, but one doubts that an ideal developmental stage is even a reasonable assumption.

Only slightly prior to the Middle Jōmon period does one find the first stages of an unbroken sequence, and then in figurines so primitive and plain as to be most likely a new beginning entirely, quite unrelated to earlier examples. From the Middle Jōmon period on, in the Kantō, Tōhoku, Chūbu, and Hokuriku, and in the Late and Latest periods in the Kinki and farther south, they begin to materialize in quantity, even — though rarely — in profusion. It is no surprise to find fragments of as many as fifty in a single site. Numerically speaking, the Chūbu, Kantō and Tōhoku rank the highest, and later cultural periods were on the whole more productive.

The Middle Jōmon period, a stage especially well characterized in the central regions, is the first complex and highly cult-oriented period in Japanese prehistory. This culture overflows from the lower mountains toward the Japan Sea coast and in the other direction into the western parts of the Kantō Plain. Its primary influences are therefore felt to the west and east of its hearth. Areas to the north and south do not respond in the same manner in spite of the vigor and originality of the culture. In an indirect way, the seeds it sowed in the Kantō Plain were later transplanted to the Tōhoku; through some hybridization certain minor features lived on.

The pottery of the earlier half of the Middle Jōmon period, known as the Katsusaka type in the Kantō Plain, takes its cue from the exorbitant ornamentation of the vessels in the mountains. Decoration may then completely overshadow shape. There is a new freedom in modelling forms, an obvious delight in the manipulation of the clay, which explores a great variety of shapes, yet may at the same time be trying to give some kind of symbolic meaning to them. Such an attitude encouraged the making of additional objects in clay, not the least of which are those of cult value. Bulk and mass, heavy and ponderous décor, suggestive motifs — these characteristics of the pottery and its decoration are

7

shared by the figurines. Similarly, the technical traits of low-fired reddish clay and frequently prominent grit tempering are to be seen in both.

The pottery itself is an expression of a dynamic and robust society. Their communities were the first large settlements of the Jōmon period. Thirty or more pits of houses is not unusual, and it may have been these mountainous people who were the inventors of simple cultivating techniques and who then included the making of figurines in their artistic repertory as a device for enhancing natural yields.

At this time in the coastal zones, where the kitchen middens have preserved the evidence, the people lived in oval-shaped pits with a hearth, made canoes and used harpoons, and kept many rectanguloid or fiddle-shaped axes on hands. The dead were buried in the shell-mound, often in a flexed position, and the children very occasionally in large inverted jars. Dogs were kept as household pets. But the people of the plains at this stage seemed less concerned with magical symbols. It may be that they were basking in the security of abundant sea foods and a comfortable climate, taking nature more for granted. They were introduced to these cult objects by the lower mountain dwellers. Phalli, a counterpart to the figurines, are one of the symbols which spread out to the Kantō from the central region, and will eventually be fashioned in all sizes, in both clay and stone.

In the Late Jōmon period a further settling of the people gave time for improving pottery firing methods and widening the selection of vessel types (spouted pouring pots, the earliest of the phallic-spouted pouring pots, small bowls, so-called incense burners, and effigy vessels). Decoration was to a great extent standardized throughout most of the country to cord-marking within zones, and systematically repeated motifs begin to appear toward the close of the period. Otherwise, the evidence is continually mounting of increasing community cooperation and ritual; it is best implied through the large circles of stones in north Japan. More elaborate harpoons were in use.

Smaller, polished axes show up in many sites, although they are greatly outnumbered by rough ones. Earrings, body ornaments, amulets and such like paraphernalia also point to greater social stability and a rising interest in personal magical protection.

By the Latest Jōmon stage the pits of dwellings tend to be square. A trend toward surface living is the result of better building techniques and a warming climate. The fishing industry was carried on widely, often beyond normal coastal limits, and sea food gathering went on apace, large communities leaving vast mounds. The considerable size of some shell-mounds is not a new phenomenon, but the numerous skeletons found in such mounds as Yoshigo in Aichi prefecture furnish evidence of larger groups and more systematic collective burials in this cultural framework. Shell-mounds in the north generally contain far more bones of animals. Hunting remained relatively easy — wild boar especially were plentiful — and any kind of agriculture was late in arriving and less attractive as long as food supplies were otherwise ample.

There is rather much ramification to ritual in this Latest Jōmon period. Here I am speaking of the Tōhoku district in the late centuries B.C. and undoubtedly lasting into the early centuries A.D. New vessel types ★Fig. 3 are to be seen: miniature cups and containers, pedestalled bowls, plates, bottles, flasks, and open-topped incense burners. Closed-topped burners and phallic-spouted ewers, neither actually an invention of this period, now flourish on a large scale, and all thrive in an atmosphere which favors quantity over size. These and other shapes may be burnished black or painted red. Most of the vessels are now rather small and neat, and made with thin walls of clay in a grayish color. ★Cat. 30 Segmented shapes are common, especially for pouring pots. An almost complete lack of handles distinguishes these little pitchers from the larger ones of the Late Jōmon period.

The phallic stones may now be smaller, usually not more then 30 cm. in length, have decorated heads and be pointed at the other end. There are polished knives,

Plate III Painted pottery vessel from Togariishi, Minami-ōshio, Toyohirachi ward, Chino city, Nagano prefecture. H. 40.1 cm. Middle Jōmon Period. Togariishi Archaeology Museum

8

cleaver-like stone implements, carved stones, and a greater variety of body ornaments in bone, deer horn, shell, stone and clay. With all of this profusion of pottery and fetishistic objects, one would be correct in anticipating comparatively more figurines. And in respect to the figurines, it is a spectacular phase, a remarkable witness to a climax of traditions in use, technical production and artistic accomplishment.

II. THE MAIN CHARACTERISTICS OF THE FIGURINES

The same well-spring which engendered the pottery of the time also produced the figurines; it need hardly be said that the ornamentation of figurines is therefore approached in much the same way as that of the pottery. Because of an ever-present predilection to decorate, the typology of the pottery is most useful in determining the chronological position and approximate provenience of any given figurine. The range of decoration will tend to discredit generalizations which by their very nature are prone to overlook the individual character of a product that comes from the hands of household potters, yet we may at this point work from the broader view toward the more specific.

General statements as to what the figurines are not come more readily to mind. In countries where ritual and thought patterns were more mature or more ancient, or were accompanied by higher speculation on the metaphysical world, realistic representation, gestures and unusual poses were often in order. This is not the case for Japan. The Japanese figurines are fundamentally non-realistic, are primitive in their rigidity and frontality, and are rendered in what might be called an essentially linear artistic approach to surface and questions of detail. Suggestive gestures designed to enhance the fertility nature of a figurine are generally absent; hands supporting the breasts, hands on the hips, a hand near the sex triangle, wildly dancing poses, sculpturally treated twisting bodies and similar advanced representations would be quite out of character. The majority are conceived strictly in a biface manner. Toward the end of the Jōmon period the hollow figurine makes its appearance. At this juncture decoration is able to follow the form of the figure, yet it is a rather rare example which makes thorough use of this op-

tion. Many still follow traditional ways of ornamenting both sides, as though neither were related to the other.

The Jōmon figurines belong to an early thought stage in which the decorative and realistic are undifferentiated. The non-realistic approach, seen essentially in the dominance of decoration over the representation of literal human form, in other words, is the mark of a cultural level beyond which the Jōmon people never advance. Despite wide variations, including shades of the realistic (and one may see northern and southern distinctions here which will be dealt with later), by and large the abstract elements in both shape and decoration seem to outweigh the literal. The decoration may reach extremes. In certain areas, at certain times, a philosophy of "horror vacui" prevails. Surfaces may be fully covered with cord-marking, punctating, incising, grooving, or applied designs in clay, this kind of elaboration especially notable in the Latest Jōmon period in the Kantō and Tōhoku. The figurines develop in the central regions and in the north toward this ultimate in decoration—not away from decoration, as might be expected if religious thought were progressing. What one does sense is an increasing awareness on the part of the makers in the artistic possibilities of the statuettes, a trend which may illustrate a settling into traditional thought patterns in regard to the meaning of the figurines.

Some systematic repetition of motifs appears on pottery vessels during the Late Jōmon, and evolves into the customary decorative system in the Latest period. This is to say that a simple rhythmic repetition of a motif around a vessel is recognition of the full use of its form. It now brings into play a decorative device which was rare and at best only accidentally achieved in earlier Jōmon pottery. This same artistic and technical sophistication characterizes the decoration of the figurines in which awkward shapes and irregular surfaces were often ingeniously circumvented. The uniform repetition of motifs may be in part a reflection of a routine dependence upon the cyclical phases of nature, habitual to a Neolithic society, in which the annual discharge of the duties associated with cultivation inspired a program of stylized, metronomic motifs.

Groups of almost identical figurines are virtually unknown. Variety rather than similarity is more normal, and sanctuaries where votive figurines were made or to which they were brought to meet the needs of a cult's adherents have yet to be conclusively proved as existing in the Jōmon period. One possible deviation from this rule will be discussed later, but the figurines still have variety. Jōmon figurines are usually recovered singly, although many may be found in a whole site. Here again an exception may be made for the dwelling at Yosukeone which contained the community's statuettes, but as a general rule this holds.

Most discoveries of figurines are not in locations which can be identified as ritual sites. Inadequate archaeological techniques until recent years may be partially to blame for the poor knowledge of their context, yet by and large this is the case. Most figurines may therefore be considered as mobile symbols, unattached to fixed spots or hallowed locations sanctified by the presence of some higher power.

Stylization in the treatment of figurines in many early cultures does not prevent emphatic attention to sex marks. Japanese examples are customarily only moderately marked, if at all—barring some very obvious exceptions which I would call atypical—and the sex triangle is conspicuously absent in almost all cases, or even any suggestion of genitalia. The protruding abdomen is a dominant feature of the Middle to Late Jōmon periods, and retained in conventional ways after this date. Nipples are common, pendulous breasts are few in number, but numerous examples will have no sign of breasts whatever. Enlarged posteriors are part of the formula of the Middle Jōmon period in the Chūbu region.

Breast-marked plaques are well known in other areas of the world. The inclusion of bulges was the standard device for allowing quick recognition of such objects as female. On the positive side, Japan has its fair share. Normally simply outlined, and often scarcely human in shape, they are provided with a pair of torso lumps. Other instances in which the surface is perfectly smooth have left the makers with the choice of indicating breasts by linear decoration. Some exercise of the imagination is often required to see these as breasts, but far less so in examples where spirals are incised in the right places.

Human inhumations in Japan are rarely preserved outside the limits of shell-mounds, but by good fortune several hundred have been found in Jōmon period kitchen middens. While these show that the mode of burial was by no means standardized and might take the form of elongated or flexed bodies lying on either side, front or back, they also show that red ochre was frequently employed to paint the bones, and offer evidence for the practice of secondary interments. This is especially the case in the Tōhoku region, and with the bones of children. The same red paint was used on numerous figurines; the later the figure the more probability it would be affected by the practice. Deterioration in the ground has taken its toll, as has excessive washing after discovery, but many are richly covered from head to foot, and close inspection will reveal paint on a very high proportion of others. In several cases it would appear that only the upper part of the figurine had been coated in this way.

Fig. 1 Figurine in process of excavation; left, before the removal of two slabs; right, exposed figurine. Amataki, Shimo-shitasaki, Kindaichi village, Ninohe county, Iwate prefecture

Fig. 2 Pottery vessel from Kami-nishijō Minebata, Shiojiri city, Nagano prefecture. H. 21.6 cm. Middle Jōmon Period. Matsumoto City Museum

Fig. 3 Carved phallic symbol in tufa, from Togariishi, Minami-ōshio, Toyohirachi ward, Chino city, Nagano prefecture. H. 23.9 cm. D. of head 11.7 cm. Middle Jōmon Period. Togariishi Archaeology Museum

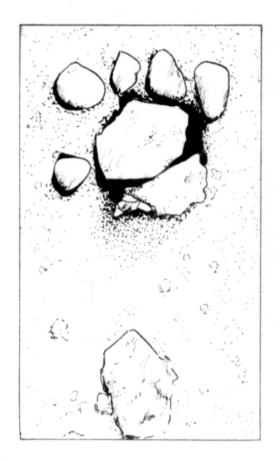 

Figurines tended to become more elaborate in outline and shape and, in broad terms, gained in size over the centuries. Underlying such changes may have been their widening use, from individual to family symbols. The demand for charms of an easily portable nature was never reduced, however, and plaques increased in quantity as the figurines became more difficult to transport. There was no complete abandonment of little figurines, but needs were revised to include smaller, simple types.

Unusually smooth and slick surfaces are attributed to considerable handling and fondling of the flatter figurines and plaques. The extensive polishing of some of the later hollow ones would be due to artistic interests rather than extensive manipulation by a devotee. Most Middle Jōmon examples, fired at a low temperature and often with crumbly surface, do not lend themselves naturally to such kind of physical contact. Where this contact is most apparent is in the specimens of the Late and a few of the Latest periods, when technical improvements of higher firing and thinner walls were instrumental in producing dense, compact clay and hard surfaces.

One extraordinary figurine in the Tokyo National Museum contains a small stone like an umbilicus baked into its distended abdomen. Its smoothness and that of the surrounding area leaves little doubt as to the constant massaging which it received.

Fig. 4   Pottery vessel bearing human figure, from Idojiri, Fujimi-machi, Suwa county, Nagano prefecture. H. 51.2 cm. Middle Jōmon Period. Idojiri Archaeology Museum

Fig. 5   Detail of pottery vessel with four rim peaks, from Location 4, Idojiri, Fujimi-machi, Suwa county, Nagano prefecture. H. of vessel 34.3 cm. W. of rim projection 7.3 cm. Middle Jōmon Period. Idojiri Archaeology Museum

III. THE CIRCUMSTANCES OF THE FINDS

The majority of figurines in modern collections are old finds which were gathered long before contemporary archaeology put a premium on the context of the discovery. Post-war finds, however, are beginning to fill the gaps in knowledge on the circumstances surrounding these discoveries. Those figurines which have been recovered from special deposits form only a small percentage of the total, but they have, as a result, gained a unique degree of importance in the over-all study.

Even the circumstances of these special deposits are far from similar, leading one to speculate on several different possibilities for arrangement. In the greater number of these deposits the figurine is laid horizontally at a shallow depth and encircled by stones, as though simulating a burial. It may then be covered by one or more stones. The resemblance to a number of later Jōmon period human burials in which the remains were isolated by a ring or oval of stones is quite obvious, and one recalls the examples of stones being placed on the chest or at the head of the deceased, or a clay vessel deposited at the head. These burials, however, cannot be looked on as typical in the Jōmon period, nor does one have the entire picture, for the discovery of burials outside of shell-mounds are rare, and the majority of figurine deposits of this kind do not come from shell-mounds.

The bow-legged Satohara figurine was a part of such an arrangement. Nine large stones composed a rectangle about 150 cm. in length within which the figurine had been placed, its head pointing almost due north, all lying a little less than 100 cm. below the modern surface. Somewhat similar schemes have been discovered in the prefectures of Yamagata, Iwate and Miyagi, the number and size of the stones as well as the depth of the deposit varying in each case.

Approximately a dozen deposits of this sort—figurines lying prone, stone-surrounded or cist encased—have been recorded. These are few in number for the Middle and Late Jōmon periods and are found chiefly in the central region and the Kantō, but the practice was more generally adopted by Latest Jōmon, particularly by the people of the Tōhoku area.

The discovery which is here illustrated in two stages Fig. 1 of excavation was made by a Meiji University expedition in 1958 when digging the corner of a trench in the Amataki site in Iwate prefecture. A figurine of the Latest Jōmon period, of a Kamegaoka type to be specific, had been consigned to the earth in broken condition. Partially surrounding it were five river stones and covering it were two flat slabs. After removal of these slabs the figurine was found to be lying face up, slightly below the level of the stones. The site yielded other clay figurines along with a number of stone plaques.

In pit-dwelling number 1 of the Tochikura site in Tochio city of Niigata prefecture, a Middle Jōmon headless figurine had been placed with its base up at *Pl. II the top of a filled in post-hole of this house, and then partially surrounded by broken pieces of pottery. One

Fig. 6 Pottery vessel from Location 4, International Christian University, Mitaka city, Tokyo. H. 25.4 cm. Middle Jōmon Period. Coll. I.C.U.

Fig. 7 Detail of pottery vessel with single rim projection, from Togariishi, Minami-ōshio, Toyohirachi ward, Chino city, Nagano prefecture. H. of vessel 32 cm. L. of "bird's head" 5 cm. Middle Jōmon Period. Togariishi Archaeology Museum

16

assumes that the house had required some rebuilding, hence the moving of the posts, but the position and relationship to the sherds leave little doubt as to the deliberate character of the arrangement.

At the large Middle Jōmon site of Hiraide, with its numerous pit-dwellings of this and later periods, the figurines were all found in a single house, a round pit measuring almost six meters in diameter. This house had been destroyed by fire. The group consists of three heads and three headless bodies, that is to say, all are Cat. 5 broken. The three heads are of the subhuman type. These figurines, however, are not enough alike to lead one to believe that they were all made by the same individual and that this was his residence. Many houses here had standing stones on a kind of platform, and have also yielded stone "plates" in the excavations. This particular house doubtless served a special purpose, perhaps for the diseased or, more likely, a parturition house, as will be discussed later.

The head of a figurine was found in a jar at Yosukeone, a subsite of Togariishi, the jar a product of the Cat. 7 middle stages of the Middle Jōmon period. The vessel itself stood on a stone slab in the corner of the pit of dwelling number 8. Nearby was a bucket-handled vessel, a rather unusual type of suspension vessel usually thought to have been made for ritual use.

At the stone circles of Ōyu in Akita prefecture, where two large rings of thousands of stones, each with another circle within, appear to incorporate extensive cemeteries, individual graves were marked out in rectangular shape inside the rough limits of each circle. *Figs. 24, 25 A fragmentary female figurine lying face up was found among the stones. Ōyu is one of the most elaborate ritual sites of the Jōmon period so far discovered in Japan, although it may yet be eclipsed by another set of circles recently under excavation farther north in Aomori prefecture. While such circles of stones have generally been believed to be creations of the Late and Latest Jōmon periods, another discovery of such circles with earlier pottery may obligate a re-evaluation of their significance in Jōmon times.

In any event, the planning and the scale of the circles, and the moving of the stones are evidence of the most elaborate community enterprises of the Jōmon period. Set apart in each case from the main circles is a "sun-dial" arrangement of a standing menhir with horizontal stones radiating from this upright like the spokes of a wheel. The relation these "sun-dials" have to the larger circles may point to a calendrical meaning—the sun-dial term is merely a descriptive one—and may suggest that, along with stone worship, cult practices based on solar positions, were carried out here. The Ōyu circles, and the few other similar groupings of stones in other sites, are an unmistakable sign of the existence of a community ritual center, the rites centered around burial practices. The figurine here is rather plain, broken across the waist. The details of the face are feebly rendered, while the modelling of the torso is clearly female.

Ōyu has other portable remains of a ritual nature. Small, long-necked spouted vessels, unlike anything else found in Japan, may have satisfied libation needs. Clay objects of uncertain identity are also probably to be looked on as having been in some way utilized in the rites.

The large, bell-bottomed figures from the central region and the Shinshū area are usually found apart from other archaeological remains. They represent a class of the largest figurines and are the only ones which have complete stability and stand alone without some kind of human encouragement. Examples may be furnished with an opening in the top of the head. One in the National Museum has a partial clay base which runs around the interior like a wide lip. This is perforated with a series of round holes, made as though to provide a means of covering it with another material, stretched and tied across.

There has been some disposition to look on these figurines as bone containers since the time one was found with powdered bones both inside and out, the bones mixed with the soil around in an area extending about a meter in diameter. These bones are believed to

Figs. 8, 9 Figurine from Sakai, Fujii-machi, Nirasaki city, Yamanashi prefecture. H. 16.5 cm. Middle Jōmon Period. Sakai Remains Museum

be those of a child or children. But it is also recognized that this figurine, found at Nakayashiki in Kanagawa prefecture, comes from outside the normal zone of distribution of these figurines and may not be wholly typical. The size of the bell-shaped statuettes and what seems to be their isolation from the residences of a community site may mean that use was made of them at sacred spots, and that in such places they had a greater degree of permanence than was normally the case with Jōmon figurines. *Cat. 24

Fig. 10 Headless figurine from Togariishi, Minami-ōshio, Toyohirachi ward, Chino city, Nagano prefecture. H. 8.9 cm. (Enlarged.) Middle Jōmon Period. Togariishi Archaeology Museum

IV. LOCAL FEATURES OF THE FIGURINES

*Cat. 2 Rare as figurines of the Early Jōmon period are, they still outnumber those of Earliest Jōmon. The very few examples are flat or have a slight stomach protrusion, and are roughly rectangular in outline with rounded top and small projections at the shoulders. These correspond to the Moroiso pottery type in the Kantō, in a time period which comes toward the end of Early Jōmon. Only five were recorded for this as late as 1961, two of these for the Kantō and three for the Tōhoku. Statistical statements may soon prove to be false and can hardly take into consideration the multitude of unpublished examples which are in collections all over the country, yet the purpose here is to underscore the scarcity of figurines at this time. An average length of these might be judged to be around 7 cm. One example with crudely formed short legs and feet which widen out from the pelvic area, is lacking any real suggestion of the hips themselves but has a very slightly distended abdomen. The hip region is flattened along the back and decorated with a pair of fine, double lines roughly paralleling the contours.

Simpler and flatter shapes are more preferred in the north. Objects coming from Aomori city and the Ichiōji shell-mound in Hachinohe city are much like triangular plaques with rounded edges and slightly curved outlines, the breasts and what may be taken as the navel indicated as small lumps. The heads of these are missing, but if one may judge from slightly later examples, these heads resembled feebly defined blisters along the upper edge, and the features may have consisted of nothing more than a vertical ridge to convey the idea of a nose.

The infrequency of figurines throughout these early periods, and the marked maturity in the succeeding stage, that is to say, the production in quantity coupled with some consistency in type, lead one to suppose that the connections between these Moroiso ones and those of the Middle Jōmon period are minimal, if at all, and that Middle Jōmon types owe their existence and development to another set of factors generally distinct from those responsible for the figurines of the Earliest and Early periods.

THE MIDDLE JŌMON INNOVATIONS IN THE CHŪBU

It was in the high central region, the Chūbu, where the cult took genuine birth, apparently in the great community centers of Nagano prefecture and thereabouts. It was then from here that it spread, presumably through the Shinshū district, into the present prefectures of Yamanashi, Kanagawa and Tokyo, the southern half of the Kantō Plain. It also reached the west coast about the same time.

Two aspects of this cult, because of their mutually influencing nature, cannot be considered inseparably. There are, of course, the figurines themselves, but in a surprising number of pottery vessels there is also the inclusion of an animal-like head in the elaborate decoration along the rim. In more rare cases this head is

Figs. 11, 12   Figurine from Chōjagahara, Ichinomiya, Itoigawa city, Niigata prefecture. H. 30 cm. Middle Jōmon Period. National Museum, Tokyo

lower, down on the wall. Since the facial details of the figurines and rim-heads so often tend to be alike — the rim-heads a little more consistent in type — the two need to be viewed as two facets of the same cultic manifestation.

Katsusaka is the pottery type in the Kantō Plain in which the central mode of decoration is mirrored. In Nagano prefecture it is the Togariishi type with sub-divisions, a type named after the large site near Chino city. As has already been remarked on, it was at this stage in the cultural development that early signs of maturity in fertility representations may be observed. Stone phalli in considerable range, from a size usable as a grinding tool to a size impractically large except perhaps for ceremonial grinding only, have been found in the sites, occasionally right in the pits of dwellings, and would now indicate a better understanding on the part of their makers of the role played by the two sexes in the processes of fertility.

Called *sekibo* (stone clubs) in Japan, one of tufa from Togariishi is equipped with "eyes" on the enlarged head above a somewhat oval-shaped shaft. Clubs at the Togariishi sites measure from 15 to 40 cms. in length, and many here resemble mushrooms. Additionally, long stones simply smoothed into slender shafts and natural stones of suggestive shape have been recovered from these sites. Of special interest at Togariishi are flat stones, rather much resembling tablets (like the Chinese symbols of rank), which were found standing on clay platforms in several pits of houses.

From Yamanashi prefecture come large, circular plates of clay or what might be called low stands, each 20 or more cm. in diameter, bearing a number of holes in the walls. These are preserved in places like the Idojiri Archaeology Hall and the Sakai Remains Museum. Their use is uncertain, but one assumes they were supports for sacral containers or cult objects, or were used as display surfaces for some sort of offering.

A special type of vessel appears in this region for which the context of the discovery suggests a ritual use, as do the details of the vessels themselves. Customarily large in size, punctured with small holes at the rim above a clay ridge, these may have a segmented body, but the surface itself generally remains largely undecorated. This in itself is significant in an area where overpowering quantities of plastic décor are of primary concern. The decoration on these is made up of ribbons of clay shaped into loop handles, oval and zigzag patterns, leaf-like motifs or, even in rare instances, a stylized human form. These vessels have often been termed containers of red paint, and a number have been found to bear paint on the exterior. The rim was apparently designed to receive a lid, perhaps to be tied on, or possibly the holes were intended for the purpose of securing a suspension net. The large illustrated jar has red paint inside to its very rim. Most interesting are the painted "eye spirals", the region of the "nose", and the strips of red running parallel with the four large handles in the middle zone where these are not restored. ★Fig. 2 Fig. 4 Pl. III

Such designs come tantalizingly close to being recognizable forms. These oblique references — as one might call them — do not come out and specify but merely suggest, and these too vaguely to know whether anything at all is actually intended, or if so, whether it falls into a human, animal, avian or reptilian category. There are enough of these to allow the statement that we are not dealing with a minor phenomenon. The decoration itself is in so many ways suggestive, yet more than this, one seems to see in the rims the heads of birds, snakes, and animals, often in both frontal and profile views, or examples of semi-human forms. Within the oval shaped ridges of just the run-of-the-mill décor, zigzag and notched incisions may appear strongly vulvar, although the effect is offset by the customary horizontal direction of the ovals. ★Fig. 3; Fig. 5 Fig. 4

Whether these suggestive forms should be read as meaningful symbolism, however, is a perennial argument which, until lately, found most of the debaters choosing the negative side. Recent suggestions that snakes at least are represented are beginning to gain attention. If this is true, it may add further argument to the evidence for an embryonic stage of agriculture.

Fig. 13   Head from Sakai, Fujii-machi, Nirasaki city, Yamanashi prefecture. H. 7.7 cm. Middle Jōmon Period. Sakai Remains Museum
Fig. 14   Head and torso of subhuman figurine, from Misaka-machi, Higashi-yatsushiro county, Yamanashi prefecture. H. 25.5 cm. Middle Jōmon Period. National Museum, Tokyo

A number of fanciful shapes at Togariishi are called snakes' heads. An examination of these, coupled with the experience of excavating on the I.C.U. campus a Fig. 7 stone bird's head near a vessel of this date bearing a design with a vague likeness to a bird, has led me to look on these as more akin to birds than snakes, espe- Fig. 6 cially where one purports to see a kind of cock's comb and a sort of wattle. One Togariishi vessel even has a pair of "heads" facing each other.

Figs. 8, 9 Figurines of simple shape are almost always present *Cat. 5, 6, 7 in some form. But typical of this time are the squat and heavy-set, corpulent bodies in which the breasts are moderately indicated, the abdomen and hips greatly emphasized and the posterior flattened above and strongly distended in the lower buttocks. Surface decoration is not normally extensive and may consist of indentations and grooving in a stylized way. The quality of the clay and temperature of baking will vary quite considerably. Examples may be low-fired, reddish in color, of coarse, grit tempered clay, or may *Cat. 4 be dark brown, of rather pure clay, and smooth surfaced.

Variety is always present and any discussion of all details would be tedious and endless. A discovery of Fig. 10 about three decades ago in which the exact location and circumstances of the find are not now remembered, is the pot-bellied, headless figure in the Togariishi Archaeology Museum. The right hand is affixed at the waist, while the left arm, shaped like a spiral, is said by some observers to be holding a jar in the crook of the shoulder or hand. Whereas this may actually be only an inarticulated pose of the arm — for the overlay of the right hand on the lower arm would *Cat. 9 seem to be graphic demonstration of the maker's problems — the difference in position of the two is in itself worth noting for its relative rarity. In characteristic fashion a line runs down the torso and abdomen and is curled at the end in order to mark the umbilicus.

Figs. 11, 12 The large figure in the Tokyo National Museum, once with full round head, has some features of this period — the stubby, upraised arms, short legs — and

some of the Late Jōmon period — spiral grooving and slightly spread legs. Except for the modelled and hollow head, which should be rather late in date, the figurine is flat. The sex triangle is quite uniquely outlined. We may be faced with several Middle Jōmon traits preserved in this region and used in combination with an early type body and a late type head. The grooving is deep enough for Middle Jōmon, but the plasticity of the hollow head (as far as one can tell) appears far more advanced.

Numerous fragmentary heads of this period range from semi-human through subhuman to animal-like in their details. They therefore have much in common with the rim-heads. Whether more or less human or not, the eyebrows are usually arched and connected with the nose. A stronger slant to the teardrop eyes or sharper point to the snout strengthen the zoomorphic character. Often a large spiral of clay behind the peaked head is worked in as a continuation of the loops and apertures of the normal rim ornamentation. Parallel lines below the eyes have inspired the nickname of "tear-shedding type".

Vertical holes in both heads and bodies seem to have been made by thin sticks which were used to hold the sections of a figurine together. Several examples have tiny perforations running from one end to the other, and heads may have as many as four complete holes. In some instances suspension by means of the openings would be quite possible, but the majority of holes would appear to have resulted from a structural device — the fragmentary nature of these figurines witness to it falling short as an ultimate answer — of joining the sections.

Farther to the west, in Niigata prefecture, the silhouette common to the Tōsan examples is preserved, but the plasticity is missing. Plaque-like instead of three-dimensional, the roundness of a protruding abdomen may be suggested by parallel incisions and linear decoration.

The farther into the Kantō the more the moderation, is a common phrase for the Middle Jōmon period. The

Figs. 15, 16 Headless figurine from Sakai, Fujii-machi, Nirasaki city, Yamanashi prefecture. H. 16.4 cm. (Enlarged.) Middle Jōmon Period. Sakai Remains Museum

lines of communication passed chiefly down the valley from Matsumoto city toward the coast. Yamanashi prefecture claims many fine figurines which illustrate the scope of this modification. The sinister looking feline, kept in the Tokyo National Museum, is of impressive size and workmanship. The two arms were in different positions. The shoulders give the effect of heavily braided hair hanging behind, while the back of the head is formed like a doughnut, in a perfectly circular ring of clay. The finishing is fine, the clay dense, the surface hard and the object heavy.

Some refinements have already crept in. Delicate surface scratching in free, irregular patterns on the big-footed figurine from Sakai, Yamanashi prefecture, are more likely to be Kantō inspired. When discovered, the figure was partially surrounded by three stone slabs and missing the right leg. The leg was retrieved later by a primary school student about four kilometers away, and joined to the body. Truncated arms are thrown up and back in a dance-like pose. The rump protrudes strongly, adding extra balance to further enable the figure to stand alone. The familiar vertical line and engraved loop around the enlarged umbilicus may be seen. In contrast to the short, obese, shoulder-arm, waistless figure which is heavily weighted in the feet, the slender shape of this type, the almost sensual stance and network of engravings show how a widely divergent approach has been made compatible to the interests of this area. Among the examples of the region, the magnified feet, the low-slung posterior and the small breasts are popular traits.

RIM-HEADS

Many rim-heads exist, but only a few are still preserved in place on the luxuriantly ornamented rims of vessels. These few, however, demonstrate how such heads were worked right into the decoration, in most cases without recourse to anything more than the usual repertory of loops, ridges, peaks and perforations. One head to a vessel would appear to be all that was called for and,

if one must judge by the few intact, the decoration is similar to that of any other vessel. The distribution of the vessels with rim-heads is comparable to that of the pot-bellied figurines and isolated animal-like heads.

The rim-heads almost invariably face inwards, the back of the head fused into one of the usual four castellations of the rim. Similar faces worked into the decoration on the wall of a vessel will, of course, be shown looking out rather than in. There is no special regard for size; the smallest or the largest vessel may have these wall-heads. One example is a crude miniature of the large ritual vessels with rim holes. The twelve holes and the otherwise absence of decoration tie this tiny one in with the large ritual type mentioned earlier. On four circular protrusions are to be seen two faces and two spirals, the side-by-side faces, for all their simplicity, recognizable as belonging to the animal-face category by their eyebrow lines and slanted eyes. The vessel turned up during the cultivation of a field in 1925 and nothing is known of its archaeological context.

Rim-head faces are pointed, the teardrop eyes are usually strongly slanted, and the nostrils are small vertical punches, the mouth open and deep. On the whole it might be said that they have a naive, child-like, amiable expression, if not that of a low-intelligenced human, then to be regarded as bordering on the sub-human. Most resemble rodents — rabbits or squirrels — or more slightly, felines. As a matter of fact, rodent and feline features vie with each other for prominence, and some examples even include canine characteristics. This slight variety once led me to suggest there was here an incipient form of totemism, a practice which never reached an adolescent stage before it must have been superseded by a stronger, obliterating cult, this successor illustrated by an anthropomorphic rather than a zoomorphic approach. These would be diametrically opposed traditions whose distinctions would be far sharper in a society of more elaborate organization. The differences here are not great, nor would they be great as long as there is a low level of selectivity in symbolism resulting from unsophisticated religious ideas. An ex-

*Fig. 14

Cat. 10

*Figs. 15, 16

Fig. 18

*Fig. 17

Plate IV Figurine from Shiizuka shell-mound, Edozaki-machi, Inashiki county, Ibaragi prefecture. H. 12.1 cm. Late Jōmon Period. Osaka City Art Museum

treme example, but not far from home, is the Shang-Chou dynasties' animal-style art. The reasoning from animal style to later human style is not difficult to trace in this case, but in Japan perhaps the distinctions are too vague to be adequately perceived by the same kind of reasoning. In any event, the subhuman character of this rim-head style is soon abandoned in favor of a more purely human approach.

The connections Jōmon pottery may have with the Asian continent are primarily those of its shared northern interest in cord-marking. Other than this, demonstrable connections are few and tenuous. I would like, however, to be able to explain the rim-heads and the "painted vessel style" of this Middle Jōmon period, dated in the vicinity of 2900 — 2500 B.C., as of foreign introduction. This is suggested only with certain obvious reservations.

Jōmon pottery is never considered to be a product of a painted pottery culture. Many sherds from random sites bear red paint, but, except for the group we are dealing with and the very late examples of the Tōhoku which probably came under the influence of Chinese lacquer, no patterns are included. When actual painted decoration appears, one has a right to look for sources in another tradition.

The painted designs go with large open surfaces on vessels which otherwise have very little plastic décor, these open surfaces seeming to be quite out of character with the great emphasis on over-grown sculptural effects. One notes immediately the contrast. The painted designs, however, are few. The "spiral eyes" are the most elaborate. The only natural conversion from painted designs in this plastic atmosphere would be a conversion to applied clay patterns, but this might be done while the subject matter is still retained and the large, unbroken, paintable surfaces are still preserved. Hence, it might be suggested that the spread-eagle figure on the pot from Idojiri may be a Jōmon modification of the skeletonized, zigzag anthropomorphs on

a small number of Chinese Yang-shao painted vessels. There are also the painted "eyes" on Chinese vessels. A rather recent discovery is a similar vessel, from Fudasawa, Fujimi-machi, Nagano prefecture, which has lost the torso and arms of the spread figure, although the abdomen and legs are still intact. The zigzag arms terminate in "fingers", not unlike the geometric, akimbo Chinese examples. Like China, these Japanese vessels bear only one anthropomorph each. The Fudasawa vessel, in contrast to the Idojiri one, shows its decoration to be more of the stock Jōmon type. The figure is less flattened and the lower half of the vessel is covered with cord-marking.

Might the rim-heads also be connected with the Yang-shao cults? The distance is difficult to account for in any case, but one recalls the Chinese heads on serrated "lids", with flattened faces painted in radiating lines, of subhuman appearance. A snake rises up the back of the neck and over the head. Short "horns" project above the temples. These "lids" have ophiolatrous connotations—the belief on the part of some of the Japanese archaeologists that the snake in the mountainous Middle Jōmon region materializes in the suggestive shapes has already been mentioned, although the rim-heads themselves are certainly less so.

The time correspondence may be satisfactory. Recent writers have more astutely avoided offering absolute chronological schemes since Andersson's boldly projected sequence was written and rewritten in the 1920's. Despite the lack of new evidence on absolute dating, it may be that an early third millenium B.C. date will hold up for the Yang-shao material.

The painted pottery lacks any possible prototypes in Japan known to me. One can be less definite about the rim-heads. In the Early Jōmon period, however, there are only naive little projections which look as though eyes and mouth were punched in as afterthoughts. Several of these are on Moroiso type pottery, that is, they are attributable to the end of the ★Fig. 4; Fig. 19

Fig. 17 Incomplete pottery vessel with rim-head in place, from Togariishi, Minami-ōshio, Toyohirachi ward, Chino city, Nagano prefecture. Maximum D. 23.5 cm. Middle Jōmon Period. Togariishi Archaeology Museum

Fig. 18 Rim-head from Hosaka, Hosaka-machi, Nirasaki city, Yamanashi prefecture. H. 11.8 cm. Middle Jōmon Period. National Museum, Tokyo

Early Jōmon period, and are found more in the Kantō than in the Chūbu. The faces may be pointed — the illustrated one resembles an eyeless horse, with nostrils and mouth indicated, the effect doubtless accidental. It is difficult for me to see that the advances and standardization shown by the Middle Jōmon rim-heads could have been entirely based on these pathetic efforts, and I have been led to the conclusion that outside influences were responsible for the phenomenon.

★Cat. 13 MIDDLE JŌMON IN OTHER REGIONS

Outside of this abnormally strong culture concentrated in a wide belt across central Japan, few other figurines fit this time period. The pot-belly, enlarged but-
Cat. 12 tocks, and stump limbs work their way into the southern Tōhoku, where they are well represented in Fukushima prefecture, having circumvented the Kantō. The plainly modelled figure with navel stone belongs to this stage. The back of its head is pointed, and is perforated by three vertical holes. They could have served for suspension of the figurine.

This is the period of the so-called Entō pottery (Cylindrical) in the upper Tōhoku. Entō is a widely produced group of rather large jars of more or less tubular shape, the surface neatly cord-marked in coarse, often feather-shaped indentations.

Middle Jōmon figurines in north Japan are from shell-mounds, from the productive Sannai site in Aomori city and from south Hokkaidō. Most are still simple in shape and rather plaque-like, but have the newer features of single-strand cord-impressions applied much like incised designs. The nature of these figurines is not very different from Early Jōmon examples in the region. They spring from the same tradition, but have incorporated new cord-marking techniques for which the Tōhoku is well known.

LATE JŌMON PERIOD FIGURINES

During the Late Jōmon period the Kantō absorbed all it was culturally prepared to accept from the Tōsan region and went on to multiply the types. The shell-mound producers now adopted the habit of making figurines as a part of their way of life and forged ahead in the developments. It may be that early cultivation techniques were moving into the lower plains, where use could be made of the wealth of water sources. Large shell-mounds were by-products of semi-sedentary living. Improvements were devised in the methods of baking pottery, and a vast diffusion took place of a specific approach toward decoration. Called *surikeshi* Jōmon in Japan, literally meaning "erased cord-marking", it was a way of treating the surface with cord-marking between outlined zones, whatever over-shot the outlines then being rubbed off with the fingers or a spatula. Impressive refinements lend a handsome beauty to the best work. The popularity of this method has no equal in Japan; it occurs from one end of the country to the other, from Hokkaidō to Kyūshū, having moved out of a strong center — either the Kinki or the Kantō — and penetrated even remote and isolated regions. The extent of zoned cord-marking speaks for conditions which brought more tribal groups together than had up to this time been customary, and may even suggest a stage of greater fusion of these groups. Significant for us is what comes to be a more general acceptance of the figurine cult at this time, in wider and more distant parts of the country.

Toward the closing centuries of this Late Jōmon period the shell-fish eaters along the Kantō coast were the most ardent practitioners of the female figurine

Fig. 19 Rim-head from Idojiri, Fujimi-machi, Suwa county, Nagano prefecture. W. of sherd 6.7 cm. Early Jōmon Period. Idojiri Archaeology Museum

Fig. 20 Head and torso of figurine from Shiizuka shell-mound, Edozaki-machi, Inashiki county, Ibaragi prefecture. H. 11.5 cm. Late Jōmon Period. Osaka City Art Museum

cult. From some of the shell-mounds which attracted notice in the early years of archaeological work in Japan—Fukuda, Shiizuka and Tachigi in Ibaragi prefecture—has come in appreciable quantity an especially well known Late Jōmon type. For convenience, I will call these the "ridge-face" type. These are particularly prevalent toward the end of the period and, while not limited entirely to shell-mounds, they do appear there in abundance and seem to have been preferred by, if not actually the invention of, seaside inhabitants.

The type has its unmistakable features. The face of the figurine is oval to triangular, the lower jaw heavily ridged from ear to ear. Eyebrows may be a horizontal strip of clay rather than the earlier arched ridge, this strip then indented and connected with the nose. The eyes are nothing more than heavy ridges, as is the mouth, and the latter marked by tiny circular punctates. These indentations are a special trademark of the shell-mound figurines. In respect to the rest of the figure, the shoulders slope, the tips of the arms flare out slightly, while the waist is now a little more elongated. Legs, too, are longer than those of the Middle Jōmon figurines. Any indicated breasts will normally be hemispherical, but are occasionally pendulous. While faces often seem to be on the anthropomorphic fringe, it may not be incorrect to say that the bodies are more human in proportions than what one had been accustomed to in the Middle Jōmon period.

In the Kantō, where a linear approach was always more traditional, the moderately protruding abdomens may be applied lumps of clay instead of the plastically built and integrated bellies of the Chūbu. Such belly blisters frequently break off. This bump may even bear its own decoration, be grooved and appear rather vulvar. A vertical, notched ridge, the "frontal backbone", often leads into it. The back of the figure, the region most susceptible to the current décor, is covered with zoned cord-marking.

Such mask-like faces are hardly less disconcerting than the feline examples of Middle Jōmon, but not unprecocious with the turned up hands. Symbols of evil spirits have been suggested, along with facial masks and tattooing around the mouth. The Japanese term is *yamagata*, mountain-shaped, a descriptive title only. Many, from Tachigi shell-mound especially, are oval rather than pointed. They are, either oval or triangular, frightfully direct and personal, whether thought to be masked or unmasked. Masks themselves in clay have yet to be made. They may have existed in some other material. But this head shape here could well be derived from the rim-head and independent figurine head shapes of the mountains. It may therefore at this juncture have little to do with reality. ★Pl. IV ★Fig. 20

Variations on this theme have the usual breadth. Worthy of note is the faceless figure from the Fukuda shell-mound, its front and back distinguished from each other chiefly by breasts and a vertical clay strip. For a type in which so much emphasis has been placed on the face, the elimination of the face here—under the Mexican hat, other features remaining constant—seems almost a throwback to a Palaeolithic idea and may be an attempt to recapture a more basic meaning in the figurine. Fig. 21

The almost inevitable groove or vertical strip, virtually never on the back of the figurine, led Munro in 1911 to feel that the spinal cord was perhaps represented, and to think that there may have been a concept, as the Ainu have, of the spinal column as the "seat of vitality"[1]. One soon discovers a concentration of all the basic symbols on the front of the figurine; the back, once the protruding buttocks are dispensed with, serves little more than a decorative purpose. ★Cat. 14

If the triangular head is a borrowing from the mountains, it may be keeping alive a scheme which is abandoned far inland by the time the ridge-face type was current along the coast. A heart-shaped face replaces the triangle in the mountains. Proportionally large, projected forward and tilted, it is attached to the shoulder by a bridge, looking as though it were being pulled back by this loop of clay. The bridge is a handy device for picking up such a figurine and is, technically, ★Cat. 15, 16 Pl. II

Fig. 21   Faceless figurine from Fukuda shell-mound, Ōsuga village, Inashiki county, Ibaragi prefecture. H. 9.5 cm. (Enlarged.) Late Jōmon Period. Osaka City Art Museum

34

indispensable in reinforcing the neck, for few thin necks, as these are, could be expected to support the heavy, off-balance, jutting heads.

*Figs. 24, 25

Meaning here must have overruled practicality. There appears to be an absurd insistence on the projection despite the technical difficulties involved.

The inspiration for these may be attributable to large handles of spouted vessels, where bridge-like connections are well known. An occasional handle has face-like marks, but handle tops were certainly not generally thought to be suitable places for faces. Such bridges do facilitate the portability of these figurines. One from Fukushima prefecture has a head rising off a body actually shaped like a handle or a bone. A vertical hole runs through the end of the intact stump arm. Its red paint is not original and its blackening is thought to have been the result of a modern fire (of its one-time owner's house?). Simpler ones without projected head may still include the loop behind.

*Fig. 26

Fig. 22

Pl. II; *Cat. 23

The Satohara figurine's face is concave, the eyes strongly protruding, the latter probably derived from the ridge-face type. The shoulders are wide, the epaulettes handsomely spiralled. This sort of incision work exists side by side with zoned cord-marking, and appears not infrequently on the same object. The long slender waist widens out into hips, the weight then put into the arched legs and the exaggerated stance. Parallel grooves and spirals adorn the back. While the head to shoulder bridge could well have been used for suspension, special effort was made to enable the figure to stand.

*Cat. 24

It is this tilted heart-shaped face and head to shoulder bridge which connects the Satohara type with the *kokeshi* doll variety. Among the several examples of the latter, one from Inariyama shell-mound in Yokohama city is illustrated. The head rises off a roughly tubular base. Parallel lines undulating between vertical rows of holes form its decoration. Here again the breasts are small, closely spaced, hardly more than nipple size. The "skirt" forms a stand for these condensed features and must be recognized for what it is

Fig. 23

intended to be—a device to allow more permanent installation of the object.

The skirt is then the connecting link with the bell-bottomed type of the central mountains. Zoned cord-marking is a clue to the date of the latter, but there is a good chance such cord-marking hung on more tenaciously in the mountains than elsewhere, spanning the Late and Latest periods.

The powerful facial expression—as though the mouth is laboring to speak—is again rather mask-like. Deep wrinkles radiate concentrically from the mouth; the eyes may be similarly outlined. Eyebrows and nose are once again joined. The arms, turned down and under, differ from the ridge-face figurines' flared arms, and accentuate the strength of the shoulders. Holes may run through the ears and the lateral lobes behind the head; the Tokyo National Museum statuette has small holes at the ends of the arms.

The figure found at Sakai, Yamanashi prefecture, came up in 1879 in the course of road construction. At that time it was looked on as a tutelary deity and donated to the Enmeiji, a local Buddhist temple. Kanagawa forms a part of the western Kantō and is a little far from the center of manufacture of these bell-bottomed examples, but Nagayashiki, where the bell-bottomed bone container was found, is in the same prefecture.

The size of these "skirted" figures averages the largest for the Jōmon period, usually in the vicinity of 30 cm. Their relative non-portability, if compared with other figurines, is unquestionably of paramount importance in their use and thus their purpose. Found in isolation, as they are said to be—one admits to slender evidence—they may not have been employed for interior needs but rather as public fertility symbols. If one deduces this correctly, a significant step has been consolidated. It is the step of moving from private to public attention, to a more fixed "sanctuary", from individual to wider group use.

Quite provincial, but to me a related object, is a small rectangular figurine from Ibaragi prefecture in

Fig. 22 Handle-like figurine from Aburai, Adachi village, Adachi county, Fukushima prefecture. H. 18 cm. Late Jōmon Period. National Museum, Tokyo

the eastern part of the Kantō. It does stand alone, but only precariously. A neck and head protrude, the head tilted in keeping with the times. Strongly undulating lines on the back are also of this period.

By way of illustrating the deeply entrenched traditions in the central mountains, a small "animal" headed object was found with Late and Latest Jōmon pottery rather than the Middle Jōmon pottery with which one would expect it to be associated. Now missing its arms, the back is decorated with an incised, partial spiral, and it bears red paint on the shoulders, back of the head and back only. Unless by some slim chance it was preserved for long as an heirloom, it is an abbreviated continuation of the frequent Middle Jōmon animal-like type. The nose is pointed, but the eyes are horizontal; the shoulder ridges (which lead into a deep chest hole), however, are derived not from the Middle Jōmon font but from somewhat later examples.

LATE JŌMON IN THE TŌHOKU

The prefectures of Fukushima and Yamagata lie across the routes which join the Kantō with the upper Tōhoku and make up a region where influences from the central mountains, the Kantō Plain and the far north come together. These prefectures, and to some extent Miyagi, are frequently the scene of hybrid forms and, to a lesser degree, the context for types which have their own individuality.

One type which may have originated in this region and then moved north, if one may judge by finds from Aomori prefecture, is the crouching figurine; its feet are drawn back to the thighs, the shoulders hunched forward. The arms or elbows rest on or near the knees. The foremost croucher comes from the outskirts of Iizuka in Fukushima prefecture. Several features leave little doubt as to where it may be anchored in time: the triangular shape of the headgear, puffed out eyes and mouth, and the cord-marking in zones connect it with the ridge-face figurines from the shell-mounds. But the flexed position is entirely foreign to the Kantō,

and the attempt at sculpturally articulating the limbs ★Cat. 18 in so complex a pose is the earliest known effort.

Found in the orchard of the Ohara family in late 1952, it was left unrepaired for several years while considerable debate ensued as to how its parts should be assembled. As it was done, the left elbow rests on the left ★Cat. 21 knee, while the right arm reaches across and through the opening; by so doing a slight disjointing occurs at the left shoulder. The bottle-like shape at the end of the right arm has been considered by some observers to be a jar held in the hand of the figurine. This projection is identical to the other wrist and hand, however, and need be nothing more than an extremely awkward rendering arising out of sheer lack of experience in advanced modelling. I would venture the opinion that a jar-holding figurine — the Middle Jōmon pot-bellied figure notwithstanding — is out of character at this and a later date.

The Iizuka croucher has been through the repair mill, but some red paint is still to be seen around the eyes. The wide lobes on either side of the face seem to contain the outlines of ear adornments, either rings or plugs, which are on the increase in popularity after this time. The right elbow and appreciable parts of the hips are extensively restored. The much restored, rounded abdomen is unquestionably correctly rebuilt, but there is no way of knowing whether vulvar marks once existed. I presume they did not, since they rarely do in the zone cord-marked types, but it goes without saying that original clay here might provide a useful lead in the interpretation of these figures. One breast only is intact.

This particular figurine is balanced; it sits without aid. But the same cannot be said for the one from Kamegaoka in Aomori prefecture, and a second from Cat. 25 the same prefecture is too badly broken to allow satis- ★Figs. 27, 28 factory judgment in this regard. The latter two average Fig. 29 only about 11 cm., and are thus no more than half the height of the large Fukushima example. The question naturally arises as to whether they were manufactured to be shown as sitting, and therefore how successful

Fig. 23 Tubular figurine from Inariyama shell-mound, Yokohama city, Kanagawa prefecture. H. 20.4 cm. Late Jōmon Period. National Museum, Tokyo

they were in this respect. The tight cramp and the prayerful position of the Kamegaoka figurine have been mentioned as arguments in identifying these as models for simulated burials. Flexed skeletons have been found of this date, lying either on the right or left

*Fig. 30 side, the front or the back. I have elsewhere expressed an opinion that these may possibly symbolize a childbirth pose, a view which I still favor as reasonable. Nothing seems recorded on the circumstances of their discovery, leaving here an unfortunate blank where context might shed light on their meaning.

Fukushima's products frequently exhibit their own

Cat. 26 brand of originality. A flat, dark brown, squat example from Monda village bears crude, rudimentary details on a rounded face. The roughly rectangular body is simply extended to form the legs, these legs shaped by an arched crotch which is probably a distant reflection of the more stylish Tōsan figures. Front and back bear similar incising, but the punched marks are limited to the front side

*Cat. 27 only. Horizontal grooves decorate the widened back of the head. Stump arms and surface marking are primary clues as to its time of manufacture.

The upper Tōhoku still produces on a modest scale at this stage. It may be that some of the well known Kamegaoka types of pottery, so prevalent in the La-

test Jōmon period in the prefectures of Aomori, Iwate, Akita and even in Miyagi, get their start toward the close of this period. Fine, multi-directional cord-marking is characteristic, and is normally confined within wavy lines. Examples may also be typified by ridge-eyes on a faintly heart-shaped, slanted face. One recognizes here a collection of altered features introduced to the Tōhoku from farther south.

The very few figurines from Hokkaidō obligate reference to individual pieces. Too few exist to speak of types. Here again, on this developmental level, traditions moving up from farther south fill a cultural vacuum. The open, parallel grooving, in this case running over the head to the ears, vaguely suggests the bell-bottom type. Truncated arms jutting-out laterally may be fossils from the Middle Jōmon. Outlines that are almost straight or only incidentally broken, creating an uninspired shapelessness, become an increasingly northern feature. But mixed traits dominate; borrowing is rampant. From Muroran city on the northeast edge of Uchiura Bay comes the brown figurine, its body appearing flat except for a small perforated protuberance on the back of the head. A profile view, however, shows it to be curved forward from the waist down. Tiny holes run through the ears.

THE LATEST JŌMON PERIOD:

THE KANTŌ

It is not to be wondered at that recognizable types take on slightly more homogeneity toward the end of the Jōmon period. As they progress in the direction of greater complexity in shape and decoration, the accumulation of detail provides more relevant information by which they may be classified. The successors to the

*Pl. v ridge-face figures from the shell-mounds in the east Kantō are weighted down with detail.

There is a tendency to push the ridge-face figurines forward into the Latest Jōmon period, a move which I

grant as reasonable. The connections between these and the type to be dealt with are largely camouflaged by the intense interest in extravagant surface ornamentation, yet connections do exist despite the great advances made in sculptural rendition and magnified stylization.

Saitama and Ibaragi prefectures were the cradle of the type. Equipped with a proportionally large head, shoulders and small stump-arms shaped like cones protruding from under the shoulders, these figurines have a short waist which widens out sharply into angular hips, and abbreviated feet. Ridges outlining the rounded

Figs. 24, 25 Bell-shaped hollow figurine from Koshigoe, Maruko-machi, Chiisagata county, Nagano prefecture. H. 36.6 cm. Late to Latest Jōmon Period. National Museum, Tokyo

or heart-shaped face are extended to include the eye-brows, and give every indication of a greater stylization of the ridge-face scheme. The eyes and mouth are slightly concave discs of clay. Massed clay on the head may be intended to represent bound up hair, the most common arrangement rising in three peaks. Nipples are often shown along what resembles a plunging neckline, and the traditional vertical groove is occasionally present. Cord-marking fills open areas, especially the back. The flat back aids in creating an erect, unapologetic pose, the details themselves artificial and doll-like. A bizarre accumulation of projected cones and flared "wings" adorn the back of the head.

The distribution of these figurines is so close to that of the ridge-face type as to lead inevitably to the conclusion that the two types are inseparable. Although not strictly confined to shell-mounds, they are most often to be found there. Such mounds had already yielded earlier ridge-face figurines: Fukuda and Tachigi in Ibaragi, Shimpukuji and Kofukasaku in Saitama, and Yoyama in Chiba. Additional localities in greater Tokyo have contained more, and examples have been found in scattered sites as far south along the Tōkai as Toyohashi city in Aichi prefecture. A handful of the distinguishing traits are occasionally noticeable in the central mountains. The Tōhoku, on the other hand, finds very little adaptable to its needs.

Despite the patent danger of accepting too literally features which are rendered in a decorative manner, I feel that we are dealing here with figurines which reflect the way their makers beautified their heads and bodies exorbitantly, perhaps painted or tattooed their faces, wore ear plugs, and put up their hair in fanciful arrangements. Flat, broad tops, like a disc laid on the crown of the head, adorn several, calling to mind the later "mortarboard" hairdos worn by female *haniwa* figures. Costume ornaments are also implied, including the possibility of necklaces, bracelets and perhaps even anklets. Earrings are consistently worn, and many actual examples of clay earrings have been dug up in these Kantō sites and elsewhere. Such rings, at first

small solid plugs, later became substantial in size and were decorated in openwork. These were forced into a perforated lobe, illustrating a custom still known to women amongst certain tribes in southern Laos, for instance.

As has been mentioned above, conventions survive from the earlier ridge-face type, including the facial outlining, the shape taken by the shoulders and arms, *Fig. 31 and the spasmodic use of zigzags along the upper hips. The belly protrusion has become thoroughly decorative. By means of several concave segments, it projects Cat. 29 to a low-set button which might double as an umbilicus and vulva. Handsome workmanship shows the abdomen off to the best advantage.

These figurines consist of heavy, dense, usually dark brown clay. Almost all were at one time painted and many are still thickly covered with red ochre. Pl. v

The fine figurines are scarcely surpassed in artistic interest and workmanship, yet it may be precisely because of their calibre that the crude and elementary examples appear in such an extremely poor light. This is not to say that essential typological features have been sacrificed; they have been minimized by the degeneration in quality, however. One has an impression of astonishing latitude in precision amongst these figurines, as though the standard in key sites was far too high to be matched elsewhere.

It may be that the unique Janus-head with a bridge Fig. 32 connecting the foreheads is to be ascribed to this period. Its home is in the foothills, but the heavily ridged eyes and ear plugs were acquired through contacts with the eastern Kantō. An open mouth is no novelty to the lower mountains. Quite instructive is the fact that the Janus-head was recovered with at least fifty earrings *Cat. 28; Fig. 33 in a place which is thought to have been where earrings were fabricated. The earrings of this head are on conspicuous display — like a manufacturer advertizing his wares — here resembling bolts holding the back-to-back faces together. Any attempt at a mental reconstruction of the remainder of the figure is fruitless. Few other objects serve as a guide, but the loop is reminis- *Fig. 33

Fig. 26   Head and torso of figurine from Nagano prefecture. H. 13.4 cm. (Enlarged.) Late to Latest Jōmon Period. National Museum, Tokyo

cent of the much larger, Middle Jōmon, handled ceremonial vessels.

THE KAMEGAOKA TYPES

Nineteenth century discoveries at the site of Kamegaoka in northwest Aomori prefecture gave this center an early prominence and saw the dispersion of much of its material to collections in Japan and the outer world. The Kamegaoka remains were so abundant that public and private collections were able to grow fat on its yields and still leave enough to decorate the rooms of farmers in the area and stock a local museum. The influence of this locality is immeasurable, but the fact that Kamegaoka was never dug extensively by archaeologists looking for chronological sequences in the more modern years of archaeology has caused many an archaeologist to shy away from classifying its ceramics for typological purposes. Substitute sites have been less productive and the resulting typological scheme for the Latest Jōmon period in the north is, to this writer, less than satisfactory. In the process, Kamegaoka has been deprived of its significant position.

The major northern types are almost invariably represented at Kamegaoka. Two currents, the latter perhaps evolving toward the close of the period, most likely as a progressive reaction to the other, are moving on the one hand in the direction of increased size and elaboration of detail, and on the other toward strong diminution of size and reduction of detail. This latter appears to be meeting the market for the smaller, portable, amulet-size figurines. Other than this, the major northern types exhibit only secondary derivative features. Their own character is essentially so innate and intrinsic as to have obliterated most traces of potential eclecticism. But they are not to be looked on as an isolated phenomenon; rather, they must be a summation of everything the figurines have been and have meant, yet by and large they mask their origins so well as to stand independently as a powerful expression at the climax of the cult.

We may deal with four main types which I will designate for convenience as follows: (1) realistic type, a type related to the crouched figurines already referred to; (2) square-shoulder, straddle-leg type; (3) goggle-eye type, including its relatives which may have all the traits excepting the large eyes, and (4) triangular torso type.

The realistic type is an offshoot of the crouching figures which were made in the north in the Late Jōmon period. A flexed one comes from Kamegaoka. The illustrated example, however, is not quite so obviously cramped, for the knees are here bent in what may be described as a squatting position. A guess might be that it was more intended to be installed on a low pedestal. Kantō Plain features show up in the rounded shoulders, incurved arms and flared hands, but this kind of over-hanging, pendulous breast is part and parcel of a new realism which views the stomach not as an abstract mass but as a fleshy surface, while the body then conforms to surprisingly natural proportions. The head is missing; it may have offset the strangely realistic appearance — the fully crouched figurine from Kamegaoka is also headless — and one can only surmise that the head was rather close to the second type to be described, the figurines with square shoulders and wide-straddling legs. A "necklace" could pass as the hem of a costume, but the costume itself has vanished. This statuette is singularly well finished, smoothed and highly polished. Tiny indentations of cord-marking in one direction around the hips and between the legs are the work of an experienced, sure hand.

Few characteristics in earlier northern figurines have prepared us for the appearance of nudity and accompanying realism by this time. Even the new arts entering south Japan with the early Yayoi culture contain nothing which would stimulate this change. The crouched figurine, the generic type here, would hardly seem to have in it the makings for advanced realism, although it does represent a pose requiring muscular action, which is more than can be said of the stock ginger-bread types.

Fig. 27 Crouching figurine from Higashi-yuno, Iizaka-machi, Shinobu county, Fukushima prefecture. H. 21.5 cm. Late Jōmon Period. Coll. Mr. Ishichi Ohara

In any event, the two courses now comprising the epilogue to Jōmon figurines include an advance to a "horror vacui" degree of decoration, as seen especially well in the goggle-eye type, and what one believes to be a reaction to this extreme, here recognized in the realistic type.

Figurines with square shoulders and straddle legs are well known in the prefectures of Aomori, Iwate, Miyagi and Yamagata of the Tōhoku. The distribution of these (Type 2) is therefore more north and east, and extends as far south as the region of Matsushima Bay where one was found in the Satohama shell-mound. They illustrate unexpected uniformity, as though all were made within striking distance of where the type was devised; hardly a single example can be isolated as transitional or peripheral.

Hollow, made of thin walls, these figurines stand alone on large flat pads, the legs set wide apart so as to give balance. Bloated legs spread far beyond the width of the waist; quite characteristic is the way in which the hips and upper thighs are entirely merged. The hip zone is frequently cord-marked even if ornamented with parallel, shallow grooves. For all the long history of female figurines, this is the only type in which the vulva is consistently indicated. An arc above, completed by a vertical line within, is sufficient to mark the sex.

The National Museum's figurine, illustrated in color, has a crescent-shaped puncture running laterally between the legs. This is accompanied by a patch of cord-marking, leaving little doubt as to its intentions. The figurine still bears spots of red ochre on its back. A bad habit of restorers of several decades ago — modern years have not been free of their influence — shows up through their passion to produce a complete figure. Heads and bodies, whether from the same figurine or not, were found sufficiently compatible to be combined. This one would seem to be such a composite freak, for its head is a fraction too small for the proportions of this type.

The ridge-faces of the Kantō have furnished decisive traits here. Ridges forming eyebrows, eyes and mouths are heavily indented. The head may be slightly tilted; the flange-like ears bear small punctures. Out of the broad, usually squared-off shoulders drop short arms, turned in or out. In some cases they are incised at the tip to represent fingers. Indented ridges running from shoulder to shoulder and falling to the navel demonstrate a connection with the goggle-eye type. Large areas of the body and legs remain entirely undecorated, ★Cat. 31 as though having taken a leaf from the realistic type's book, and on these the dark brown clay is polished to a brilliant finish. The breasts, either as a small circular ridge, tiny lumps or slender hanging cones, are, in almost all cases, forced out to under the armpits by the plunging neckline. A feature now missing from most is the odd, ribbon-like headgear. It is, however, well within keeping of the interest shown in headgear in the Kamegaoka types and, indeed, with figurine types of the Latest Jōmon period.

The faces are snobbishly tilted, the nose up in the air. These figures stand of their own accord. If one were to be installed on a rather low place, such as an earthen platform in a dwelling, it would look forward and upward simultaneously. Installation on a low level, therefore, might be partial explanation for the common practice of setting the face at an angle.

The group of figurines which conjures up the greatest number of connotations with Kamegaoka and the ★Pl. VI north is the "goggle-eye" type. At least one spectacular example from Kamegaoka itself exceeds 30 cm. in height. The average is smaller, perhaps 15 cm. or less. Cat. 32 The large figures are hollow, and all feature heavy decoration, either as cord-marking outlined by indentations or as deep, angular cutting reminiscent of wood carving. The very few remnants of carved and lacquered wooden objects from the Jōmon period are in themselves evidence of a mature wood-working craft.

These figurines differ from Type 2 by not being designed to stand on their own, but the legs are in much the same advanced stage of elephantiasis, and are quite devoid of decoration. The smaller figurines correspond more closely to normal human proportions. The larger

Plate v Figurine from Shimpukuji shell-mound, Kashiwazaki-machi, Iwatsuki city, Saitama prefecture. H. 20.4 cm. Latest Jōmon Period. Coll. Mr. Takeo Nakazawa

ones are short and squat, and even a trifle ludicrous as though waddling along blindly due to the discomforts of heavy clothing and myopic eyesight.

Costumes are suggested here, by hem lines, cord-marking and terminal rolls of cloth. Yet accompanying these are the customary indications of breasts. There can be little question but that the colder northern climate conditioned the outlook of the Jōmon inhabitants—greater nudity is the corresponding consequence in the south—but implications of clothing are not entirely new, and the simultaneous rendering of what would seem to be both clothing and sex marks normally hidden under clothing, means nothing more than an adherence to the fundamental symbolic nature of the figurines.

The head attracts most attention. Over-size as it may be, clay is massed on top, and a huge pair of eyes virtually obliterate other facial features. Resembling goggles, these are often outlined in cord-marked ridges and tipped with small ear-lobes. The roughly triangular shape of the head may owe something to earlier types in the Kantō, but the same can be said for few other details; the irregular openwork of the headgear, for instance, is quite unlike Kantō hairdos. Contemporary vessels known as incense burners, which are capped by a cone-shaped, perforated top, are a related phenomenon. Such vessels have been found in some quantity in the north, but are not plentiful in the Kantō.

Might it be possible that this headgear actually signifies fire? The degree of responsibility on the part of the Ainu for the Jōmon culture is a fruitless argument, but it does seem quite probable that very late Jōmon in the north was largely the work of these tribal people. One is naturally at a loss to determine the antiquity of their myths, but I take it that these northern figurines are prototypes of the Ainu fire goddess. She is the deity of the hearth who protects all life, watches over the infant and guides the youth into adolescence and manhood. She is a ward to the diseased and the comforter of the dying.

A now limbless body kept by Tokyo University is a member of this group. Characteristically (for the open-headed figures) big breasted, it displays intricate decoration with curvilinear designs in cord-marking. The umbilicus (or vulva, or both) is shown by interlocked curves in low relief, with punching which specifies the pubic region. The object almost qualifies as a human-shaped vessel, but is unfortunately fragmentary. It is important as a graphic illustration of the elaboration of surface decoration of this date. Both red and white paint were used, the white sometimes appearing in a layer over the red. The brittle, thin, gray clay is typical of the rather high-fired ceramics of the Latest Jōmon period in north Japan. *Fig. 34

Shogoro Tsuboi (1863—1913), first professor to hold a chair in anthropology at Tokyo University, described these "eyes" as goggles, used in northern regions for protection against the brilliant reflection of the sun on the snow. The idea has remained steadfast, and it is difficult to challenge since such figurines are found in the north only. But one discrepancy might be the fact that snow goggles are not used in either the Tōhoku or Hokkaidō today, and the climate has not changed enough since the Jōmon period to show their use was warranted then. One fragmentary figurine (and I doubt if Tsuboi could have ever seen it), little more than a head, from Akita prefecture, now in the collection of Meiji University, is the only example which to this observer genuinely resembles slit skin pulled taut over a frame. The shades of stylization in the others reduce the likeness by differing degrees. *Fig. 35 *Fig. 36

Snow goggles may have been introduced from farther north, but into circumstances in which they were not needed, and were thus quickly incorporated into the decoration of the figurines. It seems to me, therefore, that essentially (in the Japanese islands) these were considered to be eyes, and could well have been enlarged for the purpose of communicating with the soul. The "window of the soul"[2] is known in the Far East and south Pacific region in historic times. It is often thought that the hollow figurine itself results as much through symbolic needs as for practical reasons — as a shelter for the soul. I would lean toward a symbolic interpretation of these eyes, in the belief that, in so far *Cat. 35

Fig. 28 Side-view of the crouching figurine (Fig. 27)

as stylization still outweighs literalism and has customarily done so, the fundamental symbolic nature of the figurines is never seriously challenged by acquired realistic features, for these descriptive details are quickly transformed into symbolic values[3].

The smaller figures with almost ordinary eyes have been looked on and not without good reason as made prior to the largest examples in which the eyes are especially emphasized. The culmination of the motif may have taken place right at Kamegaoka. If a convincing way of proving this could be discovered, it might be possible to rule out once and for all the snow-goggle idea, and thus consider these "eyes" as the ultimate in stylization of a rising motif[4].

★Cat. 38
Cat. 36
In general terms, the greatly reduced and simplified figures which fall within the Kamegaoka orbit are modest versions of this type. They may follow the red painting or black burnishing technique of contemporary clay vessels. Vestiges are to be seen in the bumps

Cat. 37
on the head, ridges in the place of costume edges, and the shape of the outline. Examples of these have come to light as far south as Shizuoka prefecture (which reached the southern Tōkai by skirting the Kantō), and were copied in Nagano prefecture or carried there and

★Cat. 39
to other parts of the central region. The workmanship is not necessarily crude. Some are finished in the most meticulous way.

One feature which I have already touched upon is the open-topped head. Where the headgear is intact, it is completed by a conically shaped, open-work peak.

★Cat. 40
There is frequently, however, a wide hole in the top of the head, an opening which is surrounded by an out-turned lip edged by small crescents of clay arranged like *magatama* lying on their backs.

★Cat. 41

The final type is not necessarily the last to materialize. Type 4 is distinguished primarily by a triangular

Cat. 38, 39
torso. Consistency within this type is not its crowning attribute, presumably because it has drawn, at least to some extent, on a variety of sources. Perhaps these

figurines might even be called free interpretations of the "owl-face" type of the Kantō, but sizable alterations have given them their distinctive personality. Parts of the face are customarily defined by ridges. There is the familiar tilt of the face, the usual differences in headgear, but in particular a turban-like band and a saddle-topped tube. The hips have been narrowed and the shoulders broadened, the physique assuming almost masculine proportions which are, to say the least, extraordinary in north Japan. The shoulders may be rippled, the arms nothing but small vertical cones.

The popular form of surface decoration of this type is wedge-shaped punch marks. These punctates cover the head, chest and back and both sides of the hip region of the figurine from Ikaraigaseki, Aomori prefecture. Other, almost identical examples adhere to this same decorative device. The stiff rigidity reminds one of a steel vest terminated at the shoulders by a relief spiral. Such a figure will stand alone, but its stability is at best precarious.

It is possible to include the turban wearing figures in this type by comparing the shape of the head, ridging of facial features, stump arms, outlines of the torso, and proportions of legs and feet. The group is represented in the illustrations by a remarkable example from Yamagata prefecture. The thrown-back shoulders and athletic stance, along with the strongly marked hips, follow the fundamental formula closely, yet only a small number of examples meet this standard. Heads now separated from bodies often retain enough of the turban to simplify the problems of identification.

More removed from the basic type is the Heruke (Iwate prefecture) figurine, and fragments of others. These are all less sophisticated in proportions and posture, and are rather crudely incised in lieu of cord-marking. Refinements have given way to greater vigor, now visible in the way the shoulder ridges merge with the nipples, the head is hunched forward, and heavier punctating pock-marks the surface. These still

Fig. 29 Headless figurine from Kamegaoka, Kizukuri-machi, Nishi-tsugaru county, Aomori prefecture. H. 19.6 cm. Late to Latest Jōmon Period. Institute of Anthropology, Tokyo University

Fig. 30 Detail of vessel bearing human figure, from Tokoshinai, Susono, Hirosaki city, Aomori prefecture. H. of vessel 22.5 cm. Late Jōmon Period. National Museum, Tokyo

tend to retain the triangular head, which by this time seems quite meaningless; to this is added very little extra headgear. A variation worthy of note is the clear definition of the sex triangle.

Ginger-bread types never disappear completely in the north, especially in the smaller figurines. Even an occasional large figure will be solid, in an archaic technique which is often associated with cord-marking. The large figurine from Tateishi in Aomori, averaging 2.2 cm. in thickness through the body, is cord-impressed all over, after which it was hard-baked and finished to a glossy smoothness. The massive shoulders, somewhat triangular torso and overlapped terminal curves, with correspondingly slight hip proportions, relate it distantly to the family under consideration. Eight shallow holes have been punched into the "hat" and two in the ears.

This same solid technique may be seen in a composite figurine, a much removed cousin of the straddle-leg type. It bears the last of the Kamegaoka designs, as though it had been made during a stage of crystallizing Kamegaoka patterns which are not unlike the *eau courante* motif on pottery, bronze bells and wood carving of the Middle Yayoi period, and perhaps even came under influences from regions to the south of the Kantō. The region in which it was unearthed, the modern prefecture of Fukushima, looked to other areas for its mainsprings of inspiration and then proceeded to fuse the appropriated strains.

Lastly, despite the lack of typological patterns in Hokkaidō, certain cultural pockets fashioned figurines of considerable originality and distinctiveness. Muroran is one of the most consistently thriving centers. Broad shoulders, ridges plunging to the circular navel, and wide-spread legs are akin to the goggle-eye and other Kamegaoka types. The shoulders appear to have been covered by a shawl and the hips by a skirt; these parts are then decorated with extremely deep-grooved patterns of rather irregular spirals. The figurine is hollow and is perforated with numerous holes. Five may be counted around the head, including one in the

back. Others are on the top (which is partially fragmentary), at the ends of the hands, one for the umbilicus, one between the legs, and on the soles of the feet. Fine cord-marking has been applied to the headgear, eyebrows, shoulders and hips. Traces of red paint are still to be seen around the neck.

BORROWINGS FROM THE NORTH

*Fig. 37

The fully hollow technique, in which the figurine has thin walls and three-dimensional form, was perfected in the north if not invented there and reached its finest level of development in the figurines from Kamegaoka and other sites. It is widely assumed that the technique has northern origins and that other regions attempted to reproduce it. This is a relationship which should be thoroughly reassessed in the light of what contributions these other regions may have made to the Tōhoku. Open-headed examples from the Kantō reveal walls of such figurines to be thick and uneven, far inferior to northern workmanship.

*Fig. 38

Quite remarkable for its fully hollow arms and legs is the figure from the Fukuda shell-mound. Complete except for minor breakage around the upper part of the head, its stability can be satisfactorily judged. As is, it is barely able to stand alone, but would gain stability, for instance, if the legs were filled with sand. Small holes enter the sides and crotch, and are apparently there for technical reasons. The crotch hole is not in any way connected with the decoration; one may draw from this the conclusion that little significance was placed on it. Holding to a type of ornamentation that belongs to the Late Jōmon period and even retaining the reddish-brown color of the clay, the chief criteria for placing it in the later stage are the archaic decoration and mediocre technique, the latter running a poor second to that of the north.

Figs. 40, 41

*Fig. 39

A figurine from Itakura, Gumma prefecture, is closer to the northern hollow types. The head is a full sphere, wider in diameter than the body, and open as though the top were simply sliced off. The head then actually

Cat. 42, 43

Fig. 31   Red painted figurine from Konosu city, Kita-adachi county, Saitama prefecture. H. 18.2 cm. Latest Jōmon Period. National Museum, Tokyo

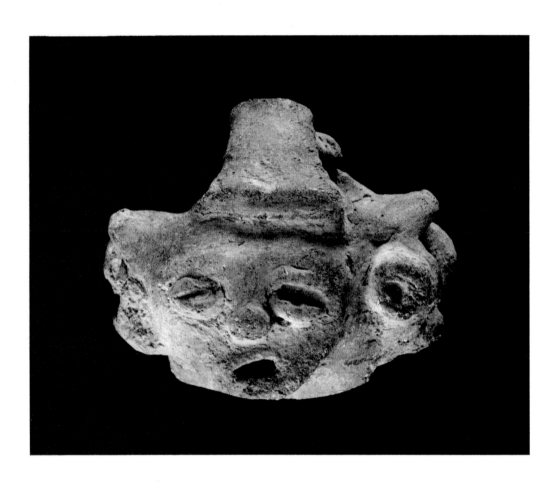

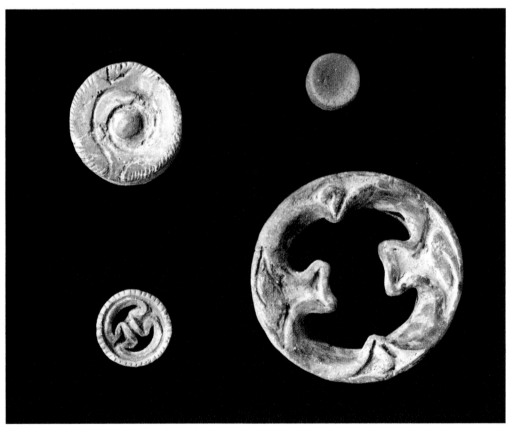

resembles a globular vessel set on a neck. The face is attached like a slanted, clay plate, the details of which — tear shedding, open mouth, ridge-eyes — are earlier characteristics, some obviously most persistent. Bulbous legs are probably made in imitation of northern types, and the neck, indented shoulder and hip ridge are based on the suggested hemlines of a garment in the Kamegaoka figurines.

Punctures make up the mouth and a small opening between the legs. Having judged such an opening in the Fukuda figure as resulting from technical considerations, consistency would call for a similar judgment on this one. It lacks all association with the decoration.

The ornamentation of rather irregular, more or less interlocked, circles might well be called a degenerate Kamegaoka design, although the same cannot be said for the decoration of the Fukuda figurine. Kamegaoka designs circumvented the eastern Kantō in their progress south, moving through inland, central valleys and reaching the west side, crossing the Chūbu and appearing as far south as the great site of Kashiwara.

Cat. 37 Northern objects which are unearthed farther south — or such close replicas as to be indistinguishable from actual northern products — are most likely to be small portable objects along the order of amulets. A handful of these appear out of their normal distributional context. In the main, these are of the highly simplified variety in which a curvilinear outline is greatly exaggerated, the front and back are almost alike, and the face is unarticulated. The object from Shiojiri, Nagano prefecture, is a good case in point; virtually indistinguishable from examples found farther north, it still claims a vestige of the thick northern costume in the radically broken outlines. These little figurines rarely exceed 6 cm. in length, and were presumably held to a small size so as to be convenient talismans, especially useful for travellers.

FIGURINES IN SOUTH JAPAN

The figurine cult was never one of major importance in west and south Japan in the Jōmon period despite good representation of the Jōmon culture in those areas. The sites are proportionally fewer in number, but numerous pottery types are known and within these, "southern" characteristics have been recognized.

Figurines appear at a late date. I know of none in southwest Japan which may with any satisfaction be called Middle Jōmon, and it is generally conceded that even those which are modelled after Late Jōmon types (largely a provincial version of the ridge-face type) are in reality later in time. Hence it is conceivable that virtually all of the southern pieces belong to the Latest Jōmon period, that is to say, to the stage immediately preceding the appearance of metal, rice and associated continental cultural introductions.

With the exception of a small number of incomplete pieces from scattered sites, the Kinki has little to offer outside of the amazing collection of scores of parts from the Kashiwara site, unearthed during the clearing of an athletic field. The Kashiwara Shrine forms the focus of ancient cult practices which were elevated in national significance during the Meiji period and greatly intensified during WW II. Behind the promotion of Kashiwara as a national shrine lay efforts to bring the origins of the state into sharper perspective and strengthen the ancient legends of the establishment of the first emperor's palace in the vicinity. A date equivalent to 660 B.C. was arrived at for the foundation of the kingdom by adding up the recorded lengths of reign of the long series of early emperors which appears in the *Nihon Shoki* (Chronicles of Japan, written in A.D. 720). A natural hill, Unebiyama, was equated with Emperor Jimmu's tomb. Next to this, during the Meiji period was built an enormous shrine in an attractive

Fig. 32 Double-faced head from Location 2, Ikebukuro Ōhana, Sakai, Fujimi-machi, Suwa county, Nagano prefecture. H. 4.8 cm. Late to Latest Jōmon Period. Idojiri Archaeology Museum

Fig. 33 Clay ear-rings from Location 2, Ikebukuro Ōhana, Sakai, Fujimi-machi, Suwa county, Nagano prefecture. D. of largest 5.9 cm. Late to Latest Jōmon Period. Idojiri Archaeology Museum

style, probably on the site of a much smaller one. Emotional expression projected new meaning into the area during the last war, and Kashiwara became a mecca of pilgrimage second only to Ise in the Kinki region.

There is little question but that this huge yield of figurines which includes rather crude animals in clay and was brought to light with great quantities of pottery and a number of wooden frames for wells, the latter most likely of an early historic date, signifies the area had a unique cultic importance. The wells were sacred, employed as the recipients of offerings. Ritual at Kashiwara is obviously an ancient practice; its inception is to be traced back at least as far as the last millenium B.C.

The figurines at Kashiwara may have served as votive offerings, made in large amounts over a considerable period of time. The ridge-face type is not uncommon, although its details are abbreviated and often feebly defined. The extent of Kantō influence is evident in these. Far more popular, however, are the plaque-like types in which the over-all shape is rectangular with rounded corners and the top is terminated in a head-shaped projection. Surface ornamentation is deemphasized; it may consist only of simple grooving. The physical traits of the figurines are shared by the pottery vessels: brown to gray colored surfaces, often smoke blackened, and heavily grit-tempered, coarse clay. Decoration on vessels includes several simplified versions of Kamegaoka designs, found here at their most distant point of diffusion from the Tōhoku cradle.

A feature common to many figurines is a depression in the lower back in the region of the buttocks. Middle Jōmon examples in the Chūbu occasionally have a slight hollow above the sharply projected posterior, but a connection between the two areas in this regard is doubtful. For a feature which runs so contrary to nature's endowments, a local reason may be necessary. The pendulous breasts of the illustrated example are atypical; simple little bumps usually serve the purpose. Broken examples often reveal a technique of inserting

pegs of limbs into sockets, a technique known in the Chūbu, where it was used (only rarely) in the application of breasts, to the torso. Connections with the central mountains may be closer than would at first appear. Cat. 20

The single full figurine from Kashiwara — there are complete plaque-like examples — is the most realistic, but is in all likelihood a composite figure, the handiwork of an ambitious restorer many years ago who put the head of another (probably larger) figurine to this body. This was not an uncommon habit among early and even later but rural restorers. Made of the usual coarse, gritty clay, the surface is hard and has a rare glossiness for objects from this site. Cat. 44

Farther south, the scattered nondescript fragments in the Inland Sea suggest less the existence of local practices of the cult than they do the rather intermittent intrusions by practicioners from farther north.

These intrusions are more apparent where remains of figurines from about a dozen sites in Kyūshū bear both southern features (the effect of nudity, well formed breasts, hollowed out buttocks) and northern features (shoulders and arms a continuous curve, protruding abdomen, shaped legs). A strange array came from the Mimanda site in Kumamoto. Ridge-faces are represented; the back of the head may be scooped out in a way not infrequent in the Kantō. One of the most distinctive is a partial figurine of dark, highly polished clay with pot-belly and single leg. It bears hatching along a fine line, entirely around the top of the legs and from navel to crotch. The buttocks are a concave oval. The remaining fragments from Mimanda are relatively characterless, being simplified pieces which are difficult to associate with other types and have few distinguishing features of their own. The site is of supreme importance because of its yield, but the context of these discoveries was never adequately published. *Fig. 42 / Cat. 45

The Nakatsu Minami High School in Nakatsu city of Ōita prefecture was the scene of a discovery of undecorated figurines on its land, of rough surface, unsophisticated workmanship, nude, with bust of sizable proportions and a larger than navel-sized abdomen *Fig. 42; Cat. 46

Fig. 34 Hollow figurine from Monō county, Miyagi prefecture. H. 26.2 cm. Latest Jōmon Period. Coll. Mr. Masasuke Kusumoto

*Fig. 44 protrusion. The results are relatively close to reality, but it must be sheer accident that a somewhat similar stage was reached by another type in north Japan at the close of the Jōmon period.

Decoration on southern pottery tends to be modest and sparing. It is not unexpected that a similar economy of expression appears in the figurines. They are suitably adjusted to a warmer climate and have been used to illustrate the most elementary symbols of the cult by avoiding all the surface falderal so prevalent in the Kantō and especially the Tōhoku. I take these plain, simply descriptive, pregnant female figures as the truly characteristic type of Kyūshū, largely uninfluenced by the interest in surface trivia which dominates the making of late figurines elsewhere.

STONE AND HORN FIGURINES

Stone figurines do not follow the types in clay as closely as one would suppose, presumably due to the difficulty in rendering so much superficial detail in stone. The relatively few stone figurines which are known are largely from late periods and hail from the north. In particular it was the Kamegaoka clay types which supplied the local inspiration, and the result is rather like the much abridged clay examples.

Stone plaques at times show impressive workmanship, yet by and large, even in sandstone, the novelty of carving the material seems not to have been fully overcome. Always there is greater abstraction, as may be illustrated by the treatment of the goggle-eyes, the chief feature of the type which lent itself most, as difficult as it was to reproduce in stone.

Geological conditions tend to destroy most materials in Japan; sculptures of the human form are quite rare in materials other than clay. Stone figures comprise only a handful. Two tiny horn figures may represent how another material responded to the current modes in clay. Traces of a triangular head are here.

Carved in openwork, the smaller has far more articulation in the arm and fingers suggested on a hand than is customarily accorded a clay figure. I assume the feet were turned out to be seen in profile. The larger of these two from the Numazu shell-mound in Miyagi prefecture is considerably more abstract. It was armless, and is so shaped as to imply it may have been intended as an ornamental comb or body decoration.

CLAY PLAQUES AND SIMILAR OBJECTS

Flat clay objects with regular contours, describable as plaques, appear almost as early as the figurines themselves, and develop in quantity in direct proportion to the increase in size and fragility of the figurines. There is thus an evolution which parallels the figurines themselves, and can be well recognized by the similarity in decoration.

In these plaques, all indications of human features are subordinated to the regular outlines of the object. Plaques may be round, circular, oval, oblong and rectangular. Square ones are rare and, to the best of my knowledge, multi-sided examples do not exist. In the category of figurines, I have included simply-shaped objects with any one or more of such features as a projected head, narrowed waist and contour breaks at the shoulders. On the other hand, plaques may bear the notched Kamegaoka outline or the ragged Tōhoku edge, for neither of these break the essential shape of the object.

Plaques find themselves caught up in the competition for the bigger and the better, and their makers often succumbed to the same temptation which saw enlarged figurines (for whatever purpose) being produced toward the close of the Jōmon period. They cannot, therefore, be looked on as exclusively small-scale substitutes for the magnified figurines—a purpose for which smaller figurines always did exist—but

Fig. 35   Hollow figurine from Ishinadate, Rokugo-machi, Senboku county, Akita prefecture. H. 17.8 cm. Latest Jōmon Period. National Museum, Tokyo

Fig. 36   Hollow figurine from Sarugamori, Tokoshinai, Susono, Hirosaki city, Aomori prefecture. H. 12.7 cm. Latest Jōmon Period. Institute of Anthropology, Tokyo University

they obviously were more easily manipulated than the larger, hollow figures and, being solid, offered the advantage of greater durability.

Scores of plaque-like objects have come to light, from the simplest of discs to the most intricately and magnificently decorated large rectangles or ovals. These objects readily fall into three categories: (1) examples with clearly defined human faces and at times more elaborate body features; (2) examples on which only eyes and perhaps a nose appear, all other details fused with the abstract decoration occupying the surface; in some cases, the entire plaque may more or less resemble a face, and (3) examples which carry only abstract decoration; all human features, if they existed, are swallowed up by the ornamentation.

The first type reproduces facial characteristics of figurines of a corresponding area and time in which they are found. The second type is closely associated with the goggle-eye Kamegaoka figurines. The third type, not unlike the first, has wide representation.

Examples are known where perforations resemble eyes, spirals mark the location of breasts or navel, and a hole indicates the position of the umbilicus or the vulva. All of these are more suggestive than specific. But appearing almost without fail is a sharply defined backbone line. The most finely executed plaques adhere faithfully to the contemporary style of pottery decoration, at a time when the ornamentation techniques had been remarkably refined in the Kantō and Tōhoku.

The increase in number of plaques as one proceeds north is phenomenal. Stone plaques follow suit, and are understandably more prevalent than stone figurines. Despite more experience with the simpler plaques, it still remains a recognized fact that stone carving was never Jōmon man's *forte*. Uneven incising techniques and flat relief are customary, the latter perhaps handed down from the Late Jōmon period in the Kantō. The outlines of the relief in either technique reveal clearly the time and approximate provenience of the plaque's manufacture.

HOLLOW "PLAQUES", TURTLE-LIKE OBJECTS, AND MUSICAL INSTRUMENTS (?)

As might be expected, once the hollow figurine was produced, the hollow "plaque" appears. Technical demands required perforations in the walls as they had in the figurines. The distribution of such objects is not confined entirely to the Tōhoku; an occasional one is unearthed farther south, in a range much like that of the hollow figurines. ★Fig. 45 ★Fig. 46 ★Fig. 47

Often taking strange, nebulous shapes, they are, so to speak, neither fish nor fowl. The arched, decorated top assumes some resemblance to the shell of a turtle and has thus lent the name "turtle-shape" to the greatest number of this type. Examples in the Kantō may have "fins" comparable to projections on pottery vessels of the Angyo types of the Latest Jōmon period, or they may have ragged edges composed of tiny lobes, similar to the ornamental rims on vessels of the Kamegaoka types in the north. These excrescences seem to add to their turtleness (and reduce their value as hand-warmers!), yet even these, and this includes the large ones of 15 cm. or more in length, require some exercise of the imagination to believe that they are more than only accidentally reminiscent of turtles. ★Pl. VII ★Cat. 47 Cat. 48

The majority have a pair of holes, one in one end, the other along the top toward the opposite end. These meet technical requirements, but their fixed relative position indicates they are there for a functional reason. This arrangement allows these objects to serve as a whistle with varying degrees of success. Figs. 48, 49

The limitations as a musical instrument are obvious — as they were for any instrument of considerable antiquity in its initial stages — but conceivably they filled a need in a ritual of limited scope. To these might be related the clay "rattle" from Yamanashi prefecture, a pottery ball, now repaired and filled with nine (according to Mr. Shimada, the organizer of the collection) small pebbles. At least one other rattle has been reported, this one from the Musashi Plain west Cat. 49

Fig. 37   Figurine from Tateishi, Ajigasawa-machi, Nishi-tsugaru county, Aomori prefecture. H. 19.3 cm. Latest Jōmon Period. Osaka City Art Museum

of Tokyo, and such objects possibly served as percussion instruments in ceremonial activities.

Cat. 50   The oddest of these hollow zoomorphs comes from the Shimonumabe shell-mound in Ōta ward of greater Tokyo. Made of brown clay with large blackened areas and composed of thick walls, it is both beaked and finned, perforated at the ears, peaked at the head, and pointed at the tail. Pointed tails are not unknown in other examples, but whether it should fly, swim or

*Cat. 51   crawl (or perhaps all three) is a moot question. No one can say whether it is going or coming, standing or lying. It is clearer what it is not than what it is; it makes no noise. Its ear holes might allow it to be suspended, or perhaps to be supported in a net.

MASKS

The mask-like character of so many figurines' faces has introduced us gently to the existence of actual masks by the Late Jōmon period, fashioned in a variety of sizes in clay. The relatively few which are known are almost exclusively from the Tōhoku, but a simple mask without surface decoration, approximately the size of a human face, came to light in Nagano prefecture. Most, however, belong to the Kamegaoka

Fig. 50   manifestation of Latest Jōmon, in a size considerably less than that usable by an adult.

The range of approach is rather broad. The finest, preserved in the collection of the Anthropological

Fig. 51   Institute of Tokyo University, is equal to any other work done in the north. It bears angularly-cut relief, in cord-marked, spiral-like and sinuous patterns, all elegantly carved in the habitual way. Only the nose, here projected, may be said to have received different attention because of the nature of the object.

The masks are roughly cone-shaped, concave in the back and perforated near the ears. It is conceivable that the largest were actually worn. Possibly they became more symbols of wooden ones which may have been

*Cat. 54   in use. The Ainu of the Kurile Islands carved masks of wood, although generally bare of decoration. In any event, Ryūzō Torii was probably correct when he assumed the custom of making them among the Ainu was most likely very ancient[5]. It seems feasible to me that the masks were utilized in mimicry antics, associated with an early shamanistic-like ritual, the clay models then used as signs of the trade, kept by the actor.

A number of clay noses and isolated ears have been found in approximately the same distribution as the masks. These are close to human size and may have merely substituted for full masks. They are well formed, normally devoid of decoration, and are widened out in the upper part toward the eyebrows. A back view of the concavity of the nose appears strikingly vulvar, and some observers have voiced the feeling that these objects are strongly phallic, although no special pains seems to have been taken to provide this effect. Most have several perforations by which they could be attached to the face or to the remainder of a mask in some other material. I suspect that the final effect, however, was simply achieved by painting the exposed parts of the face.

ANIMALS

The subhuman to zoomorphic nature of the figurines— a sort of interlude in itself—disappeared with the close of the Middle Jōmon period. The customary bipeds of later periods prove this beyond a shadow of a doubt, despite occasional resort to coarse and debased human features. Genuine quadrupeds are a late phenomenon, and are in no way related to the periodic suggestions of lower life which have already been noted on pottery vessels—shapes that resemble the head of a bird, the head of a snake, or even rim configurations carried as far as to suggest the head and snout of a wild boar.

The quadrupeds are drawn directly from the close daily contacts Jōmon man had with animals. The majority are boars, bears and dogs. Deer are surprisingly absent. Wild boar may outnumber the others. Of several known, an average might be estima-

Fig. 38   Figurine with traces of red paint, from Hihara, Mishima village, Ōnuma county, Fukushima prefecture. H. 27.4 cm. Latest Jōmon Period. National Museum, Tokyo

ted at around 7 cm. in length. Dogs were certainly popular, and are generally smaller in size. Bears fit well into the northern cults. The monkeys, one from Aomori and a head from Miyagi, are rather realistically portrayed.

Animals were rarely manufactured outside the Tōhoku with the chief exception being the extraordinary Kashiwara site. Often rather crude, they are frequently so roughly modelled as to range from difficult to impossible to identify. Among those in the twilight zone are the turtle-shaped objects already mentioned. One is called mole-shaped; the long, rocket-shaped kind with fins and snout is called "praying mantis-shaped."

Unless deer are too poorly rendered to be recognizable, deer do not appear because they were not the game in the north when clay models were in vogue. The wild boar, whose meat was prized but the hunt of which called for the greatest feats of skill, may have been reproduced with due respect for its ferocity, as though behind the production lay the expection of gaining a psychological advantage over the beast, as well as replenishment of the species. The stones in Akita prefecture which bear engravings of salmon might at first seem beyond the scope of comparison at this particular point, yet these too may have been carved for

much the same purpose. As a symbol of a magical-control-cult, however, little evidence remains today to suggest that it was very widespread. If it existed in more elaborate form, it probably did so in markings on rocks or on the ground which were unable to survive the passage of time. ★Fig. 38 ★Fig. 52

Bears were hunted and eaten. The Ainu bear cult of today is a major tourist attraction. It may have little more meaning than financial gain at the present, but it involves a three-day ceremony after which the bear is finally slaughtered. The killing of the animal is looked on as rendering it a service, one of releasing it from its captivity of this world and dispatching it to a superior world where it can join other higher spirits in surroundings far more attractive than any this earth has to offer. The ceremony is of uncertain antiquity. ★Figs. 48, 49 ★Fig. 50

The house dog was already a family pet by the Middle Jōmon period, as is proved by the many meticulously buried canine bones in shell-mounds. It was a small, family-type dog, like the modern Shiba, adequate for guarding the premises and intelligent enough to be trained for hunting purposes. A little clay replica of a dog was found in Iwate prefecture. Its erect neck and head are remarkably descriptive despite the rudimentary nature of the modelling. ★Fig. 53

Plate VI Figurine from Tokomai, Morita village, Nishi-tsugaru county, Aomori prefecture. H. 19.8 cm. Latest Jōmon Period. National Museum, Tokyo

V. THE MEANING OF THE FIGURINES

Interpretations of the Jōmon figurines have passed through every conceivable gamut, from the first report to the Anthropological Society made by Kotaro Shirai in 1877 to major recent studies by Teruya Esaka[6] and Yoshimaro Noguchi[7]. The customary nineteenth century ideas are embodied in Shirai's analysis. The figurines could be toys used by children, decorative objects produced for their artistic value, or statuettes fashioned to represent the higher spirits. It was another twenty years before the suggestion of amulets was recorded, this by Entaro Ōno just before the turn of the century[8]. In 1911 Munro called them effigies of the dead in his massive study, *Prehistoric Japan*[9]. Ryūzō Torii, whose anthropological surveys led him far afield, spoke of them in the language of the European Neolithic, and viewed them as symbols of the Mother-goddess, associated with earth cults and the procreative processes of nature[10]. Ichirō Yawata harks back to Ōno's concept of their use as amulets with magical meaning, noting especially the intentionally broken examples as probably employed in sympathetic magic to cure diseased portions of the body. He points to the persistence of the practice of fondling an amulet while praying for recovery, or for preservation from disasters. As Mother-goddesses, he suggests they could be considered apart from agriculture, for female figurines are known to have been made by certain food-gathering societies. Modern uses of talismans might be the survivors of the clay and stone amulets of ancient times, then as now the simplified forms of the figurines[11].

Nishioka's study of phallicism has led him to look on the figurines as part of a general early phallic cult[12] and, indeed, I would comment that the shape of several when seen from the reverse side is obviously intended to be phallic. There are decorated clay phalli, which to this observer are complementary objects designed to express the male generative force at a time when the society becomes more settled and the operative principle of the male is more clearly understood and accepted.

Teruya Esaka has for the first time made an extensive and well documented study of most of the known figurines and all related objects. Largely descriptive, one point of note is his insistence on the female character of all the figurines, adopting the attitude that the figurine became so much a part of custom that its very nature and meaning were taken for granted. Careful delineation of the sex features was not necessarily a prime requisite[13].

Yoshimaro Noguchi has rendered the service of surveying all written theories and stressing the validity of those which argue for the use of the figurines as talismans, primarily as charms in the healing of disease, and as representatives of the Mother-goddess[14].

I have already outlined the circumstances of the finds, and have devoted some attention to careless disposals and careful deposits, to recurrent emphases and the frequent subordination of sexual features. We have touched on obesity, mask faces, headgear, eyes, surface decoration, and have described technical changes from the solid to the hollow types. Additionally, we

Fig. 39 Figurine with traces of red paint, from Japan Ironworks Co., Rinsei-chō, Muroran city, Hokkaidō. H. 19.0 cm. Latest Jōmon Period. National Museum, Tokyo

have considered the abandonment of the early sub-human features in favor of fundamental anthropomorphic characteristics, the attempts to make standing figures, and the increase in quantity in correspondence with the augmentation of other ritual equipment.

These modern theories are not in disagreement with each other. To these I would add a further one, as well as a judgment as to where the emphases lie and at which junctures wider uses are being made of the figurines. My interpretations are prejudiced by a belief in the practice of a minor form of agriculture during and after the Middle Jōmon period; that is, not necessarily widespread nor continuous farming, but an exploitation of the cycles of nature which accounted for the transformation that came over the religious practices of the time. It is a point with which few Japanese archaeologists will agree.

There is little room for argument over the use of the figurines as fertility symbols. Breasts are generally indicated on the oldest examples, witnessing to the birth of female features as the fertility idea first takes material form. The Middle Jōmon types, in which a distended abdomen merges into broad hips and buttocks are stressed by quaint conventions, are procreative symbols, clearly illustrating human pregnancy. Others, not indubitably female, lacking all but the general outline of a human figure, might be used as a case in point for argument against the Mother-goddess theory. I concur with Esaka—not in the sense that all are inevitably female, but that definition of the distinguishing organs eventually seemed unnecessary. This trend is coupled with the rise in importance of the cult in coastal areas, in which one sees a new regard for facial details and surface ornamentation. In one respect the diffusion of the cult is coordinated with a generally progressive stylization which accompanies an eventual addition to the culture of other fertility symbols.

The fertility figurine, as it assumes the role of Mother-goddess, does so not only for human increase but for all aspects of nature. Upon the replenishment of the animal and vegetable life depends the survival of the human race. Hunting societies devised magical rituals which were carried out prior to the pursuit, and their concern with the depletion of stocks and nature's ability to rejuvenate itself was registered in several ways. Early man's intimacy with nature made him feel a part of it. He could not separate his survival from nature's productivity, hence his constant attempts to gain nature's aid in the endless battle for existence.

The arguments both pro and con the presence of a simple form of agriculture in Jōmon Japan are as yet inconclusive. This is partially due to the limited ecological studies in and around archaeological sites and the lack of sifting of the soil for the required evidence. In the lower mountains where agriculture is most likely to have developed, conditions are the poorest for the preservation of perishable evidence. The profusion of sea foods along the coast did not encourage the search for additional forms of subsistence, and the abundance of animal life in north Japan also provided less incentive for the pursuance or discovery of auxiliary food sources. The remains in the Jōmon sites seem to suggest less plentiful game in southwest Japan which, if true, may explain why sites are proportionally less dense in that direction.

The appearance of extensive communities, or at least spots occupied for a considerable length of time; figurines; stone "clubs"; large clay vessels, a few obviously for ritual use; associated ritual objects of undetermined use; rim heads; pottery painting; suggestive decorative patterns on pottery, most of which seem to appear about the same time, are all too coincidental to this observer not to be a part of a substantial change in the mode of living[15]. It may be that an introduced form of agriculture was slowly but surely dissipated in the context of rich natural resources, so that the total Middle Jōmon manifestation as it appears in the lower mountains had no particular reason for diffusing or being accepted fully by neighboring people.

I grant that the steatopygous characteristics of Middle Jōmon figurines are thought of as being as-

Figs. 40, 41   Hollow figurine from Fukuda shell-mound, Ōsuga village, Inashiki county, Ibaragi prefecture. H. 27.1 cm. Late to Latest Jōmon Period. Coll. Mr. Yoshio Taniguchi

sociated with a primarily hunting society and one which comes into close contact with animals. They might well be an offshoot from some remnant Palaeolithic ideas, although the source is most difficult to trace. The only other arts remotely resembling a Palaeolithic type are the stones in north Japan, centered in Akita prefecture, on which salmon have been outlined. Through the presence of pottery in the vicinity, these are believed to have been engraved around the Late Jōmon period, although a later date is quite conceivable. They have to do with seasonal catches of fish, and are quite likely the material remains of a ritual held prior to the major fishing season, as the salmon swim upstream to spawn.

Settled people became group conscious through problems arising out of land division and claims, and express their reliance on or expectation of benefits from natural forces. As the male of the species participated more in local activities and in manual labor, and took a part in group planning, there is a corresponding recognition of his role in the fertility processes and the inevitable appearance of symbols to show this. These male symbols illustrate the awareness of this partnership, but do not supplant the female symbols—the maternal is the permanent life-giver—and reveal the understanding early agricultural people had of the complementary character of the creative powers.

The appearance of stone phallic symbols with the Middle Jōmon figurines is strong testimony for the feeling of a close bond between the inhabitants and the soil. It may mean an initial broadening of the fecundity concept into a concern not only for human fertility and off-spring but for increase throughout all of nature. The preoccupation with daily subsistence leads to attempts to relieve the difficulties and tensions brought on by childbirth and the uncertainties and fears associated with death. Even a minor form of cultivation directed attention vividly to the way the earth gave up its fruits for human consumption. A planting rite was both a return to the soil of its yield and an invitation to Mother-earth to repeat this yield. Death and burial rituals came to be associated with all forms of increase, and the fading of vegetation in the winter followed by its re-emergence in the spring doubtless greatly encouraged the notion of an after-life with accompanying attempts at preserving the human remains[16].

The archaeological evidence might therefore be used to imply these figurines were not only aids in childbirth but broader symbols of nature's production at this stage in cultural development. The Hiraide house containing the community's figurines may of course suggest its occupation by a privileged person, but is more suggestive to me of its use as a parturition hut, employed for childbirth purposes. There are the phalli, the standing stones, the rim heads (grain protectors?), the various ceremonial vessels—all found in the sizable Middle Jōmon communities. The ritual had many facets and, in the desire to foster fecundity, several types of objects were brought to play on the major objective.

The distended abdomen soon defers to other features in the Late Jōmon period, but is not yet dismissed as it was in the north. It is frequently a neat hemisphere only, when seen in the eastern coastal region to which it was transmitted from its inland source. Supplementing the types of this Late Jōmon period are the crouching figurines. While these may perhaps be childbirth symbols, they could well have been designed for simulated burials, although nothing is known in detail of the circumstances of their finds. But special deposits are acceptable evidence of this facet of the total cult, and flexed human burials are a mode of interment well attested to by this time in the shell-mound environment. Simulated burials have usually been ruled out on the assumption that the Jōmon society was non-agricultural. I have, however, taken the accumulated evidence as indicative of a simple form of plant cultivation. If these are simulated burials, advances made in the funer-

Fig. 42   Figurine from Kashiwara Park, Kashiwara city, Nara prefecture. H. 8.3 cm. Latest Jōmon Period. Yamato History Museum
Fig. 43   Stone head and torso of figurine, from Komukai, Nanbu-chō, Sannohe county, Aomori prefecture. W. 11.9 cm. Latest Jōmon Period. Coll. Mrs. Misao Takamatsu

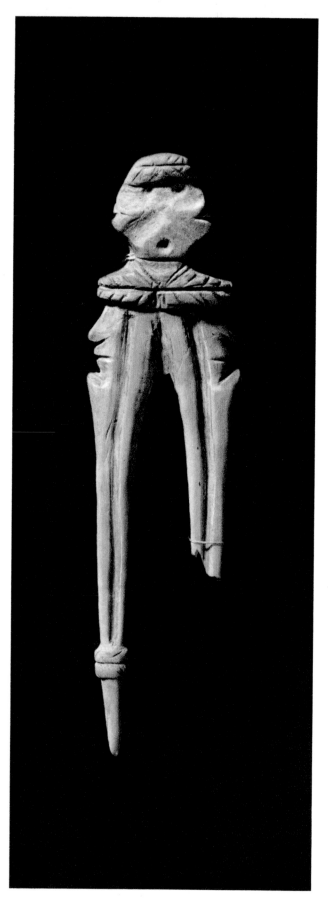

ary ritual have added connotations of fertility. The crouching figurines have prominent breasts and retain considerable emphasis on the abdomen.

I suspect that, along with the observance of the custom of simulated burial, a parallel use of figurines is made in practices utilizing sympathetic magic. Most of the stone-surrounded figurines and the greatest number of red painted examples belong to the Latest Jōmon period. It may be during this stage that the notion takes genuine hold. The distinctions in use to which the figurines were put is by no means sharp, but it is doubtful whether the obviously pregnant types were involved in practices designed to check disease or forestall dire calamities. One means of releasing the spirits trapped within a diseased individual could be carried out through breaking the figurine at a prescribed point. Yet simple breaking alone may not have always sufficed. The case of the separated figure, the leg found about four kilometers distant from the body, might be construed to mean that a complete separation of the parts was more desirable. Paper objects, incidentally, take the place of ancient figurines at Shinto shrines today, and are employed in similar ways in efforts to cure the sick.

The data speaks for a spread of this practice along with simulated burials in the last millennium and a half of the Jōmon period. Secondary burials are even more in evidence during these late centuries. Bones bearing red ochre, in particular bones of the upper half of the bodies of children in north Japan, demonstrate at a minimum a belief in the preservative agency of the paint and its similarity to blood, and at a maximum the life-giving nature of the substance which it signifies and some vague hope for rejuvenation. Burial in shell-mounds, in the *débris* of the staple itself, was restitution to nature and a primary route to renewed life.

The general absence of grave-goods means the Jōmon people had scant idea of an after-life. An occasional stone on the head or the chest or near the remains infers Jōmon man registered his fear of the dead in ways best known to him—bequeathing this fear perhaps as a legacy to the Ainu—but he did not normally break human bones nor did he intentionally dismember them. Cremation, which is often associated with sky cults of the sort represented in Japan by the Sun Goddess, does not actually come in until patronized by Buddhism around the eight century.

The only recognizable collective burials of the Jōmon period, in the sense of being confined within clearly defined zones, are the stone circles of north Japan. Such community cemeteries presumably attracted seasonal gatherings for the celebration of fertility rites. The arrangement of the stones, the standing menhirs and their relationship to the circles, and the female figurine found among the stones at Ōyu, point to community projects designed for continuing community ritual use. The "maypole" dance participated in by Izanagi and Izanami, the propagators of the Japanese islands according to the earliest mythology, after which a Pillar of Heaven was erected in the center of the land, an island in the eastern part of the Inland Sea, immediately comes to mind when considering these circular groups of stone.

Farther north are the Kamegaoka vessels with phallic spouts, and the small pointed stone shafts with carved heads, perhaps employed in planting and fertilizing rites.

Major advances were made on two inter-related fronts toward the end of the Jōmon period: the figurines were considerably enlarged in size, and certain types were made to stand alone. Despite increasing interest in pure ornamentation, the specificity of the detail gives them real personality. Conceivably they were thought to have their own soul, the opening in the top of the head (common to one type only) permitting the spirit free access to his abode. The later idea of the Shinto shrine—empty and void, but habitable—is not so different from this. The large figurines, beyond

Fig. 44 a and b   Carved horn figures, the larger with traces of red paint, from Numazu shell-mound, Inai village, Ojika county, Miyagi prefecture. H. of larger 8.2 cm. (Enlarged.) Latest Jōmon Period. Coll. Mr. Masasuke Enomoto
Fig. 45   Fragmentary plaque from Yumada, Iwai-machi, Sashima county, Ibaragi prefecture. L. 11.3 cm. Late Jōmon Period. Institute of Anthropology, Tokyo University

the stage of personal amuletic use, are on a household scale and, when compared to Yayoi period vessel heads, may be said to be on the threshold of an even broader, community-wide significance.

Technical changes alone would not have accounted for the plasticity of the later figurines. Rather, the demand for new uses forced technical improvements to meet these needs. The bell-bottomed figures, which rank as the largest all-round type, are said to be found in isolation to other artifacts. There is more than an outside chance that they acted as tutelary spirits at a primitive sanctuary, to which individuals and perhaps groups of people were attracted who had specific fertility desires. In respect to these, we might recall the one utilized as a bone container, and remind ourselves of the modern shrines scattered over the country at which barren women have habitually worshiped.

Human-headed vessels or even vessels bearing a full human form on the vessel's wall may render special protective services to whatever contents they may hold. Later, in the Yayoi period, such examples are known to have borrowed their inspiration from Jōmon prototypes; they were in all likelihood guardian spirits of grain. The nebulous archaeological evidence from the Middle Jōmon period and the following centuries still discourages a similar interpretation at this time.

The fully standing figure is on a scale too large to be exclusively personal. It is comparable to the penates, the household deities, and may be the origin of the Ainu guardian, the goddess of the hearth. Superficial features must reflect, however hazily, certain types of costumes, ways of putting up the hair, styles in body ornaments and practices of decorating the face. The *haniwa* of the Protohistoric period provide proof for this, although in a stage of much more generalized symbolism. I would suggest the existence of evidence for masked dances, fancifully costumed performers, exotic coiffures, necklaces, and earrings, as seen in the Latest

Jōmon examples chiefly, and in particular those from the Kantō, but almost equally so in examples from the north. Still living are Ainu women who were tattooed around the mouth in their adolescent days. The figurines imply considerable antiquity to the practice, and one may trace at least face painting if not scarification in the human-headed vessels of the Yayoi period, and certainly face painting in the Tomb period. There was probably no break in the continuity of facial decoration in ancient times, and Japan presumably shared a practice not uncommon among primitive peoples.

Masks, separate noses and ears, although life-size, are not in themselves very practical. Nevertheless, they suggest disguises used by actors in the ritual. The inland, heart-shaped faces sport large noses (i.e. the Satohara figurine with arched legs), but the coastal, triangular-headed ones normally do not, in spite of the fact that both areas produced figurines which look masked. These face pieces added the grotesque element, successfully achieved in the later Buddhist period dances, but, in contrast to other countries, they are entirely human and are not in any way intended to identify the actor with a bird or animal. Were one dealing with the Yayoi and Early Tomb periods, the religious outlook would certainly be called shamanistic; at this stage its designation is less sure, but regardless, there is little evidence in Japan of the use of animal or bird costumes, a case in which Japan stands in contrast to Siberia, south China and southeast Asia.

By way of summarizing the significance of the figurines, I view them as symbols of the all-embracing, procreative powers of nature, produced and used to effect more plentiful natural increase. An incipient form of agriculture may have given rise to their proliferation in the Middle Jōmon period. Where the pregnancy of the figurine is most apparent, human fertility and childbirth were of primary concern. When specific reproductive features are diminished, human

Fig. 46   Plaque with eyebrows and nose, from Tomioka village, Shibata county, Miyagi prefecture. L. 8.2 cm. Late to Latest Jōmon Period. Institute of Anthropology, Tokyo University

Fig. 47   Stone plaque from Numazu shell-mound, Inai village, Ojika county, Miyagi prefecture. L. 14.5 cm. Latest Jōmon Period. Coll. Messrs. Genshichi Endō and Soshichirō Mōri

Figs. 48, 49   Hollow clay object in turtle-shape from Tōhoku. L. 8.5 cm.; maximum thickness 2.7 cm. Latest Jōmon Period. Coll. Dr. Sueji Umehara

illnesses were to be alleviated; but reduction to conventions is an ever-present tendency and may show the figurines to have become part of a way of life in which they express less individual but more collective faith in their effectiveness. In any event, the simulated burials, more common toward the end of the Jōmon period, should be interpreted in greater breadth, as indicative of ceremonial interment, as though of a spirit, to further appease the powers of nature, make restitution and encourage greater abundance.

Fig. 50   Clay mask from Kamegaoka, Kizukuri-machi, Nishi-tsugaru county, Aomori prefecture. H. 10.8 cm. Latest Jōmon Period. National Museum, Tokyo

Fig. 51   Clay mask from Aso, Nanakura village, Kita-akita county, Akita prefecture. D. 14.5 cm. Latest Jōmon Period. Institute of Anthropology, Tokyo University

VI. YAYOI PERIOD FIGURES

During the half millenium of the Yayoi period, Japan witnessed the establishment of several of its crucial systems, adopted the cultivation of rice throughout traditional areas to as far north as the middle Tōhoku, became metal-producing, employing bronze ceremonially and iron for menial occupations, and gave distinctive burials in the form of cists and jars to those who could afford more than the usual fare.

Among those preferring jar burials were immigrants from Korea who followed the continental practice of depositing personal belongings with the remains of the dead. These goods, which were of Chinese manufacture or were copied after Chinese types and were perhaps carried down from the colonial region of north Korea, included bronze mirrors, bronze daggers, jade rings and glass beads.

North Kyūshū, where the buried foreign articles are found, becomes the first major power center in Japan. It was at this time composed of what the Chinese called "kingdoms", a collection of tribal groups often led by a shaman who was, at least in many instances, a woman. The existence of the female mediums, it may be said in retrospect, paved the way for the general acceptance of Japan's supreme deity as a female personification — the Sun Goddess.

In a new agrarian society, where nature's spirits often seemed fickle and not always benign, the ceremonies were all-important. The medium's tasks included sponsoring rites designed to insure abundant harvests. Early bronze weapons brought in by travellers from Korea served as models for Japanese types. In the re-making of these for domestic use the weapons were converted from their original utilitarian purpose to meet strictly symbolic needs. The Japanese-style weapons are large, wide-bladed, low in tin content, and brittle. Often unearthed in groups, distributed throughout Kyūshū and the Inland Sea, they were interred as means to gain protection of the land from human predation and natural calamities.

There is little question but what spearheads had fertility connotations by the time they were being cast in a handful of workshops in Japan. The oldest traditions attribute the fabrication of the Eight Island Country to deities in heaven stirring the waters below with a spear. Drops of brine from the spearhead created the land formations. Later references may describe magical spears as standing in the ground with points turned up.

The conversion of weapons to peaceful uses at this stage speaks for the exercise of power primarily by religious leaders. Cultural pressures inevitably pushed the population centers forward once the explosive force of the continental milieu had reached Japan and had introduced features of the sedentary life. Expansion of rice-producing land through the Inland Sea, the Kansai and even well beyond the Kantō, gave the fertile Yamato Plain of the Kansai a new centrality, in a location which was greatly enhanced by adequate access by both land and sea. These religious rulers were deeply involved in securing the maximum of welfare for their people through various magical means.

One facet of the religious program may be seen in

Fig. 52   Monkey from Tozurazawa, Susono, Hirosaki city, Aomori prefecture. H. 9.9 cm. (Enlarged.) Latest Jōmon Period. Institute of Anthropology, Tokyo University

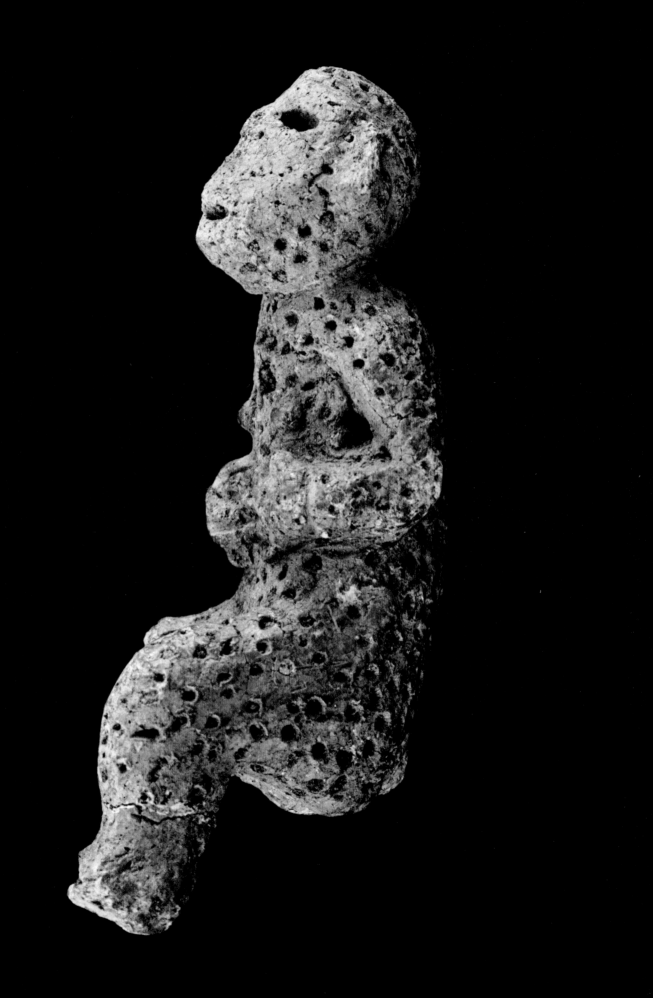

the making of bronze bells which were at first cast in workshops along the Inland Sea. Small and initially rather poorly cast, they increase in size and quality as the idea is picked up in more easterly areas.

These bells represent the major investment of the wealth during late Yayoi, as the concentration of power was shifting from the Inland Sea into the Yamato Plain. Sensing this migration, early historians employed by the Yamato rulers in the eighth century sought to grace the succession of leaders with an aura of antiquity. They reached back into Yayoi centuries for the beginnings of the state, although the date of 660 B.C., the traditional one for the raising of the imperial banner on the spot marked today by the Kashiwara Shrine, is clearly a date before continental traits begin to make themselves known in any quantity in Japan.

The story is told of a descendant of the Sun Goddess, posthumously called Jimmu, the first emperor, making his way by sea from southeast Kyūshū to the straits which open into the Inland Sea, then proceeding at the head of a fleet to the vicinity of Naniwa (modern Osaka), sailing around the Kii Peninsula, skirting the impenetrably dense mountain ranges in the south, moving up the east side to the neighborhood of Ise, and returning a short way to finally strike out across the land, overcoming the fading opposition and building a palace and establishing the nucleus of a state.

★Cat. 30 Yamato historians must have gathered together numerous local legends, strung a series of tribal rulers end to end (whether Yamato or not) in an unbroken chain, and in this way were able to present a detailed picture of vivid activities the broad outlines of which are not contradicted by archaeology. Jimmu remains as the personification of leadership of an expanding tribe, and his trek eastward is the symbol of the cultural current. He represents happenings of around the first century A.D. The major removal of authority to the Yamato region is a *fait accompli* by the end of the second century, where it remains despite serious challenges to its unity in almost all later prehistoric and early historic centuries, whether tribal warfare or slightly more refined family

feuds with Buddhism's future one of the stakes.

This is not to suggest that the final century of the Yayoi period witnessed the formation of the Yamato state. Yet there was, however, the creation of a strong economic base for an ambitious and vigorous tribe which now occupied a strategic area and was able to tap the raw manpower of the plain's farming communities. The major drawback to the Yamato state, as it discovered so often to its regret, was the unfortunate distance it found itself from all major foreign sources of supply. Troops were often tied down in Japan simply trying to hold these lines open, instead of being dispatched to carry out foreign policy as the Yamato rulers would have wished.

The emergence of the Yamato state is a fourth century phenomenon, coming well after the close of the Yayoi period and a century or more after the first of the large tumuli were built. The appearance of these tumuli marks the end of the Yayoi phase.

Yayoi pottery is the companion of rice, moving along at what seems to be a coordinated pace, sweeping the old figurine cult before it. Bronze cultic paraphernalia substituted for wider community rituals in which most of the people may have participated at crucial times of the year. Few elements of the old Jōmon culture were adaptable to the new Yayoi needs. Cord-marking on pottery was picked up north of the prefecture of Shizuoka, and cord-marking within zones on a vessel's surface is not uncommon in the lower Tōhoku. The human-headed vessels, traceable as far back as the Late Jōmon period and perhaps even then used as grain containers, furnished the inspiration for lids, caps or faces near the rim of a jar in this Yayoi period. Examples have been found in such prefectures as Ibaragi, Fukushima and Kanagawa, and indeed, perhaps this is a region where some primitive form of agriculture may have eventually taken hold. Not many human-headed vessels have been preserved from the Jōmon period and hardly more from Yayoi times, but several recent discoveries of Yayoi examples have contributed to a more comprehensive view of the type.

Fig. 53   Human-faced quadruped from Numazu shell-mound, Inai village, Ojika county, Miyagi prefecture. L. 8.5 cm. Latest Jōmon Period. Institute of Archaeology, Tōhoku University

Face painting and scratching, especially around the eyes and mouth, are often seen within sharply defined zones, while cord-marking is reserved for the body of the vessel or, in the case of the largest, is also used along the rim. Perforated ears are customary. This particularly tall vessel was dug out of a pit in the company of three complete jars, in a setting which had the earmarks of a ritual deposit.

Just how the small heads on tubes were used is difficult to say. The trunk of the Kaminojiri example is incomplete, and the top of the head is broken. It is thus impossible to know whether it was a closed or open tube. The shoulder stumps, one might add parenthetically, are a Jōmon vestige. I have found no arguments against the use of these vessels as grain containers. Despite the relatively small size of most (and I suggest that this in itself shows the Jōmon heritage), there is a disconcerting degree of human expression—what might be called a blank, ominous glare, or an elderly, patronizing gaze—showing they are obviously the product of a long tradition of bestowing genuine per-

sonality to the visage. Far more expressive than the later, abstract *haniwa*, they reveal a distinct cleavage between the Jōmon-Yayoi and the Tomb period traditions. It is quite likely that these may be taken as symbolic protectors of the vessel's contents, something along the order of a guardian deity.

Anything by way of actual figurines of small size in the Yayoi period is exceedingly rare. Eight figures averaging about six cm. in height, all quite amorphous and flared out so as to more or less stand on a flattish base, came up with other ritual objects at Kofuji village, Fukuoka prefecture, in southwest Japan. The workmanship is so crude, the shapes so unmodelled, and the eyes and mouth produced by the simplest of punched holes, that there is no way by which they may be related to the Jōmon background. They impress one as having come from a traditionless environment. Like all Yayoi figures, they are sexless, for the specific notions of fertility of Jōmon times have become more generalized, in circumstances now giving new significance to the face.

★Cat. 55

★Fig. 54

★Fig. 55

Plate VII   Clay plaque from Fukuda shell-mound, Ōsuga village, Inashiki county, Ibaragi prefecture. L. 16.6 cm. Late Jōmon Period. Coll. Mr. Tsuneichi Inoue

82

VII. THE GREAT TOMB PERIOD AND THE HANIWA

HISTORICAL AND CULTURAL OUTLINE

Since the earliest dated Chinese mirrors recovered from tombs have been found in the tumuli of the Kinki, it has been assumed by Japanese archaeologists that the first of the mounded tombs were constructed in that area, and that adoption of the practice in other regions soon followed. A mirror from the Chausuyama Tomb in Osaka, for instance, bears an inscription corresponding to the year A.D. 240. This tomb is composed of a large circular knoll from which projects a lower, rectangular barrow. It is an early example of the "square front, round back" (*zempō-kōen*) type of tomb which English books have referred to as keyhole in shape. European writers may use "en calebasse" or "en coquille Saint-Jacques".

Archaeologists also tend to go on the assumption that Chinese mirrors had heirloom value in Japan. The discovery of a Chinese mirror with what appears to be native articles of a much later date is the evidence for this idea, evidence which is reinforced by several instances and related situations. Chausuyama must be one of the earliest tombs, but it would hardly precede the end of the third century or the beginning of the fourth.

To the Yayoi social situation has been added the mounded tombs, the tribal rulers having acquired a new-found capacity for marshalling the labor force needed to erect these monuments to their vanity. In the early stage their persuasive methods, however, do not appear to have been strongly bolstered by military might. No weapons, nor replicas of weapons with the possible exception of stone knives, are found among the grave-goods. Like those in or near Yayoi jar burials, the mirrors in the mounds are still foreign.

The majority of grave-goods of local manufacture are stone copies of metal, clay and wooden objects. These include mirrors, bracelets, clogs, chisels, pestles, vessels, sheathed knives, axes, spindles, and so on. The sheathed knives could well have been used for carpentry. Of particular interest are a small number of stone batons, perhaps used as shamanistic symbols and implying status. Some of these replicas would be cheaper in the original materials of wood and clay, but obviously less durable and lasting. An underlying fact must have been a shortage of metal for such luxuries as grave-goods. These replicas are generally of greenish steatite and often bear remains of red ochre.

The burial itself was usually carried out in a wooden coffin near the top of the mound in a trench. More advanced would be a simple form-fitting chamber composed of rough stones covered by crossing slabs, all not much wider than the coffin itself, though frequently considerably longer. Liberal application of red paint may sometimes be seen in and around the coffin as well as on the inner surface of the stones.

What we may here call for convenience the Early Tomb period is, in the Kinki region, approximately the fourth century. Toward the conclusion of this period the Yamato state was on a firm footing, its position probably aided by the arrival of warrior groups who

Plate VIII *Haniwa* dog from Kamibushi, Sakai-machi, Sawa county, Gumma prefecture. H. 46.3 cm. Late Tomb Period. National Museum, Tokyo

brought for the first time military accouterments to Japan to be used as such.

The fifth century constitutes the Middle Tomb period at least in the Kinki, and represents a stage of consolidation of tremendous royal power, the marks of which were hardly surpassed even in later Japanese history. Colossal mounded tombs of this date accompanied by numerous smaller mounds lie like mountains in the open plains. The projected part of the tumulus has been enlarged to at least the width and height of the knoll, and moats habitually appear as part of the tomb's monumental splendor. The tombs attributed to late fourth and fifth century rulers are the largest of all. They may be seen in the vicinity of Furuichi city and from there south and west toward Osaka. Armor, weapons, including straight iron swords, and, before the century is out, quantities of horse trappings, were all deposited within the tombs, pointing to the new character of the ruling nobility. Locally made mirrors are often copies of Chinese types, but less frequently, different enough to be called typically Japanese.

The supremacy of the Yamato state was made possible through both conquest and trade with the southern kingdoms of Korea. Japan consequently found an ally in Paikche, the more culturally-inclined kingdom in the southwest. Known in Japan as Kudara, it sent over men learned in the classics and later dispatched writing instructors. In the middle of the sixth century came Buddhist statuettes and scriptures, followed by architects, metal artisans and all the experts who enabled the Japanese to erect temples.

Silla, in the southeast, remained almost continuously at war with Japan, desperately attempting to preserve its mineral wealth from Japanese seizure. Japanese records refer to Silla's subjugation in suggestive statements often framed in terms of tribute of shipments of iron and copper ores. But Silla's natural resources aided its rise to an eventual domination of all Korea, preceded by the expulsion of Japanese troops from its shores. Japanese references claim a colony in south Korea, a

part of the coast, known as Mimana. Korean accounts seem to discredit this control of Mimana, but there is convincing evidence from the Japanese archaeological viewpoint to lead one to feel that the association was so close as to have been nothing less than an area under Japanese jurisdiction, its governor appointed by the Yamato ruler. Mimana was tenaciously held not only as a trading center but as a sort of buffer zone, and at length little more than a beachhead.

The era of greatest prosperity comes after Japan's most notable successes against the Korean kingdoms. Both Paikche and Silla succumbed to Japanese attacks around 391, opening the way for the century of elaborate tomb building, presumed by this writer to have been impossible without unusually favorable international conditions. The tombs erected by emperors Ōjin, Nintoku and Richū, successive rulers probably of the late fourth and early fifth centuries, are all on a colossal scale. Many years were required for each and tens of thousands of men were involved.

After these affluent years Paikche remained on good terms with Japan. Silla would not lie down and be counted out; it revived to present an incessant threat to Japan. It was attacked again in 465, and in subsequent generations exerted continual pressures on Paikche, forcing the latter to send periodic missions to Japan in quest of relief. One of these missions brought the Buddhist gifts in 552. But the unstable mood in Japan forced the postponement of promised reinforcements and only ten years later, that is, in 562, Mimana was lost to Silla.

Japan enters a new chapter in its history, the story now woven around the dramatic events of Buddhism's adoption. From an early touch-and-go stage to the later, broader realization that Buddhism equalled cultural advances and sophisticated civilization, it passes the test of conflict with the traditional deities and emerges to play a complementary role. The compatibility was formalized in 645. Internal difficulties not diminished, Japan's foreign power faded fast. In 660 Paikche, still beleaguered a hundred years after its first

Fig. 54 Pottery vessel topped with human face, from Osakata, Shimodate, Makabe county, Ibaragi prefecture. H. 68.5 cm. Late Yayoi Period. National Museum, Tokyo

gifts of Buddhist objects had been received, again requested aid. Troops were mustered and dispatched the following year, but Silla was on the march; the Japanese army was defeated and virtually decimated. Scattered remnants withdrew in 663, cutting Japan's direct connection with Korean affairs for more than a millenium.

This digression is given here to explain one aspect of the economic foundations of the Yamato state, although it has carried us far beyond the Middle Tomb period with which we were dealing. The fifth century sees the peak of individual power both reached and eclipsed. The *Nihon Shoki*, the eighth century Chronicles of Japan, speak of Nintoku reigning for eighty-seven years and starting his tomb in his sixty-seventh. His three-moated mound, covering some eighty acres, illustrates an investment of monumental proportions.

Iron weapons preceded horse trappings to Japan, but certainly by the end of this period the horse-archers were sweeping the country. In their mobile way, well equipped as they were with weapons and ruling techniques, they established themselves in key positions in the old centers. As they moved out into more recently developed communities, they ruled with vigor, dominating the Late Tomb Period.

Korean immigrants wrought significant changes to the cultural patterns in Japan during this century. One view holds that several elements arrived about the same time, presumably introduced by rather large groups of arrivals led by mounted warriors. Their impact was registered in Japan within the span of perhaps a single generation. Most notable are the horse trappings, the stone passageway tombs, the gray pottery known as Sue, and the practice of decorating the walls of tombs.

It may be that a small group from a decorated tomb area settled in north Kyūshū and perpetuated the custom, but without recourse to trained decorators they were forced to rely exclusively on local talent. Stylistic contact was thus immediately lost with the peninsular tombs. As a matter of fact, something along this line may have happened twice, once in which the earlier mode of both carving and painting the wall was put into effect and again when the later practice of painting only was adopted.

Horse riding spread over the country, creating a new field for economic monopoly. Extensive use was made of the Tsukushi Plain of north Kyūshū and the Kantō Plain in the northeast as breeding grounds. The power struggle between Iwai, governor of Tsukushi, who built the largest keyhole tomb in Kyūshū, and the central government, during which Iwai was able to prevent the prosecution of the war in Korea, is manifest demonstration of such an economic and military monopoly. It ended when Iwai was killed while resisting an attack by government troops. One reason for the new-found strength of the kingdom located in Gumma prefecture of which the many concentrations of tombs in the lower mountains are evidence, was doubtless due to a thriving breeding business in the Kantō.

Passageway tombs, that is to say, those with a stone corridor opening into a chamber often preceded by an antechamber, were first constructed in north Kyūshū. Wall decorations tend to go with this type. Following this passageway plan, and occasionally even including more than one antechamber, local rulers built tombs to their tastes and the availability of materials and skilled workmen. The Sue pottery would probably have been in use by the middle of the century, for its kilns were sufficiently reputable for Emperor Yūryaku to order his own tableware from centers in the Kinki region. But this gray, hard, highly fired pottery, was less intended for the use of the living than it was for the dead. It is the common ceremonial ware found often in substantial numbers in the corridor or chamber of the tomb. Organizations not unlike guilds, called *be*, were responsible for most of the crafts and trades, and the *be* of Sue pottery was continually active in meeting the demand for mortuary vessels. Especially popular were libation vases.

Be were in fact smaller categories of *uji*, the main social unit, and were more or less hereditary occupations whose workers were scarcely more than serfs with little choice of vocation or freedom of move-

Fig. 100

Fig. 55 Clay tube with head, from Kaminojiri, Takasato-machi, Kawanuma county, Fukushima prefecture. H. 18.2 cm. Late Yayoi Period. National Museum, Tokyo

ment. The success of the imperial designs were in part due to the highly organized society. *Uji*, roughly clans, were patriarchal in nature, each respecting its own deity, the *uji-gami*. Allegiance to the head of the Yamato clan, the emperor, was through local chieftains whose rewards were undoubtedly liberal as long as loyalty was maintained.

Wall decorations in tombs could not have had more than a nominal start in the fifth century, perhaps appearing first in the general region of Kumamoto city or to its south. They tend to serve dual purposes in the succeeding century, substituting for the much reduced production of grave-goods, in particular for bronze mirrors, and having at the same time their own peculiar symbolism. As the importation of Chinese mirrors tapered off rapidly after the third century, the slack was quickly taken up by Japanese workshops. During the fourth century mirrors were for the most part fairly faithful copies of Chinese types, showing progressively more imagination and often becoming quite distinctive by the fifth century, embodying local features and including decoration altogether unlike any conceived by the Chinese.

The Late Tomb period, the sixth and seventh centuries, overlapped with the fitful advances being made by Buddhism. Diminishing returns in foreign policy and the inevitable levelling off, or even decline, after the early burst of power-consolidation, coupled with greater diffusion of the wealth yet discontent among outlying rulers, were responsible for a florescence of the more native arts. In a sense, this is a new degree of indigenization in the arts.

Smaller tombs were built, more gourd-shaped for the keyhole type, or often simply cut into the face of a rocky cliff in a trend encouraged by the making of passageway tombs and the idea of family vaults. This trend is a scarcely concealed factor in the eventual disappearance of mounded tombs. Stone sarcophagi,

once deposited in the passageway, were normally dispensed with, or were sometimes replaced in the regions of the Inland Sea, the Kinki and farther north by clay coffins.

Tumuli were finally discontinued in partial consequence of an edict following the imperial lament that the poverty of the country was entirely due to the building of tombs. This the way the *Nihon Shoki* reports Emperor Kōtoku's phrasing of the decree which specified burial in fixed cemeteries, modest mounds scaled down in size according to rank, prohibition of grave-goods, and complete elimination of places of temporary interment. Horse sacrifice was also proscribed.

Other factors entered in, for laws were only slowly enforceable. Most important here were Buddhism's demands on the family resources. Temples were erected for the living; few families could also afford elaborate tombs for the dead. Cremation added to the demise of the tombs, but in outlying areas they may still have been built as late as the eighth century. Tombs cut into hillsides in places in the Kantō belong to even later centuries.

The Yamato rulers claimed divine descent from Amaterasu, the highest deity, commonly called the Sun Goddess. The spread of her worship coincides favorably with the consolidation of the state, yet it also coincides with the diffusion of the keyhole tomb, the spread of the use of *haniwa*, and the popularity of Japanese-made mirrors. These are in other words, a collection of characteristic Yamato features. This sky cult, associated with the concept of divine kingship, supplanted the earth cults so well exemplified in the burial of bronze weapons and bells during the Yayoi period, at which time the spear was recognized as an early symbol of the highest celestial deity. How much later editing or telescoping of time has taken place in the literature is not always easy to say, but the mirror

Fig. 56 *Haniwa* cylinder bearing marking near rim, from Gumma prefecture. H. 50.5 cm. Late Tomb period. Aikawa Archaeology Museum

Fig. 57 Plan of Futatsuyama Tomb, Ikushina, Nitta county, Gumma prefecture, showing arrangement of cylinders and other *haniwa* objects on the mound, and outlines of passageway leading to tomb chamber

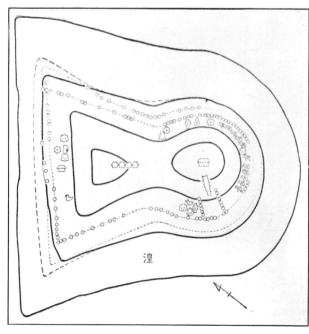

湟

does replace the spear in Yamato times, and its general acceptance is associated with the merging of smaller kingdoms into the bulk of the Yamato state.

*Cat. 66
*Cat. 72
The domestic pottery of the Tomb period is a direct descendant of the traditional Yayoi ware. Known as Haji, it is reddish, simple in shape and usually rounded on the bottom, often undecorated, and is frequently almost indistinguishable from its Yayoi antecedents. Out of this Yayoi-Haji background comes the making of the *haniwa*, the cylinders at first, then various objects and later human figures, the clay sculptures which adorn the slopes of these tumuli.

*Fig. 72
*Fig. 76 ff.
The term *haniwa* therefore designates the large body of sculptures in clay made expressly for the slopes of the tombs. They may not have appeared with the first of the tombs in the Kinki, but certainly not long thereafter, and were in use no later than the middle of the fourth century. Details of the *haniwa* chronology will be given later, following what is currently known of the general chronology of the tombs and their contents, but at this point a brief outline of the context from which they came, the course being followed by the pottery craft, and the textual background will lay the groundwork.

Fig. 56
Springing from the Yayoi-Haji tradition, they begin as cylinders designed to be thrust into the slope of a tumulus. These were ranged in rows along the bank, in such a way as to resemble a fence or to have acted as a deterrent to erosion. Most cylinders were fashioned from flat bands of clay, reinforced at the junctures, of the usual reddish color well known to Yayoi and Haji pottery alike. The surface may be strongly brushed or combed, and several circular holes are not uncommon in the wall.

Figs. 58, 60, 61, 62
The first actual *haniwa* models are now thought to have been houses. Production of these took place in the Kinki during the second half of the Early Tomb period,

Fig. 65
and before the close of this period a small number of inanimate objects such as shields appear. These repre-

sent the rising military spirit. On the whole, however, the *haniwa* are consistent with the generally more peaceable character of the Early Tomb period, to judge by grave-goods, and prefer the more ceremonial types. An illustration of this would be the use of sunshades. The creature world may also have been introduced prior to the end of this century, in this case as water birds.

The moving of the mounds in the Middle Tomb period from the hillsides to the plains with the intention of bringing them closer to living areas and keeping them more in the public eye, created a new stimulus for the *haniwa* art. More houses and a wider range of inanimate objects may be seen, presumably followed by horses and then by a limited variety of human figures. The small decrease in size of mounds during the latter half of the century slowed production slightly, but as interest waned in the Kinki, the provinces picked up the ball, opening the way, especially in the Kantō, for a flourishing business in *haniwa* in the Late Tomb period.

Passageway tombs were moving up from the southwest. Their inspiration to those disposed to use rock-cut tunnel tombs can hardly be said to have worked to the advantage of the *haniwa*. But this had little effect as far north as the Kantō. The keyhole and circular tombs of the Kantō are profuse, and often quite substantial in size. The major concentration lies near the juncture of the prefectures of Gumma, Tochigi and Saitama, but they are almost as plentiful in central Nagano and only a fraction fewer in the prefectures of Yamanashi, Kanagawa and the eastern part of Tokyo. The Kantō is, in other words, both ringed and dotted by tombs, the concentrations unusually numerous in the northern, higher levels.

In this somewhat isolated region, sixth and seventh century workshops turned out masses of *haniwa*, as the demand warranted, largely unhampered and unimpeded by the impact of the more sophisticated art employ-

Fig. 58 *Haniwa* house with door and window on one side only, from Fujioka city (former Akabori village), Sawa county, Gumma prefecture. L. 73.5 cm. Middle Tomb Period. National Museum, Tokyo

Fig. 59 Bronze sword handle from Tōdaijiyama Tomb, Ichimoto-machi, Tenri city, Nara prefecture. L. 10.2 cm. Early-Middle Tomb Period. Tenri Reference Museum

ing more expensive materials, serving the cause of Buddhism. If Buddhist art had any noticeable effect on the *haniwa* — which is quite doubtful — it could be observed only in the increased interest in natural rendering. This might be detected in the costumes and armor. The Kantō's figures have the freshness of an original art. The widest variety of human subjects, ranging from warriors to farmers and including several female types, forms a spectacular climax to the full *haniwa* evolution. Inanimate objects were not excluded, but the selection was drawn from other ceremonial furniture than those used in the Early Tomb period.

What this brief survey attempts to say at the outset is that emphases varied from period to period and region to region, and, as will be seen, even on the arrangement of the *haniwa* on the tomb. Thus, like the Jōmon figurines, as much as one might hope now as then to simplify the question, again it is equally impossible to dispose of the meaning and significance of the *haniwa* in one sweeping statement. I have been inclined to do this in prior writings, normally rationalizing it (at least to myself) as the result of limited space. No such excuse can be claimed here, and if justice is not done, lack of space need hardly be blamed.

LITERARY SOURCES

It may seem strange that the *haniwa* are referred to no more than twice in the rather large mass of early Japanese literature. The Japanese were not unlike many ancient cultures which attempted to rationalize the beginnings of many of their accepted customs so as to give them justification. This is the case with the *haniwa* and if modern historical scholarship and archaeological procedures should consider this story quite unsound, it should be remembered that no eighth century writer was the least concerned with minor distinctions between fact and fancy. Blatant myth and unembroidered fact are intermingled in the most natural way in all early literature, although I have in mind especially the *Nihon Shoki* (Chronicles of Japan), *Kojiki* (Records of

Ancient Matters), *Fudoki* (Records of Lands and Peoples) and the tenth century *Engishiki* (Engi — era name — Ceremonies). Other literature has less use to historians, archaeologists and students of early religion and some may not be as ancient as claimed. Earlier records were presumably employed in the compilation of these.

Throughout extant written material, the *haniwa* caused only enough concern to be remarked upon twice. This paucity of references has been taken as a sign of their sacrosanct character because of their connection with death and indeed, the second reference is entirely an isolated, supernatural event[17]. My feeling on this is that once explained, they no longer had any news value, and even the reasons behind the explanation raise serious doubts. They were commonplace and had no calendrical significance, nor did their use take place on fixed occasions. The *Nihon Shoki* makes constant reference to the standard celebrations and sacrifices to the gods of Earth and Heaven, but the *haniwa* do not qualify for any of these. They fit no category which interested the compilers of the early accounts.

Remarks on tombs are of the briefest and most generalized sort; in fact, they are largely geographical in nature. Rather unusual is the story of Emperor Nintoku selecting the site of his tomb on the plain of Ishitsu in Kawachi (Sakai Plain, Osaka), but historians must have thought a few comments on the largest tomb ever built well worth the space. In the note for October 18, the 67th year of his reign (ca. A.D. 379), the building of his tomb was started. His last twenty years were marked by hushed up rebellions, while he demonstrated his generosity by reducing taxes, devising means of taking care of orphans and widows, and himself set a good example of hard work by rising early and retiring late. During these two decades in which he dramatized his sympathy for the poor and afflicted, he built the most splendid of all tombs. He died on January 16 during his 87th year on the throne and was buried on October 7 of the same year. Such elementary statements are in fact elaborate remarks for the *Nihon Shoki* in regard

Fig. 60 *Haniwa* roof with four attached buildings, much restored, from Saito-machi, Koyu county, Miyazaki prefecture. L. 78.5 cm. Middle Tomb Period. National Museum, Tokyo

to tombs, although another illustrates how inseparable are truth and fiction. Emperor Sūjin's aunt married a deity who made himself known only at night. Upon her request to see him during the day, he agreed provided she would control her reactions. He turned out to be a snake, but she was unable to hide her fright, thus shaming him. She therefore had little choice but to commit suicide, which she did by stabbing herself in the private parts with a chopstick. Her tomb, according to the *Nihon Shoki*, was built by men during the day, by gods at night. Stones used in its construction were passed bucket-brigade fashion from Mt. Osaka to where the tomb was erected. It came to be called Hashi-no-haka, Chopstick Tomb, a name that probably gave to later generations a chance to enjoy a little play on words. But all said, the story is quite fantastic, quite useless archaeologically.

Wider inferences do exist concerning the cults, the period of mourning and the final burial in which are included references to a "shrine of temporary interment", and there are the requests on the part of wives to be buried with their husbands, usually given out of reasons of economy. But the literature can, on the whole, be regarded as relatively uninformative in most of these matters where the archaeologist could hope for greater precision. An exception is the description given in the *Fudoki*, written as though recounted by an old man, of the stone figures which stood on the tomb of Iwai in Kyūshū.

The explanation for the origins of the *haniwa* are worked into the narrative on Suinin, an emperor who reigned perhaps in the middle of the third century — before mounded tombs were built, if archaeological reasoning is correct. Suinin ruled traditionally from 29 B.C.–A.D. 70, living for 140 years according to the *Nihon Shoki*, 153 years according to the *Kojiki*.

Interestingly enough, only in the preceding year, 3 B.C. so the official chronology states, had the religious authorities ascertained by divination which weapons would be most efficaciously offered to the deities. From the various ones in use, it was determined that bows, arrows and swords would be most suitable, hence the practice was inaugurated by the redesignation of land and buildings in the service of the deities and, so the account continues, the offering of weapons to the deities of Heaven and Earth probably started at this time.

The emperor's brother, Yamato-hiko, died in October of 2 B.C. If not entirely fictitious, this is a date probably closer to A.D. 270. About three weeks after his death he was buried. We may pick up the story from Aston's translation[18]:

"Yamato-hiko was buried at Tsukizaka in Musa. Thereupon his personal attendants were assembled, and were all buried alive upright in the precinct of the misasagi. For several days they died not, but wept and wailed day and night. At last they died and rotted. Dogs and crows gathered and ate them.

The Emperor, hearing the sound of their weeping and wailing, was grieved in heart, and commanded his high officers, saying: 'It is a very painful thing to force those whom one has loved in life to follow him in death. Though it be an ancient custom, why follow it, if it is bad? From this time forward, take counsel so as to put a stop to the following of the dead'."

Some four years later the good intentions of the emperor were put to the test. Hibasu the empress herself, died on July 6, the 32nd year of Suinin's reign. The *Nihon Shoki* carries the story from here:

"Some time before the burial, the Emperor commanded his Ministers, saying: 'We have already recognized that the practice of following the dead is not good. What should now be done in performing this burial?' Thereupon Nomi no Sukune came forward and said: 'It is not good to bury living men upright at the tumulus of a prince. How can such a practice be handed down to posterity? I beg leave to propose an expedient which I will submit to Your Majesty.' So he

Fig. 61 *Haniwa* building of high, narrow proportions, from Myōjinyama Tomb, Asakura-chō, Ashikaga city, Tochigi prefecture. H. 98.5 cm. Late Tomb Period. Institute of Archaeology, Kyoto University

Fig. 62 *Haniwa* house with doors at ends and windows on sides, from Tobi, Sakurai city, Nara prefecture. H. 47.7 cm. Early-Middle Tomb Period. National Museum, Tokyo

sent messengers to summon up from the Land of Idzumo a hundred men of the clay-workers' Be. He himself directed the men of the clay-workers' Be to take clay and form therewith shapes of men, horses, and various objects, which he presented to the Emperor, saying: 'Henceforward let it be the law for future ages to substitute things of clay for living men, and to set them up at tumuli.' Then the Emperor was greatly rejoiced, and commanded Nomi no Sukune, saying: 'Thy expedient hath greatly pleased Our heart.' So the things of clay were first set up at the tomb of Hibasu-hime no Mikoto. And a name was given to these clay objects. They were called *Hani-wa*.

Another name is *Tatemono*.

Then the decree was issued, saying: 'Henceforth these clay figures must be set up at tumuli: let not men be harmed.' The Emperor bountifully rewarded Nomi no Sukune for this service, and also bestowed on him a kneading-place, and appointed him to the official charge of the clay-workers' Be. His original title was therefore changed, and he was called Hashi no Omi. This was how it came to pass that the Hashi no Muraji superintend the burials of the Emperors."

The actors in the play include Yamato-hiko, a younger brother of Suinin on his mother's side, and Hibasu-hime (Hibasu princess), a young lady who came from the province of Tamba in the 15th year of Suinin's reign along with four sisters. She became the empress while three sisters became concubines, but the fourth was so abominably ugly she was sent back home. Unable to face up to her rejection, she jumped from the carriage and was killed. Nomi no Sukune was a wrestler from the Izumo region called to fight the Yamato's strongest man, Kuehaya from Taima. Nomi no Sukune made short work of Kuehaya by kicking in his ribs and then his groin, and so disposing of him. He is known as the father of *sumo* wrestling, but hardly the inventor of its modern rules. Nomi was exalted to the head of the Haji (Hashi) *be*, who were then given

responsibility for the imperial burials. The honor was undoubtedly considerable and linked a common interest, for the wrestlers were themselves highly respected and regarded as power symbols, as were those whom they served.

This entire story is thought by many today to have been a fabrication of the Haji-be, the potters' guild, concocted to enhance their standing and perhaps to explain how they were almost the exclusive makers of objects for funerary use. The other guild so primarily occupied was the Suetsukuri-be, the makers of the gray pottery who could claim a better ware but were not shrewd enough to invent the corresponding prestige. All of the other guilds of crafts, whether in metal, textiles, stone or woodwork, performed their tasks for the living, not the dead. This gave some special repute to the Haji potters whose normal ware had improved little technically since Yayoi pottery got its start and who had good reason to divert attention from their mediocre performance.

Haniwa refers to rings of clay. By extension it might even include the arrangement of cylinders around the slopes of tombs. Inadvertently the story could actually be speaking of these. *Tatemono* are standing things, but certainly the term has had no modern connection with *haniwa*. It is used for buildings today.

Like all of its accounts, the *Kojiki* gives one terse version and that is recognizable only if one is familiar with the story from the *Nihon Shoki*. Suinin was 153; his august tomb is in the Mitachi Plain at Sugahara. When the empress, Princess Hibasu died, the *be* of stone coffin makers and the *be* of potters were established. The empress was buried in the tomb of Terama near Saki.

Sugahara has been identified by later historians with Amagatsuji, west of the ancient city of Nara, where a large, moated tomb can easily be seen from the passing train window as one travels south beyond Saidaiji. Except for the enlightening morsel that stone sarcophagi

Fig. 63 *Haniwa* object, probably a sword, from Tonozuka Tomb, Shibayama-chō, Sambu county, Chiba prefecture. H. 75 cm. Late Tomb Period. Shibayama Haniwa Museum

Fig. 64 *Haniwa* quiver marked with *chokkomon*, from Anderayama Tomb, Hirono-machi, Uji city, Kyoto prefecture. H. 102 cm. Early-Middle Tomb Period. Institute of Archaeology, Kyoto University

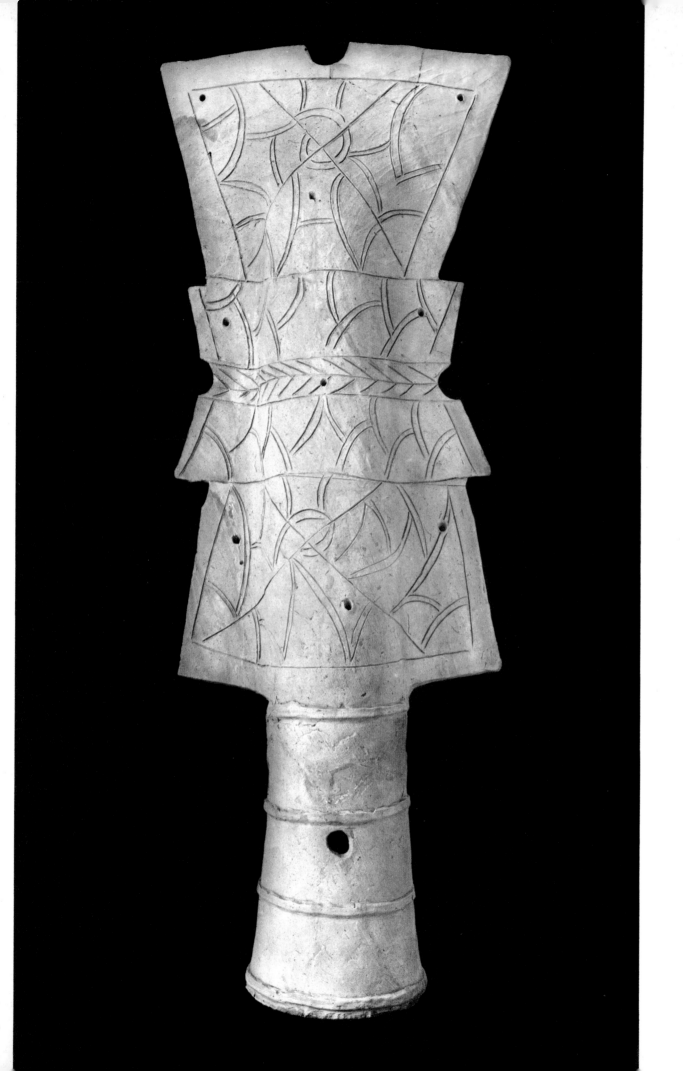

now came from formally organized workshops, there is nothing else here. Yet, without the human interest padding, it could well be more historically accurate than the *Nihon Shoki* account. Any return to this story is done at the risk of beating a dead horse, but some similarities between it and fact may yet be found.

Bearing in mind the prominence of the horse in certain cult practices in a nomadic or nomad-descended society, it comes as no surprise to find that the other reference in the ancient literature is a supernatural horse anecdote, presumably related for the metaphysical characteristics which are here attributed to a *haniwa* horse at night. Following some remarks on the origins story, we will return to the nightmarish episode of a man called Hyakuson.

The unequivocal statements in the *Wei Chih* (Chronicles of Wei) made by a Chinese writer when he described the burial of Queen Himiko of Wo (Japan) in A.D. 247 have a bearing on the question of live burial. In describing her social position, it is said she was entombed in a great mound while over one hundred of her attendants, both male and female, followed her in death. There is nothing to indicate in these accounts whether the following in death was done voluntarily or otherwise, but it matters little here. If we can believe the chronology, the humaneness of the Japanese rulers in this regard shows up prior to the time it does in Korea, for the *Tongguk Tonggam* (Comprehensive Survey of Tongguk [Korea]) does not list the prohibition of live burial in Silla until 502.

Confrontation at this point between the literary and the archaeological evidence has so far created a virtual impasse. Himiko (Pimiko) is no more than a symbolic female shaman-ruler, but such an individual of great prestige was buried during the mounded tomb period. The Chinese call this the middle of the third century. Suinin, if the tomb by any slim chance belongs to him, and his relatives who needed burying, should have been living during the tumulus period. His death may date in the neighborhood of 280, but all ten emperors preceding him are listed as having been buried in mounded tombs (*ryō* or *misasagi*). Archaeologists prefer to think that such tombs hardly preceded Suinin's time, if at all; that they were not first built where Suinin is claimed to have his but perhaps closer to present Osaka; that Suinin's tomb has a fifth century shape; that it is probably not Suinin's anyway, and had better go by a geographical name, although the popular idea is unlikely to disappear. There is clearly no distinction made in the literature as to when the tumuli come in, and as far as the early historians are concerned, the tumulus is the one and only form of burial for an emperor. Archaeologists have often come off second best in encounters with historians on these questions, but it is fruitless to enter the argument here. All one need say is that answers are still being sought. The Chinese writer in his description of the location of Yamatai, a substantial Japanese kingdom, was wrong by either direction or distance. While perhaps being a reputable historian, he was a poor geographer, and as such he opened the door to doubts on several issues.

One obvious point of disagreement between the origins story and the actual chronology is the disregard of the cylinders *per se* in the story, yet their appearance came well ahead of the models and human figures. The story compresses successive additions to the repertory into one simple occasion; but it may not be too far-fetched to suggest that the title might actually have been invented when the cylinders alone were in use.

Proof for the practice of live burial may never be found in Japan, although few would doubt that it could have existed. The tomb chambers themselves were not large enough for the inclusion of retainers, servants or slaves, and any such immolations would have had to take place outside the tomb, almost literally on the plain, as the story says. Under these circumstances one could not expect to find any remains today. Smaller tombs near large ones have been explained as the tombs of relatives—buried at the natural conclusion of their lives. The anguished suffering of those who were marked to accompany the deceased noble

Fig. 65 *Haniwa* shield marked with *chokkomon*, from Ishimi, Miyake, Shiki county, Nara prefecture. H. 119.7 cm. Late Tomb Period. National Museum, Tokyo

is a bizarre interjection; it reminds one of slaves who died with their master by starvation, or other known inhumane ways. It adds an unnerving touch, but was quite likely a device drawn in to demonstrate the generosity and kindheartedness of the emperor.

A possibility as to how such an idea could have come about if the story is fictitious, may have had to do with the inability of giving the tombs adequate care which, by the eighth century, had been discovered to be well nigh impossible. *Haniwa* heads are especially common in the Kinki. As a matter of fact, complete human figures in the Kinki are rare and I suspect that this was already the case in the eighth century when the *Nihon Shoki* was written. Pillaging of tombs reached its peak in the Nara period—after cremation had gained in popularity—and before the period was over had been so damaging to historical property that the government intervened in order to bring it under control. But the *Nihon Shoki* was written when protection of the tombs had evaporated, and ravages were at their worst. Collectors in any modern sense were obviously not restoring and reconstructing *haniwa*. I know, for instance, of no *haniwa* which shows indications of ancient repairs of the sort one may occasionally find in a Jōmon figurine. Scattered heads may have given real plausibility to the idea that the *haniwa* were an attempt at reproducing a mode of vertical burial as deep as the neck. Even a few heads as caps on cylinders—but these are atypical rather than typical—could have lent substance to the idea. Small, globular heads are somewhat pressure-resistant, thus often surviving better than larger, broad-surfaced bodies. In any event, it may not be amiss to ask whether what could then be seen of the *haniwa* themselves could not have provided a partial basis for the legend, rather than the legend have been an attempt at explaining the beginnings of the *haniwa*.

The other mention of the *haniwa*, although the name itself is not used, comes on the evening of what might be called July 1, in the year 465, during the reign of Emperor Yūryaku. It is filed as a report from the province of Kawachi, now the prefecture of Osaka. An otherwise unknown man, Hyakuson by name, was visiting the house of his son-in-law where his daughter had just been delivered of a child. His return journey led past the large tomb of Emperor Ōjin, referred to here by the given name of the emperor (also a location name), Homuda or Honda, *misasagi*. The story is reproduced literally as Aston translated it[19]:

"The daughter of a man of the district of Asukabe named Hiakuson, Tanabe no Fubito, was wife to a man named Kariu, Fumi no Obito, of the district of Furuchi. Hiakuson, hearing that his daughter had given birth to a child, paid a visit of congratulation to his son-in-law's house. He came home by moonlight, and was passing at the foot of the Homuda misasagi at Ichihiko hill, when he fell in with a horseman mounted on a red courser, which dashed along like the flight of a dragon, with splendid high springing action, darting off like a wild goose. His strange form was of lofty mould; his remarkable aspect was of extreme distinction. Hiakuson approached and looked at him. In his heart he wished to possess him, so he whipped up the piebald horse which he rode and brought him alongside of the other, head by head and bit by bit. But the red horse shot ahead, spurning the earth, and, galloping on, speedily vanished in the distance. Hereupon the piebald horse lagged behind, and, slow of foot, could not overtake the other. But the rider of the courser, knowing Hiakuson's wish, stopped and exchanged horses with him, upon which they took leave of each other and separated. Hiakuson, greatly rejoiced at obtaining such a steed, hastened home and placed him in the stable, where he took off his saddle, foddered him, and went to sleep. The next morning the red courser had become changed into a horse of clay. Hiakuson, wondering at this in his heart, went back, and, making search at the Homuda misasagi, found the piebald horse standing among the clay horses. So he took it, and left in its stead the clay horse which he had received in exchange."

Any such supernatural story cannot be subjected to rational explanation. The more or less double moated

Plate IX *Haniwa* monkey from Tachibana village, Namekata county, Ibaragi prefecture. H. 28 cm. Late Tomb Period. National Museum, Tokyo

tomb of Ōjin runs a pale second in size to that of Nin-toku, measuring 491 meters in length from the outer limits of its moats. It is not far from the Furuichi train station today, in an area administered by Furuichi city. The reddish clay of the *haniwa* created the night-time illusion of a red charger, but in characteristic disregard of fact, while the apparition might have had no difficulty reaching the mound, the piebald horse and Hyakuson himself would have had to cross the moats to do so. This is as much a Halliburton feat as the body of the story.

THE ORIGINS OF THE HANIWA

Any suggestion that the *haniwa* were influenced by Chinese grave figurines is always countered by three arguments intended to set the record straight. The Chinese figurines were used inside the tomb, the Japanese figures outside; the Chinese ones are small, the Japanese large; and the Chinese are highly realistic, often painted or glazed, and the product of advanced techniques, while the Japanese *haniwa* are relatively abstract and plain, and are made in fairly simple ways[20]. Fashions have changed in regard to these considerations, and few suggest much connection between the two today. It is often felt (perhaps more than written) that some distant association, several steps removed, does actually exist, but it is unlikely that any further discoveries will add new means of measuring the degree of relationship.

An old theory suggested that the Spirit Path figures of Chinese tombs furnished the ultimate model for the *haniwa*, and these were first seen in the stone figures which stood on several tombs in Kyūshū[21]. The *haniwa* are cheap imitations of these.

The Spirit Path-stone figure-*haniwa* evolution has long since been dismissed, but there are subtle associations between these which need not be passed off too lightly. It should be remembered, however, that the stone statues on the Kyūshū tombs are not part of an

early stage of figure sculpture in Protohistoric Japan. In fact, some statues show features borrowed from the cylindrical *haniwa*; others show a cubic approach to form, and a rare few are surprisingly realistic. Technical variety is great, and may be seen quite mixed in the many figures which stood on the sixth century tomb of Iwai in north Kyūshū, the tomb called Iwatoyama, indicating that time differences are not a factor in the stylistic variations.

It is not wrong to assume that these stone carvings were inspired by Chinese Spirit Path figures. They include men in armor, quiver-men, nude male and female figures, horses, small animals and jars, and are used more like the *haniwa* as figures for the slopes—Emperor T'ai-Tsung's tomb did have reliefs to decorate the ascent to his tomb—rather than forming an avenue of approach. But these are interchangeable with *haniwa*; Iwatoyama had both, standing side by side.

The stone figures fall within the distribution limits of the decorated tombs in Kyūshū, being concentrated in the central northern part, largely around Kumamoto city and into southern Fukuoka prefecture. Han dynasty vestiges may be seen on the wall-screens of the early decorated tombs, in the low relief decoration of circles, quivers, weapons, diagonal lines and so on, some of which suggest enlarged but irregularized stamped tiles in China and Korea. The closest contacts would be with Lo-lang in the northern half of Korea. The later tombs which carry paintings only, dealing with subjects dominated by animals and human figures, may be traceable to post-Han influences, entering Japan from a decorated tomb region in Korea. The cubic style of stone figure is most closely associated with the earlier stage of tomb decoration, but it does not disappear under the impact of later developments. As so often happens in outlying regions, including Japan, it is simply joined by the cylindrical and more realistic style, a style which follows the fundamental form of the *haniwa*.

Fig. 66 *Haniwa* helmet with hole in top, from Tottori, Yasaka-machi, Takeno county, Kyoto prefecture. L. 19.5 cm. Middle Tomb Period. Institute of Archaeology, Kyoto University

Fig. 67 *Haniwa* object shaped like a skirt, from Miyayama Tomb, Muro, Goze city, Nara prefecture. H. 75.9 cm. Middle Tomb Period. Yamato History Museum

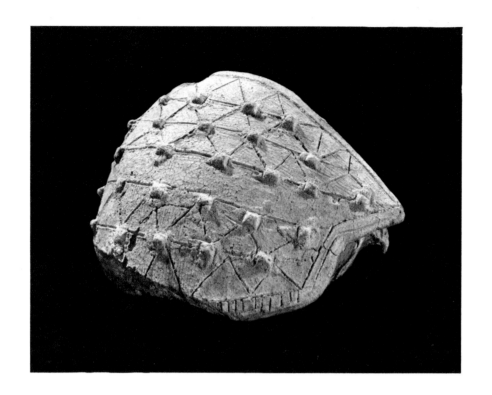

At best, however, the stone figures cannot pretend to be the forerunners of the *haniwa*. They represent a greater attempt at achieving permanence in a region where a distant acquaintance with the Spirit Path must have existed.

Reasons given for the visual effects of the *haniwa* have a close bearing on their use. Increases in size and in number taxed the workshops heavily, from the time the *haniwa* were ordered until their delivery. There must have been instances of long distance transportation. It is possible that the workshops had some mobility. The haste with which *haniwa* had to be turned out is frequently proffered in apologetic tones for their simplicity. This is to some extent true; it is more than a by-product, however, that their simplicity contributed to their portability and ultimate durability, and even to their natural visibility at a distance. This last was inevitably a prime factor in all considerations of the *haniwa*.

The Chinese grave figures are relatively small. They were made on some kind of an armature and frequently glazed or painted. Glazing at this time in Japan is no more than accidental, occasionally exhibited on a Sue vessel. Obviously no technical devices were learned by the Japanese from Chinese mortuary models. Early human *haniwa* in the Kinki are not necessarily large. They often illustrate a scale and personality that seems a little closer to the Chinese examples than later and more provincial *haniwa*.

Later, larger *haniwa* give the impression that their size was increased in concert with an awareness of the problem of visibility. As such they have more resemblance to Spirit Path figures (here again, most remote) than the early figured *haniwa*. For purely practical reasons clay figures standing on the plain leading to or around a tomb could only be expected to be natural targets for destruction, yet instances of violation of this logic do occur, leading one to guess that placement on the flat must have been in itself exceptionally significant. Those on the bank had a better chance of survival from just ordinary human traffic.

The question of visibility was of real concern. Late *haniwa* in the Kantō, for instance, were flattened out into a rather oval cross-section and, if painted, were painted on one side only. This was done with a view toward increasing visibility. Fortunately for the visual effectiveness of the *haniwa*, the tombs tended to be erected in smaller sizes after the middle of the fifth century at a time when the *haniwa* were being increased numerically, but if one assumes that the *haniwa* served as prestige symbols, to be seen right along with the tomb itself, then the very scale of the tombs mitigated against their visual value despite these minor modifications.

The large moated tombs bearing *haniwa* — and the earliest known figured *haniwa* may have come from the tomb of Emperor Nintoku — demonstrate the proportionally primitive level on which this coordination concept started. Quantity helped. The estimated ten to twenty thousand cylinders which ringed the banks in seven tiers could hardly be seen from the hundreds of yards separating the observer and the lowest ring, much less a few small human figures.

In the Kantō where volcanic deposits have laid down layers of reddish loam not unlike the color of the *haniwa* itself, a mound would almost automatically appear in this reddish color. *Haniwa* standing against this would have had a visibility level close to zero. Or, within a couple of years the mound would have been overgrown with vegetation. Some *haniwa* were toppled; most were smothered in spite of what I imagine were elaborate attempts to keep the growth cut back. At best, the *haniwa's* usefulness was greatly circumscribed by what seemed to be a connivance between nature and the natural fragility of the material. Quantity had its compensations; more than this, one is forced to conclude that their usefulness was at least half otherworldly.

All the early proponents of Chinese influences on Japanese *haniwa* overlooked the role of the cylinders just as had the *Nihon Shoki* writers long before. The cylinders are to the *haniwa* what electricity is to mod-

Fig. 68 *Haniwa* boat with seats and thole pins, from Saitobaru, Saito-machi, Koyu county, Miyazaki prefecture. L. 101 cm. Middle Tomb Period. National Museum, Tokyo

ern science. They opened the door for all later developments.

THE CYLINDERS AND THEIR ROLE IN THE ORIGINS OF THE HANIWA

The cylinders were as subject to mutation as other *haniwa*. They undergo periodic changes and exhibit local peculiarities. Their cradle and greatest concentration was in the Kinki, and they were only a fraction less popular in the Kantō and the Inland Sea region. Fewer are to be found in Kyūshū or in the north, but every region which encouraged the building of tombs also demanded cylinders to some degree. The Late Tomb period's excessive zeal for human figures was a cause of lowered interest in the cylinders. Rather few from this period are known, and those which do date to this time are usually narrow tubes of modest size.

Early Tomb period cylinders show little change in diameter from top to bottom, may average close to 50 cm. in height, and are customarily perforated with circular holes. These are elaborated in detail and enlarged during the following period to as high as a meter, and frequently provided with holes of triangular, square or rectangular shape. Not content with remaining simple, they may be oval shaped, flanged or capped like a morning glory. Some will bear scratched marks, shell imprints, hunting scenes, stick figures, ships and deer, all incised. The marks are believed to have been started toward the end of the Middle Tomb period. Such signs lack sufficient consistency to be clearly designated as makers' or kiln marks, but they may well be so, and are certainly in no way an attempt at decorating the surface.

Flanged or finned cylinders are limited to the Kinki in both the Middle and Late Tomb periods. The earlier examples present a wide, flat outer surface; later ones resemble more simply ears. The way they were used in the fifth century may be seen at the Uwanabe Tomb No. 5 located somewhat northwest of Nara city. The cylinders were sunk in close proximity to each other, flange to flange, in a way that presented to any one viewing the tomb from the plain a solid clay wall near the foot of the slope. Flanges thus make the barrier complete, but the idea is short-lived and impossible after they shrivel to decorative lobes.

Lines of cylinders on the slope were frequently interspersed by larger ones or examples with trumpet-shaped tops. Tombs were often terraced, as may still be seen today, and *haniwa* lined these terraces in some cases, though most often following the contours of the mound. This terracing contributed to the rectangularity of the front part, giving it the appearance of a ceremonial platform.

Several suggestions have been offered as to the purpose of the earliest cylinders and the evolution of their meaning, if any. One practical explanation, preferred by those who lean toward concrete rather than symbolic answers, is that they were designed to prevent the erosion of the bank. They shored up the slope in a slightly more permanent way than could be done by wooden posts. They could hardly be said to have been a saving on wood—it had to be cut so they could be fired—but they did not require periodic replacement, and were a notch higher in sophistication. *Fig. 56

The idea that they represented a magical fence, a *tamagaki*, as suggested by Gotō and followed by Kanaya[22] is the most attractive to me, partly because it appears to me that the widely spaced cylinders made little pretense at holding up the soil. The rather sandy Kinki earth might lead to minor landslides, but the denser loam of the Kantō would become no serious problem in this respect. *Fig. 69 *Fig. 56

What I conceive of was initially a cordoned off area through the use of posts, not unlike the *shimenawa*, the straw rope with folded paper streamers which surrounds sacred spots, trees, or entrances to Shinto shrines today. Early tombs were novelties. Some were near the

Fig. 69   Boat with a bank of oars on either side, incised on a *haniwa* cylinder, from Karikodake Tomb, Kurio, Otokuni county, Kyoto prefecture. L. of boat 12.5 cm.; H. of cylinder 47.5 cm. Middle Tomb Period. Institute of Archaeology, Kyoto University
Fig. 70   Moccasin-shaped *haniwa* sarcophagus for a child, from Fushimi-machi, Ikoma county, Nara prefecture. L. 71.5 cm. Middle-Late Tomb Period. Yamato History Museum

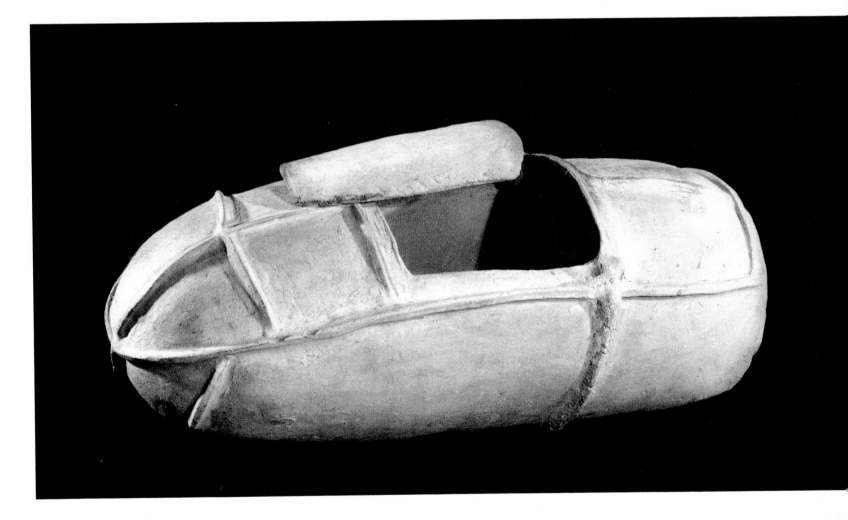

top of a hill or even tended to resemble a hill. A device might be needed to separate the sacred from the profane lest any visitor be uncertain. Greater permanence was soon desired. The perforations in the cylinders were technically useful, but could also have served for threading the rope in instances where cylinders stood some distance apart. Greater wealth and the popularity of the scheme insisted on a proliferation of cylinders, and a solid clay fence was created. The moats of the Middle Tomb period sharply define the tomb from its surroundings, but by this time the form was set, hence the ritual continued. Modifications and new attitudes toward protecting the tombs in the last centuries drastically lessened the need for cylinders, and deeply undercut their meaning.

Prior to the introduction of the gray Sue pottery from Korea there was no ware which served almost exclusively the ritual needs, nor was tomb ritual so advanced as to demand such a ware. The domestic Haji acted in this capacity when called upon to do so. Haji was the font from which the cylinders sprang, leaving little doubt that the origins of the cylinders and possibly even broader concepts in the *haniwa* are rooted somewhere in Haji history. The connection need not be labored; the Haji-be made both the domestic ware and the *haniwa*.

The Chausuyama Tomb at Sakurai in Nara prefecture, excavated in 1949, revolutionized notions about the *haniwa* in general and in particular the cylinders. No cylinders were found on Chausuyama. Instead, this Early Tomb period tumulus, with a long, low front and narrow stone chamber, had over thirty pots of Haji ware lined up in close, rectangular formation above the burial on the rounded knoll. The excavator looked on these as ceremonial vessels, inasmuch as they had all been broken before firing, and their globular shape, small necks and morning glory tops gave reason to consider them as libation vases[23].

In any event, ceremonial needs were met here. Cylinders might have taken over after this point. One writer, however, has referred to the presence of cylinders on tombs claimed to be earlier than Chausuyama[24], and others have been able to circumvent the implications by suggesting that cylinders were just not available here. Haji pots, in other words, were used in their place.

The idea that Haji libation pots are behind the appearance of the cylinders has been ardently espoused by Ueda and generally agreed to by Miki[25]. Along with this goes the assumption that the morning glory cylinders are in actuality *haniwa* pots, the direct descendants of the Haji libation vessels. A variety of other inanimate objects were used to top off a cylinder. There must be no reason why jars should not have been used in the same way. This seems to ring true until it is realized that these "jars" are associated with the rows of cylinders in most instances. Groups are not independently placed as are other inanimate objects, hence they may always retain their original significance, acting — at least symbolically — as libation vases.

The evidence for the connection is strong, yet I cannot see that the Haji libation vase and the *haniwa* cylinder are completely inseparable. Certainly the artistry is not so advanced as to be concerned with accent, variety and rhythm in a row of cylinders. If *haniwa* cylinders as a whole had assumed the libation vase role from Haji vessels, why were morning glory types still needed? The inevitable answer might lie in the strength of the tradition, yet it may not be fully convincing here. The Sue ware took over the libation duties. Many of its shapes are clearly ceremonial, and *haniwa* gravitate more and more away from symbolism in their attempts to impress and decorate.

Tomb slopes were often banked with stones in a practice which increased in frequency in time, although the evidence is now often obliterated by vegetation or has been removed in historic centuries for building or other purposes. The use of stones as dikes implies less need of cylinders for this purpose and leads one to wonder whether cylinders were ever intended to support the slope. The huge exposed stone chamber of the Ishibutai rests on a square-based platform, the sloping

Fig. 71   Hollow *haniwa* object marked with *chokkomon*, from inside Miyayama Tomb, Muro, Goze city, Nara prefecture. L. 39.7 cm. Middle Tomb Period. Private Collection, on loan to Yamato History Museum

walls of which are still reinforced with stones today.

The peculiar arrangement of the Chausuyama Haji pots and a somewhat similar scheme at another tomb but in *haniwa* cylinders is worth comparing. The Haji pots defined a rectangular area immediately over the burial chamber. This area was levelled off rather like a platform and thus made into a segregated section. The tomb attributed to Empress Hibasu-hime, which figures prominently in the *Nihon Shoki's* origins story, would seem to be transitional to the end of the Early Tomb period and the beginning of the Middle. Stone reinforcement has been found on the knoll of this tomb, with remnants of *haniwa* cylinders outside the remains of this wall. Here again was a kind of segregated platform above the burial spot. No figured *haniwa* were found — it was too early for them, regardless of the story — but in this separated section which was probably once square, were what was left of *haniwa* shields and sunshades. Recalling periodic appearances of square bases for round mounds, most of which are rather late in time — the Ishibutai is a good example — this rather little noticed combination of shapes may suggest some remote connection with the Chinese mandala. To the Chinese cosmic truths could be demonstrated in diagrammatic arrangement, in this case by using associated squares and circles. The Chinese notion of "heaven round, earth square" consists of one within the other, the former standing for nature, the latter for man. There is not much evidence of these reappearing in continual alternation in the Japanese tombs as in China, but we have been able to note cases where the square is above or below the circular mound. The one tomb, or perhaps three, in which a central mound is square and two round ones are attached to this on a long axis, may be an attempt at reproducing the same idea.

It would be impossible to attribute much understanding of these concepts to all but an infinitesimal number of people in Japan and they could not have been greatly concerned with their significance, but the more evolved combination of shapes of which the Ishibutai is not an isolated phenomenon, seems point-less if it were not derived from a source which originally saw meaning in the relationships.

Moving on to the Middle Tomb period, some seven tombs are known to have had cylinders displayed in rectangular formation on their rounded knolls[26]. These are primarily in the Kinki region and belong to the early half of the fifth century. One (Kanakurayama) is in the Inland Sea zone. All are keyhole but two, which are round. Further elaboration of the *haniwa* now includes houses and various objects, together with a few human figures. Cylinders are almost without fail a prerequisite for any *haniwa*, yet the Kumano Tomb in Tochigi prefecture, in a region which leads out of the Kantō going north, had *haniwa* of human figures without a trace of a cylinder.

Multiple rows of cylinders may often be seen in the Middle Tomb period. Three rows is not uncommon and these may run along both knoll and projection. Emperor Nintoku's tomb, where cylinders are variously estimated to range between ten and twenty thousand in number, had cylinders standing in as many as seven rows, some of these circumscribing the full tumulus. Not all cylinders are necessarily close together during this period; the great distance over which they are expected to reach sometimes precludes this.

THE ARRANGEMENT OF OTHER HANIWA ON TOMBS

The cylinders, as has been pointed out, often followed the contours of the tumulus and were occasionally employed to set off a specific hallowed spot, this latter directly above the place where the physical remains had been laid. It is not unheard of to find the cylinders on the level field around the tomb, as though literally forming a barrier for the protection of the locality. The round-mounded Kankoji Tomb in Osaka prefecture was encircled by the usual row of cylinders, but around the tomb on the flat stood a row in rectangular outline. Between this outer row and the alignment on the slope were found a *haniwa* boat and a sunshade.

Fig. 72 *Haniwa* horse wearing bells and other ornamental gear, from Chūjō, Kumagaya city, Saitama prefecture. H. 87.5 cm. Late Tomb Period. National Museum, Tokyo

Cylinders were ignored almost as much by early excavators as they were by the *Nihon Shoki* writers. Their arrangement or even that of the human figures was not an early refinement in archaeology. The first record of note comes in 1930 when the scheme for the Hachimanzuka Tomb in Gumma-machi of Gumma prefecture was reported[27]. But post-war investigations have given the arrangements and relationships all due consideration, and the majority of these which will be described here in summary form have been observed and evaluated within recent decades.

The Early Tomb period reveals chiefly the position taken by the buildings in the symbolic format. Uzuisuzuka in Nara prefecture may be the first to illustrate this. A single house rested on the crest of the knoll above the burial trough. The famous tomb at Akabori village in Gumma prefecture, also known as Chausuyama, which yielded eight buildings, is an early tomb in the outer Kantō and significantly one of the oldest. Two pit-style trenches yielded minimal grave-goods. The tomb's banks were covered with small stones.

The buildings were surrounded by a telling selection of other objects: a pair of fans and sunshades, cuirasses, a single throne, a bowl on a perforated stand and, toward the front where the projection leads away from the knoll, two cocks.

The disposition of the *haniwa* illustrates a ceremony, shown as though performed by the deceased himself. The throne is in the middle and is flanked by fans. The libation bowl is directly behind, the sunshades bringing up the rear. Birds, here sitting like a pair of lookouts, symbolize the soul of the dead and are closely connected with belief in divine guidance in the performance of duties. Additionally, out in front, they herald the morn and the early light, signalling new life in the next world for the dead.

Chausuyama boasts the finest display of buildings yet found. These represent three residences and four storage structures, one of the former of which must be the chief house since it is the only one to bear ridge logs. Three storehouses are of the same size and all are provided with gabled roofs. The fourth is smaller and its roof is hipped. Another building is so small as to have been called a shed. It stood directly behind the main building and followed its orientation. All of the other structures stood around the main building and were oriented east and west, whereas the other two buildings faced the square projection of the tomb. This remarkably regular arrangement allows a rare insight into what lines pre-Buddhist planning may have taken.

The opinion that the holdings of a wealthy landowner may be seen here has been generally accepted. The many storehouses are graphic evidence of his abundant harvests, yet at the same time the house as the abode of the dead — and certainly next-world usage was an underlying thought — is doubtless intended here.

The arrangement on the Ishiyama Tomb in Mie prefecture (Middle Tomb period) would not be greatly different from the Chausuyama Tomb just described. A number of houses crowned the knoll. Such objects as *haniwa* shields, sunshades and parts of armor were disposed rectangularly around the buildings. Cylinders aligned outside these were also placed rectangularly. Some of these cylinders bear flanges. Still lower had been installed four *haniwa* shields in military formation, facing the plain. Rows of cylinders in lower terraces seem to have included sunshades and shields.

Kanakurayama, a north-oriented, hilltop, keyhole, Early period tomb, situated in the outskirts of Okayama city, was excavated in 1952. Its total length is 160 meters. The projecting part is terraced, and the slopes are faced with flagstones. Three rows of *haniwa* cylinders surrounded the mound, the knoll of which was decorated with *haniwa* shields, hats and additional cylinders forming a square, outlined by stones.

A rich trove of ancient armor was unearthed from the Kurohimeyama Tomb, Kuroyama village, Osaka prefecture, in the investigations of 1947–49. A large, moated, keyhole tomb of about the fifth century, the discovery of twenty-four pieces of arms and armor on its floor, composed of cuirasses, helmets, neck and

Fig. 73 *Haniwa* wild boar, from Kami-takeshi, Sakai-machi, Sawa county, Gumma prefecture. H. 50 cm. Late Tomb Period. National Museum, Tokyo

shoulder guards, swords, daggers, arrowheads and knives, came as no small surprise to the excavators. *Haniwa* cylinders encircled the mound on two levels. The collected remains showed that a square plan had been used in the arrangement of one or more *haniwa* shields, hats, and cuirasses, and a sheathed sword and a house. Below the double row of cylinders on the circular part of the tomb were more hats.

Toward the end of the Middle Tomb period human figures begin to show up, grouped with the inanimate objects. One of the first such assemblages could be the tomb called Hachimanzuka in Gumma prefecture. The figures are overshadowed in number by a straight line of eight birds along the north side, which included two barnyard fowl and six water birds, and a similar line of six horses on the south side. Two more horses were grazing on the top of the knoll. All of these faced west, that is, toward the front of the tomb, except the grazing horses. Five human figures stood along the front, two more slightly higher on the slope and an eighth had been relegated to the back of the tomb. The entire group was confined to an area which had been neatly defined by a rectangle of cylinders.

The best known through wider publications is the Futatsuyama Tomb of Gumma prefecture, but it runs a feeble second in quantity to the two Shibayama tombs in Chiba. The latter lie side by side. The larger, certainly one of the giants of the Kantō, is Tonozuka, the smaller, presumed to be that of a wife, is Himezuka. An estimated eighty figures stood in one row only on the Tonozuka, and some forty made up the total for the Himezuka.

To return briefly to the Futatsuyama Tomb, a building on the knoll was accompanied by four neatly lined up near the crest of the projecting part, and a sixth had been placed halfway down the slope at this same square end. A human figure standing on the back incline of the knoll was flanked by a line of six horses on the southwest and five on the northeast, the entire group following the contours of the slope and all facing the front of the tomb. A sprinkling of human figures stood on the southwest side near the house on the forward slope, and a small number of inanimate objects at various points completed the pageant. One feature of rare significance was the double line of cylinders which jutted off more or less at right angles from the upper tier to form a row on either side above where the entrance would be to the stone passageway which leads into the tomb chamber. It is a phenomenon of striking interest in any consideration of the cylinders as spirit guides and protective barriers. A cluster of *haniwa* — two figures, a bird and a shield — was gathered at the juncture of one row and the outlining cylinders.

The area around Shibayama-chō claims four hundred or more mounded tombs and seventeen in the immediate vicinity of Tonozuka and Himezuka. Tonozuka is approximately 100 meters in length; it has a short chamber on the side of the knoll opening toward the south. Himezuka, somewhat over half the size of the Tonozuka, has a long stone corridor leading directly into the chamber, but this is not in the knoll; rather, it is on the south side of the projecting section. Enough *haniwa* were *in situ* or were found in such a way that the excavators were able to surmise the approximate position in which they stood. Their quantity is most ★Fig. 57 amazing here.

Tonozuka had three rows of *haniwa*, the uppermost and the lowest consisting of cylinders only, though mixed with morning glory examples. The south side of the middle row was also composed of cylinders. Where the knoll and projection meet were located inanimate objects and houses. A single ceremonial fan stood on the north side near the summit of the projection, and a group of men at the extreme far end on the incline of the knoll. The projection carried cylinders on its north bank except at one point where remains of three oddly-shaped human (?) bodies had been inserted. These last are too imperfect to make much of; they may be simply inept productions, yet could conceivably represent dwarfs or deformed individuals of

Fig. 74 Head of a *haniwa* deer, missing one ear, from Sammaizuka Tomb, Okisu, Tamatsukuri-machi, Namekata county, Ibaragi prefecture. H. 23.7 cm. Late Tomb Period. Ibaragi Prefectural Art Museum

Fig. 75 *Haniwa* hen, from Kyoizumi, Moka city, Tochigi prefecture. H. 54 cm. Late Tomb Period. National Museum, Tokyo

the sort who may have been kept as court jesters. Dwarfs are mentioned in the texts, and it may be worth recalling the reference to a dwarf being sent as tribute to the court in 671 from a province in the Kantō.

Tonozuka was capped with a house, fan and quiver. The arrangement was generally similar on both tombs. It is the middle row on the north side of this tomb which attracts the most interest. Eighty or more *haniwa* lined the steep slope, although the majority had fallen into the moat below. It was judged that this line followed the order of cows, wild boar, deer, a dog, cocks, other birds, perhaps ducks and a hawk. After the birds came a groom and four or five horses, followed by a group of male figures from where the line continued as cylinders. Apparently other human figures were interspersed throughout the cylinders. A visit to the Shibayama Haniwa Museum, constructed exclusively to house the remains from these tombs, will attest to the worth of the recovered material, to say nothing of the ambition of the restorers.

In a sense, an observer of one of the sixth century tombs is witness to a funeral procession done up in little models. This is most apparent for the Himezuka tomb. It could boast forty-five figures aligned on its Fig. 88 north side. Here again were horses, four in this case, led by grooms. Next stood a group of men, then another of women, the latter of mixed social levels. Out of line and near the middle was a *koto* (a stringed instrument rather like a harp) player and on the other side of the row was a kneeling man whose task it must have been to make the proper obeisances as the procession went off.

The most arresting *haniwa* were the five bearded Figs. 78, 79 warriors from the smaller Himezuka Tomb. The long beards, heavy braids of hair, and tall peaked hats lend a remarkably elderly, distinguished air to these figures, giving them a human touch which only the Kantō could do. The headgear conjures up strong connotations of what one has come to look on as Korean hats. The *Nihon Shoki* takes note of Koreans with recognized talents entering Japan, but for the Kantō speaks only of

clergymen settling in 684. It may be that they represent the heads of the local clan, or perhaps its ancestors, whose chief is presumably buried in the Tonozuka.

Quantity was stressed over quality at Shibayama. Levels of quality of surprising range are quite apparent. Where this is the case, the distant view afforded of the *haniwa* by the observer had logical advantages, for many of the figures could hardly stand close inspection. The fewer figures on the Himezuka Tomb were produced under better controls and must be the work of experienced craftsmen. Perhaps the crude ones which I kindly suggested might be intended as dwarfs are actually the work of utter novices, recruited out of sheer desperation to get a massive job done.

Rapid recapitulation from this and other evidence will show that progress in types and arrangements went from Haji ware to cylinders, followed by single buildings and then groups of buildings. As these last appear they are accompanied by shields, then other weapons, sunshades, fans, bowls and eventually birds, the first of the natural life to have been made. Subsequently the full repertory includes animals and human figures. The houses maintained their topmost position and were usually surrounded by other inanimate objects. Thrones appear singly, many other objects in pairs. After human beings become the dominant theme the precise placement of the inanimate objects, except for the buildings, seems to be far less important. Everything may go into long files of *haniwa* which follow the contours of the mound. Most figures faced the front of the tomb during the Middle Tomb period, but facing out with back to the slope was generally preferred in later situations. Humans were usually grouped processionally and without regard to rank. One case at least is known of a male and female figure which stood out at the front of the tomb, most likely as symbols of the deceased and his wife. Horses are known to have appeared like sentinels; some are within the rows, some are individualistic (Hyakuson's horse was grazing on the mound). Other animals are normally confined to the long files. Fowl were often used in

Figs. 76, 77 *Haniwa* warrior in full attire and detail of equipment, from Hōsen, Nitta county, Gumma prefecture. H. 124.2 cm. Late Tomb Period. National Museum, Tokyo

isolation or in pairs for greater effect, and in some cases were put as close to the moat as possible to simulate water-birds.

HANIWA STRUCTURES

The *haniwa* houses are the prime source of information on the architecture of these centuries. They suffice to show that major advances in the art of carpentry and building techniques had been achieved since the houses had become habitually surface dwellings and raised storehouses had been adopted in the Yayoi period. Most notable is the variety of dwellings which seems to be in use. Almost all the clay models appear to be reasonably "buildable". That is to say, despite an occasional roof whose slope is awkwardly steep or whose ridge-pole weights seem unduly many, these models give every appearance of being relatively faithful — to the point of being unimaginative—reproductions of existing structures.

Residences and storehouses alike were constructed of either boards and squared supports or thatch-covered walls and skinned poles. In effect, the former are metropolitan style buildings, urban in flavor, the latter are country houses, rural in character. These are not dwelling and storehouse distinctions as might at first be thought. The criteria for differentiation are to be found in other features, the most useful clues to which are the windows and doors. Lodgings are windowed, storehouses are not. The door of the latter normally opens on a short side, but dwellings were not averse to this, although there is some disposition to face the broad side of a house toward the south before Buddhist architecture formalized the idea and proved its worth.

Storehouses may be raised above the ground, as they had been traditionally since the first or second century A.D., or may be built directly on the surface. Roof-covered pits are known through textual remarks, and some of the isolated roofs of *haniwa* are likely to have been made as superstructure for pits.

The shape of the roof is also not related to the function of the building. Residence and storehouse roofs may be simply gabled, hipped, or both hipped and gabled. One style is roughly equally pitched on all four sides. The hipped and gabled (*irimoya*) is so prevalent Fig. 62 that it may be looked on as typical to Japan, first employed during the Yayoi period.

Roofs were of thatch or bark and ridged with a heavy pole which was depressed by short weighting logs. It Fig. 61 took Buddhist architecture of the late sixth century to introduce tile roofs. Herring-bone patterns incised on walls of houses evidently simulate matting or possibly suspended mats of woven reeds. Where this matting appears on storehouses, it may be taken as intended for heat and ventilation control or for dampening if fire threatens the building. The *haniwa* models seem to demonstrate that slanted walls were not uncommon.

A higher class residence may have two stories. Cat. 58 Single-storied houses were in widest use, and it is still apparent that pit-dwellings had not yet fully gone out of style. Separate *haniwa* roofs suggest this, but there is ample archaeological evidence to show that pit-dwellings lingered on in most provincial areas. These underground houses of the Tomb period are square in shape with rounded corners. A fireplace is located in the center and an oven for culinary needs is set against a wall, usually on the north side. Some *haniwa* houses have a bench surrounding the entire interior, in an arrangement which brings to mind the plan of the Ainu house of recent years.

One of a pair of swords exhumed from the Tōdai-jiyama Tomb in 1961 bears a gold inlaid inscription of the Chung-ping era (A.D. 184–89). It is therefore of the Han dynasty and purely Chinese. The other must be a Japanese version. It uses a roof instead of what appears to be the bird's crest or cock's comb of the Chinese Cat. 59 sword. The roof is composed of two sections. On the right is some kind of entranceway rig, perhaps a well-head. It vaguely resembles a *torii*, the sacred gate of every Shinto shrine. The more or less right-angled bar which connects with the peaked flange may be a wall ★Cat. 56 or fence.

These features recall the frequently illustrated Mirror with Four Buildings, also from Nara prefecture, on

Plate x *Haniwa* hawk from Tochigi prefecture. H. 16.5 cm. Middle to Late Tomb Period. Coll. Mr. Kaichirō Kaneda

which the structure that acts as a roof over a pit is accompanied by a parasol above the entrance and low horizontal bars marking an enclosure. The right-angled bar here looks more like a door flap propped up by a pole. The opposite building on the mirror, a two-storied residence, has a similar enclosure and is also outfitted with a protective parasol. I have in other writings called this a kind of patio. A plausible theory that has now been offered for the mirror may have some bearing on the sword[28]. It suggests that this gear represents a well located directly in front of the house. Covered pits seem to have a special claim on wells in front yards, but it should mean that these are dwellings and not storage pits. I doubt if the rig is intended to be a proto-torii, and could see little room for argument that the roof-over-pit in reality represents a shrine.

The largest of all clay houses — a roof with four small buildings attached — from one of the Saitobaru tombs in Miyazaki prefecture of southeast Kyūshū, is nothing more than the superstructure of a pit into which a ramp would lead through one of the side porches. There is a good chance that the earliest "imperial" reception halls were just this — mammoth pit-dwellings. The story of Emperor Jimmu ordering a muro to be dug and entertaining his enemies in it on the pretext of negotiating, only to have them all slaughtered at a given signal, probably pertains at least in this case to such a structure.

This so-called "palace" is a very much restored model and should be used cautiously at best for elaborate theses. The four side buildings might act as guard houses, assuming the pit were not so colossal as to need more than one entrance. They could, of course, act as coverings for windows; if so, it implies an enormous pit. A single entrance does rather well for light in the family-size, reconstructed pit-dwellings this author has been in. Jimmu is in theory a tribal leader during the Yayoi period, but other evidence could be used to imply that his chicanery was written about as though

taking place in a Tomb period context. Further literary references are to doorless (i.e. inescapable) muro, and the burning of muro.

The muro, indicating a chamber originally, was a term applied to ice houses for summer storage by the time of Emperor Nintoku. Subterranean storage was nothing new, but ice houses of considerable size, measuring three meters in depth, received official promotion at the time as a result of the discovery of one of these by an imperial prince during a hunt in the month of May. He caught sight of a hut over a storage pit and was told that ice was still resting on a bed of reeds. He took a sample with him to the court — it does not say clearly how far he had to go — and thus proved it, for without the evidence he would have been ridiculed. The mental recorders of history were properly impressed.

HANIWA ARMS AND ARMOR

*Fig. 60

It is to be expected that the great bulk of haniwa objects consists of armor, weapons and military equipment in view of the quantity of these deposited as grave-goods. In their early stage of production, such haniwa may have filled a temporary shortage of equipment that was needed for tomb consignment, but by the middle of the fifth century all indications are that if anything, a surplus existed. Unlike the houses, the accuracy of the models may in most cases be measured against the actual objects from the tombs, and attest to a faithful reproduction with only an occasional tendency to simplify, perhaps for technical reasons.

The rare sword haniwa are of a type which has not Cat. 60 normally been found amongst the grave-goods; they resemble a kind of hand-operated fire-extinguisher. On the basis of the usual absence of actual examples of the common iron sword in the haniwa repertory, a convincing theory has been offered by Gotō, a theory to which I have on the whole subscribed[29].

Fig. 78   Elderly *haniwa* warrior, from Himezuka Tomb, Shibayama-chō, Sambu county, Chiba prefecture. H. 161 cm. Late Tomb Period. Shibayama Haniwa Museum

Fig. 79   Head of a bearded *haniwa* warrior, from Himezuka Tomb, Shibayama-chō, Sambu county, Chiba prefecture. L. from hat peak to beard tip 51 cm. Late Tomb Period. Shibayama Haniwa Museum

The *haniwa* sword is encased in a broad, elliptically-sectioned sheath that widens toward the base. The exposed handle features a knobbed guard, the knobs perhaps of semi-precious stones. Such knobs in quartz and steatite were discovered in a tomb in Sakurai city, Nara prefecture, although nothing more of the sword seems to have been unearthed. The sheath for such swords must have been of leather, and whether deposited in the tomb or not, would have perished. The relative size of the handle makes the sword appear to be short, in contrast to the usual long, single-edged iron weapon of this period. The sheathing is all too complex to be merely a technical device hit upon by *haniwa* makers who were inclined to simplify their work, and the importance of its presence is to be seen in one example from Tochigi prefecture which bears large red triangles painted on the enclosing case.

Swords of this type were not in everyday use. They, along with several other objects occasionally represented by *haniwa*, served on special occasions or for supramundane purposes. Included in this group would Cat. 66, 65 be the sunshade (*kinugasa*), fan (*sashiba*), and the throne. All of these, it may be noticed, would have been constructed of large sections of perishable materials. They are more conspicuously status symbols than the conventional inanimate *haniwa*. Possession of the sword was claimed by an institution which took responsibility for its safe-keeping. While specifically a symbol of the deity, unless human nature was different, the shrine chief came to regard it as his own, and it was ★Cat. 61 reproduced to signify his position. Quite credible is the idea that this *haniwa* type is a model of the bejewelled sword preserved as a holy treasure of the Ise Shrine.

The idea is deeply entrenched that ordinary swords Fig. 63 were not copied. The Shibayama object has therefore been termed an unidentified article in the latest catalogue, possibly a sword[30]. A fan has also been suggested. The Kantō was never averse to taking liberties with hallowed traditions of another region. Novelties become almost commonplace. This *haniwa*, which was found on the front part of the Tonozuka Tomb,

has a largely complete and original outer edge to the circular part. The center hole seems quite out of scale for a fan, and, in fact, Shibayama already has one good, properly made fan. I assume, therefore that it is intended to be a ring-handled sword. As the possible exception which proves the rule, there is implied the existence of either some socially recognized taboo on the making of *haniwa* swords or so much abundance that was it pointless to model them in clay. Swords were never without their magical power to defend their owner, and were laid on either side of the remains of the deceased in the tomb. Kusanagi, the Grass Cutter, had a history of aiding the descendants of the Sun Goddess and was especially effective in Prince Yamato-dake's attacks on the barbarians. In historic times, when a reason was sought for the disease which was afflicting Emperor Temmu in 686, divination proved the culprit to be Kusanagi. The sword was then sent to the Atsuta Shrine near Nagoya.

Innumerable finds point up the profusion of these swords. *Haniwa* ones may have been superfluous. The list is endless, but several tombs can be cited as examples: Hyōtanyama Tomb, Shiga prefecture, 14; Kurohimeyama Tomb, Osaka prefecture, 14 single-edged swords, about 10 double-edged swords, and 5 short daggers; Shōrinzan Tomb, Shizuoka prefecture, 12; Kinreizuka Tomb, Chiba prefecture, 8; Nambara (Minamihara) Tomb, Kyoto prefecture, 7; Kameyama Tomb, Hyōgo prefecture, 6 long swords, 2 short swords, and 4 short double-edged swords.

The rather large object decorated with *chokkomon* preserved by Kyoto University gives every indication to me of being a sword guard. This judgment is based to some extent on the presence of the *chokkomon*, since the *chokkomon* is a pattern with a special penchant for sword handles of horn and quite fragmentary pieces of *haniwa* which may be parts of swords. Another collection contains a sword pommel of equally substantial size, apparently from the same Kanshizuka Tomb in Nara prefecture, whose flattened end is marked with the same design. It is conceivable that the two belong to the same piece. The magic of sword and

Fig. 80 Detail of the *haniwa* warrior (Fig. 81)

chokkomon combined suggest a formidable deterrent to any would-be contender.

Quivers reach massive proportions. Most are made up to resemble headless warriors holding arrows. Such quiver-men are best known through the stone statues from tombs in Kyūshū, and tomb paintings seem to show some effort was made to illustrate this type. Quivers held by these bearers are of the kind easily transported. A rare few, however, are large, ornate arrow boxes, sometimes flanged and furnished with "ears". *Chokkomon* is a familiar decoration on these symbols of a well stocked arsenal, used in the large rectangular panels or in registers across a curved surface. Actual quivers on this scale must have served at times of formal contests. In all the quivers the heads of the arrows are exposed for all to view at the top, whether the quivers are the small ones on the back of a warrior for dress occasions or on the side for battle needs. Appearance is all important, taking precedence over facility of use.

Haniwa shields also reach a striking size. Iron was doubtless preferred for shields for its obvious durability, but shields of a more wieldy sort were made of wood, leather and wickerwork. It is the larger iron shields which the *haniwa* emulate, since these had rank significance. The outlines and decoration of a leather shield was discovered through fine archaeological techniques in the Kitsunezuka Tomb in Toyonaka city, Osaka prefecture. Tall and concave on either side, it widened a little more at the top where it had an arched outline. Triangles were the chief decorative motif, the popularity of which as shield ornamentation is attested to by the *haniwa* from the Miyayama Tomb in Nara prefecture.

Judging by the frequent inclusion of triangles in vital spots in the tomb paintings, especially in the burial receptacle itself or in extreme proximity to the dead, and their less frequent appearance on anything which can be regarded as more properly designed for the living, it may be that their meaning here is along the order of regeneration. The motif is given greater efficacy through repetition and color[31].

The large iron shields, which could hardly have been ★Fig. 64 more than symbols because of their weight, were made up of iron strips cut at sharp angles and soldered to joined backing sheets. These created a pattern of zigzag lines in a way which conforms admirably to the engraved geometric art of the period. Iron shields were votive gifts according to the ancient literature. In the *Norito* they are spoken of as offerings to the gods. The *Nihon Shoki* reports that Emperor Sūjin offered eight red shields and eight red spears to the god of Sumisaka, and eight black shields and eight black spears to the god of Osaka.

Helmets as reproduced in *haniwa* tend to follow the Fig. 66 oval-shaped, ridged type rather than the circular visored, plume-holder type. Both types are widely distributed without areal differences. Iron was the usual material, but one well known example of the circular type bearing engravings of primitive birds and animals on ★Fig. 65 its bands is made of gilt bronze. It was recovered from the Gion Tomb on the outskirts of Kisarazu city, Chiba prefecture. All helmets are heavily riveted, but the zigzags on the *haniwa* helmet in the Kyoto University collection are the artistic result of the urge of its maker to include triangles for symbolic reasons.

Armor materializes in *haniwa* as the cuirass or cor- Cat. 63 selet, made of riveted bands of iron. The full slat armor, composed of small rectangular plates tied together by leather thongs, commonly seen worn by *haniwa* warriors, is more rarely fashioned as isolated *haniwa*. There must be at least one good reason for this, and I ★Cat. 62 take it to be equally good for the helmet selected for *haniwa* reproduction, and that is that presumably slat armor came in a little later, at a time when the custom of producing *haniwa* armor had been largely discontinued. The great popularity of armored soldiers takes place in the Kantō and its outer limits and is the final great outburst of *haniwa* production.

Fig. 81 *Haniwa* warrior wearing peaked cap, from Hachisu, Isezaki city, Gumma prefecture. H. 124.6 cm. Late Tomb Period. Aikawa Archaeology Museum

Fig. 82 *Haniwa* warrior in full armor, from Kuai, Nitta county, Gumma prefecture. H. 133 cm. Late Tomb Period. National Museum, Tokyo

MISCELLANEOUS INANIMATE
*Cat. 65 HANIWA

Cat. 66, 65 The best known of the ceremonial objects are the sunshade and fan. Elaborate restorations inevitably required by the sunshades may at first strike an observer as quite fanciful, but the details can all be attested to by a sufficient number of examples, most of which are from the Kansai region. This is a poletop decoration of leather or cloth mounted over a metal or wooden frame. Gotō noticed the similarity between such *haniwa* as the fire-extinguisher sword, fan and sunshade and the ceremonial paraphernalia carried in the procession which marks the periodic transfer of the "residence of the deity" from an old shrine at Ise to a new shrine in an adjoining lot. This ceremony, the so-called Sengūshiki, traditionally follows the order of procedure as described in the *Engishiki*, a book of the tenth century. An old scroll illustrates the transfer and gives a fairly clear picture of the equipment employed in it. The jewel-handled sword discussed above is one of the treasures which is transferred at this time.

*Fig. 68 The Ise Shrines follow a rejuvenation practice of rebuilding both Inner and Outer Shrines every twenty years. Reconstruction was literally impossible in periods of great national stress, but in 1953–54 the

*Cat. 64 fifty-ninth was carried out. The culmination of the custom is the ceremonial move of the symbols from the old buildings to the new ones. Once codified this event has certainly not changed noticeably in a thousand years, and parts of it may well be of protohistoric origins. Hence one may accept these as utensils of the

*Fig. 69 emerging shrine cult. They were the marks of office, and the originals themselves could hardly have been interred with the dead.

The ceremonial fans may be traced at least as far as China where they served to ward off diseases, plagues and other forms of evil. In Japan they generally took a simple, circular shape with central hole. Often used in pairs, they could set up a magical ring into which malevolent spirits dared not intrude. Two standing on

*Fig. 67

a tomb framed the magic circle and protected the deceased, acting as purifiers of the area. *Haniwa* fans may also have a serrated edge, similar but less elegant than the motifs painted on the walls of a small number of tombs.

The Miyayama Tomb in Nara prefecture, sometimes referred to as Muro-no-Ōbaka, has yielded several highly unusual *haniwa*. One of these is an enormous tube-mounted object shaped like a skirt. The top, which measures approximately the same diameter as the cylinder below, is open. Despite the need for restoration, both upper and lower edges are original and finished. What there is of it, in other words, is complete. It is too large to be the lower half of a legless warrior — composite figures do exist, but not in the Kansai to the best of my knowledge — nor is the cross-hatching customary décor for the lower tunic of a male figure, although triangles do appear on the skirts of stone figures in Kyūshū. No adequate explanations have yet been given for it.

The few *haniwa* boats which have been found come from such widely diverse regions as southeast Kyūshū and the Kansai. The largest is from one of the Saitobaru tombs in the region said to have been invaded by the ancestors of the first emperor, Miyazaki prefecture in Kyūshū. Another, much simpler one is from a tomb in Kyoto prefecture. This seems to say that whether it be coastal or more inland, the basic transportation for the island country was never lost sight of, and discoveries in the Kyoto area have surprised those who most often repeated the theme that Kyūshū's strong maritime culture gave it a monopoly on *haniwa* boats.

Wall scratchings, paintings, *haniwa* cylinder drawings and models all illustrate boats of high bow and stern, and the Saitobaru one has several benches running laterally for the oarsmen who rowed on either side with the aid of thole pins. Incised pictures on tomb walls and several textual references show that sails were in frequent use. Divine breezes assisted the Japanese ships in the invasion of Silla by Empress Jingū, the *Nihon Shoki* adding that neither helm nor oars were needed.

Fig. 83   Helmeted head of *haniwa* warrior, from Kotsunoda-mae, Serata, Nitta county, Gumma prefecture. H. of existing part 25.2 cm. Late Tomb Period. Institute of Anthropology, Tokyo University

The use of boats as *haniwa* could very well have been related to ideas having to do with the transportation of the soul after death. This is not unknown in shamanistic circles and apparently retained considerable popularity in Kyūshū if one may judge by the many reproductions of boats in the decorated tombs and such religious sites as Okinoshima, an island off north Kyūshū, where crude stone models of boats have been discovered.

Clay coffins were manufactured by the Haji guild on demand toward the end of the Tomb period in the eastern Inland Sea and the vicinity of Nara. Despite the *haniwa*'s Yayoi heritage, in the north Kyūshū region where jar burials had been plentiful, clay sarcophagi were not produced, partly because the older burial practices remained traditionally strong. Clay sarcophagi are multi-legged containers with arched lids, and are most commonly associated with rock-cut corridor tombs. Four cylindrical coffins were found grouped in the Jimbayama Tomb in Okayama prefecture. Such coffins may be long enough to hold a short adult, are ribbed, and capped at either end. The ribbing, or a banding effect on the larger examples, is common to almost all, and serves to reinforce the walls. A remarkably well preserved child's coffin in the shape of a moccasin comes from northwest Nara prefecture, just west of Nara city. The head end is blunt, the foot tapered. Its lid fits quite well. Combing characterizes the reddish surface.

Tomb interior *haniwa* include flat, hollow objects from the Miyayama Tomb. Few *haniwa* articles have any reason to go into a tomb. These are expertly fashioned and handsomely incised with *chokkomon* on one side only. Three of these, along with an undecorated piece, either stood in the corners or were laid out parallel to the inner walls of the tomb. The undecorated piece is also entirely hollow, but is arched at one end as though its projections are intended to be a pair of legs. It may have been a stand. The relative position of these is significant inasmuch as the *chokkomon*, in its most elaborate form on permanent tomb surfaces, such as the wall screens of the Idera Tomb in Kumamoto prefecture, is used to form a fully protective ring around the dead and his possessions. The *chokkomon* may have been initially derived from simple Han dynasty tomb tile patterns and similar objects and was then transmitted through Korea and kept alive for centuries by means of constant modification and variation on small portable objects in Japan, ultimately to be used extensively for *haniwa* and wall decorations in tombs. When employed this way it is intended to emphasize the orientation of the tomb, borrowing a faded leaf from the tomb designers and decorators in China and Korea. Any cosmic meaning in Japan could hardly have been in sharp focus by the time the Idera Tomb was built, and all the vaguer ideas in evolving Shinto dulled most specific religious ideas brought to Japan from Taoist China. Reorganized motifs might remain as a matter of form after those who had initially understood them had passed on.

The *chokkomon* is a design consistently associated with the dead and must be assumed to have had a powerful, magical meaning, one which allowed the dead to become a part of the fundamental order of the universe, aiding in returning him to his rightful position in relation to the human and spirit world. The *chok-* *komon* is common to several types of inanimate *haniwa*: sunshades, *tomo* (an archer's wristpiece), shields, quivers, sword handles and others. It had already passed its prime when human *haniwa* reach their peak of popularity, yet by definition there is no reason for it to appear as decoration on costumes or paraphernalia actually worn or carried by the *haniwa* figures[32].

Music making objects had their start well before the Tomb period. There were perforated, hollow, turtle-shaped objects from the Jōmon period. The Yayoi people had contributed bronze bells, but the Tomb period's connections with Korea meant the addition of several other instruments to the repertory of the sort which took considerable skill to play. These were Chinese in origin. The *haniwa* are almost exclusive evidence of the presence of these in protohistoric Japan, while the Shōsōin in Nara, the eighth century store-

*Fig. 70

Figs. 64, 65

Cat. 61

*Fig. 71

Fig. 84 *Haniwa* warrior wearing broad decorated belt, from Hirai, Tano county, Gumma prefecture. H. 114 cm. Late Tomb Period. National Museum, Tokyo

house of Emperor Shōmu's personal possessions, contains the evidence for the later, more refined developments.

Cat. 85 *Haniwa* instrument players include a drum beater, a woman holding something like a castanet, and a seated figure playing a lyre. This last is a kind of *koto*, a five-stringed instrument used by men like a wagon zither that may be related to the Yamato-goto, a six-stringed instrument. A fragmentary warrior from Tochigi prefecture has a *koto* attached to his skirt at the end of which are three spherical bells. One loose hand grasps

Cat. 67 a plectrum, and the *koto* from Ibaragi prefecture is a good replica of what the five-stringed type was like. It may have been as long as 60 cm. at that time; claims for larger ones seem dubious. Small stone, amulet-like objects from fourth century tombs resemble bridges for the strings of a *koto*. Some may actually be, but the shapes are not consistent.

The wood clapper which I compared to a castanet above was the property of female dancers who were simultaneously singers. Dancing was a woman's chore,

*Pl. 1 acting as performers at funeral ceremonies and the like. I suspect that some with cupped hands have simply lost the small baton-like clapper which was a part of their equipment.

The jingle-bells on mirrors, horse trappings, shaman's hats and elsewhere should not be overlooked in any consideration of instruments. The jingling of the

*Cat. 68 shaman's bells about his costume attracted the attention of the spirits, and the jingle-bell mirrors, chiefly a manifestation of the sixth century, served as percussion instruments in the shamanistic ritual.

*Cat. 72 In a date given as 454 in the *Nihon Shoki*, on the
*Fig. 75 death of Emperor Ingyō the king of Silla dispatched eighty ships of tribute carrying eighty musicians. They performed spectacularly, wearing white and singing and dancing as they played their stringed instruments, making their way to the scene of the funeral at Osaka.

Music and dancing were a part of court life and were greatly enhanced under Buddhist patronage. Empress Jingū, who assumed the priestly duties herself, had a *koto* player to accompany her in the acts, having decorated the *koto* with special cloth[33]. Not many years later some wood from an old and venerable ship which had been scheduled for destruction by fire refused to burn. Recognizing its supernatural nature, the emperor ordered the remaining piece of wood to be made into a *koto*. This was done and the instrument had a peculiar, haunting tone which carried for great distances, suggestive of the wind in the summer trees or water breaking against rocks.

Flutes are mentioned in the literature around the beginning of the sixth century, especially in connection with performances at funerals. This should be the Yamato-bue, traditionally native in origins, an instrument of bamboo with six holes.

Farming tools identify male *haniwa* with little question, and the number of farmers is quite surprising. As the sickles and hoes hang from the waist or are carried across the shoulder, there is probably no reason why tools should not be made separately. It happens with some weapons. Farm tools are certainly not many, however, and would probably only be conceivable in the Kantō and its fringes where prosaic subjects were not too lowly to be represented. The curious range of subjects at Shibayama includes a hoe which seems to have a hafted iron blade and slight shaping of the handle.

HANIWA BIRDS

Water-birds and barnyard fowl make up the largest groups of birds, but many lackadaisically modelled examples have doubtful family connections which has led to much confusion in identification. It seems safe to speak of geese, ducks, cocks, hens and trained hawks. The differences of opinion range from calling a bird from Gumma a turkey-cock (*shichi-menchō*)[34] to refer-

Fig. 85 Lightly-armed *haniwa* soldier, from Nakada, Koga city, Ibaragi prefecture. H. 77.5 cm. Late Tomb Period. National Museum, Tokyo

Fig. 86 Cylindrical *haniwa* with head, representing man carrying a shield, from Yokoba, Tonogawa, Tsukuba county, Ibaragi prefecture. H. 61 cm. Late Tomb Period. National Museum, Tokyo

ring to it as a young chicken (*hina*) [35]. A banded bird from Saitama is spoken of as a hawk, although it appears to sit on its turned-under legs and it carries its body horizontally. The neck rises at a right angle, and the head parallels the body. It has little in common with the well modelled hawk here illustrated, yet it is somewhat similar to the goshawk on the arm of its trainer with which this banded bird has evidently been compared for identification. I would consider it to be rather like the Sasanian ducks, and would associate it with the water-birds.

The broad underside of the water-birds is helpful in recognition, as are the much elongated necks of geese, the combs and wattles of cocks, and the postures and bearing of these other birds. Geese are best known from Saitama and Chiba prefectures, barnyard fowl from Tochigi and Gumma. A chicken from Shizuoka city has its wings restored in the shape of a saddle. Four small, simple water-birds and a cock are recorded for Okayama prefecture. A water-bird from Gumma, now missing its head and tail, bears zigzag incisions over its body and on the fore-part of the wing, but this is quite out of the ordinary, since the customary treatment is simply brushing or combing and, if the wings are not modelled, they are outlined by incising and otherwise marked by a few additional lines to feebly suggest feathers.

The majority of the birds emerge from the top of the cylinder without specific indication of legs and feet. It had proved virtually impossible to make the juncture between bird and tube strong enough if this part was unduly narrowed, but one maker in Gumma solved the problem by joining the bird to the cylinder at the usual constriction and then attaching a pair of roughly modelled feet in the front in such a way as to overlap the top band of the cylinder. This is the so-called turkey-cock.

Birds of the Kansai inspired a flourishing production in the Kantō. It may be that the original reason for their existence was lost sight of when they were manufactured in numbers, but by and large they symbolized the flight of the soul upon death, illustrating a migration of the soul. The Ishiyama Tomb bore a water fowl on the summit of the mound. It served to exemplify the apotheosis of the spirit, which was then believed ★Pl. x to fly heavenward.

Dramatic evidence of this idea was visible to many upon the death of the distinguished soldier Yamato-dake, the prince who had first subdued the Kumaso in south Kyūshū and was then commissioned to fight the Emishi infesting the region leading toward the Kantō Plain. His success was less spectacular than in the south and he fell ill after his return through Ise. Yamato-dake died at the age of thirty and was buried with royal splendor in a mounded tomb. Even before the crowd had dispersed a white bird was seen flying out of the tomb in the direction of the imperial capital. The governmental chiefs then entered the tomb and opened the coffin. It was hardly surprising to discover no body of the prince, although his clothing still remained in the way it had enveloped him. Messengers were then dispatched to follow the bird and where it landed another tomb was erected. Soon after it flew on toward present-day Osaka. At Furuichi city the white bird alit and there roosted. One more tomb was built, popularly called Shiratori Ryō (White Bird Imperial Mausoleum), historically thought of as the final resting place of Yamato-dake and one tomb of a group of many large ones only a short walk west of Furuichi train station. Three Shiratori Tombs are explained in this way, all built to accommodate the migrating soul of the prince.

White birds, egrets or cranes, may be seen on many tombs today and especially on those mounds which are set off by moats. Emperor Nintoku's tomb, south of Osaka, is a bird sanctuary and several of its trees are almost a solid white with flocks of roosting birds. Birds are credited with unusual sensitivity to change, and are

Fig. 87　Nude male *haniwa* figure, from unknown locality in Gumma prefecture. H. 58.5 cm. Late Tomb Period. Aikawa Archaeology Museum

Fig. 88　*Haniwa* groom reaching toward horse, from Himezuka Tomb, Shibayama-chō, Sambu county, Chiba prefecture. H. 97.8 cm. Late Tomb Period. Shibayama Haniwa Museum

the first to respond to ominous events. They are good omens when seen on a rooftop. Pairs appear above three buildings on the mirror from Nara prefecture which we have already called attention to, and a fragmentary *haniwa* house from Tochigi prefecture still retains one small bird called a pigeon standing on a cross-log while facing the center. These propitious birds were imitations of Chinese representations of the Han dynasty, in which it is not uncommon to see birds playing this role in low relief on tomb tiles or stone stelae.

Poems in the *Manyōshū* speak of the action of birds at times of great change, primarily in regard to the implications of death. Once tamed, according to one, birds will not turn wild in the Palace of Shima despite the departure of the master. In another, birds which inhabit the garden will stay until the end of the year. Only then will they fly away like wild birds, as birds do at the migration season when a major transformation takes place.

That birds were directly connected with ideas of resurrection is made quite clear in the frequently repeated story of the Sun Goddess disappearing into the cave and subsequently being lured out by the other conniving gods. Susano-o had so upset her that she ran into the Rock Cave of Heaven and closed the stone door behind her, thus cutting off all the light of the land. The devices accumulated by the deities after taking counsel to attract her out is a collection of all known magical symbols to which was added the most exotic dance that any deity had ever performed. The dance was ridiculous. But it took a tree decorated with a mirror, strips of cloth and jewels, recitations, the burning of fires, and this dance performed on a noisy tub by a goddess waving a spear wreathed in grass to accomplish the return of the light. One version (and not all of them include so much paraphernalia) says the gods gathered together cocks with a reputation for strong lungs and coaxed these birds into crowing to each other. It was through this episode that the cocks, which had always been associated with the light of the

new day, took on a meaning related to the coming forth from the cave, that is, emerging from the tomb, and so gained solar connections through the triumph over darkness by the Sun Goddess.

The white birds inhabiting the rice fields in the autumn are much appreciated for their destruction of rice-damaging creatures. Their presence is a sign of the approaching harvest. Kawazoe looks on the cranes which may be seen in pairs on Yayoi bells as fructifying the land as they drop rice stalks in their wanderings[36]. He identifies them with agricultural practices and Toyouke, the goddess of staple foods. Susano-o, whose crimes included slaying the serpents which had materialized from the goddess of staple foods, was a necessary instrument in nature's cycles, if the *Kojiki* can be followed. In the *Nihon Shoki*, however, it was Tsukiyomi, the Moon God, whose duty it became to kill Ukemochi, the Food Goddess, so that new life could be achieved. Regardless of the versions, the essence is that by expectoration she produced rice; from her head emerged the ox and horse; from her forehead sprang millet; from her eyebrows came the silkworm; in her eyes grew panic grass; from her genitals issued wheat and certain beans. Taking these, the Sun Goddess separated them, dry planting some, wet planting others, and so ceremonially initiated a practice still followed by the emperor today at the rice sowing season.

Haniwa makers were selective. They ignored most of the birds mentioned in the old literature. I take it that this is partly due to the international borrowings which entered the literature and which were far above the grassroots concepts expressed by the *haniwa*. Waterbirds, for instance, make a very poor showing. The texts refer to the use of cormorants for fishing and falcons for hunting. On two separate occasions a pair of magpies and a peacock and parrot were delivered at the Japanese court as tribute from Silla. In the category of birds graced with magical powers was a pheasant sent down by the Sun Goddess as a heavenly spy, and a swan which was able to restore the voice of a prince who had lost his ability to speak.

Fig. 89 Pair of *haniwa* singer-dancers, from Ohara, Ōmiya county, Saitama prefecture. H. 64 and 57 cm. Late Tomb Period. National Museum, Tokyo

The more obviously mythical birds, the Three-legged Crow and the Red Bird of the South, are derived from traditionally advanced religious ideas. Both have their background in Chinese mythology and got little farther than the literature, finding no place at all, as far as one can see, in the *haniwa*. The Three-legged Crow was a sun symbol and had made frequent appearances on the walls of the painted tombs of T'ung-Kou along the Yalu River. The Red Bird was the tutelary deity of the south and its presence is equally frequent. If it is in Japan, it can hardly be separated from any other bird.

The crow, the Yatagarasu, however, is an ever present sign of divine guidance in early mythological tales. It may have been borrowed because of its connections with solar symbolism, but it becomes a common two-legged variety in Japan. It was on constant call by the Sun Goddess when her descendant the first emperor met with insurmountable obstacles, and was dispatched to bolster his morale and lead him to victory. The fundamental concept is given visual shape on the left side of the painting on the end slab of the Mezurashizuka Tomb in Yoshii-machi of Fukuoka prefecture, where a bird may be seen near the bow of a boat. The bird perched on the crest of the tumulus did so as the soul of the deceased, yet it is conceivable that the *haniwa* bird was also viewed as a symbol of the Sun Goddess which acted as the guide for her progeny at this time of the soul's greatest ordeal.

HANIWA ANIMALS

Only a few animals are known from the Kansai, and animals did not join the repertory in appreciable numbers until the Kantō showed an interest in them. Some local preferences are apparent in the distribution of each species. Horses come from Chiba and Saitama, but the great majority are from Gumma. Wild boar are chiefly from Gumma and Chiba. Members of the bovine family are found in Osaka and Nara prefectures in the Kansai. The deer are chiefly from Ibaragi, but

do also come from Chiba, yet a small spotted deer was found in Shimane prefecture of the Izumo region. Dogs are largely from Gumma. The well known monkey hails from Ibaragi prefecture. The range of subjects for the Kantō even includes at least two *haniwa* fish, both from Ibaragi.

The complexion of art patronage has changed considerably since the artisans of the Yayoi culture had represented a selection of predatory flying insects, fish, cranes and reptiles, along with hunting scenes of boar and deer. These have to do with the gathering, preparation and preservation of food, all signs of the Yayoi preoccupation around which its religious practices revolved.

The Tomb period's preoccupations were not with the fertility of the land but with political controls through military methods. The earthy, vain, belligerent interests of the nobles had to be met by the craftsmen. And these interests they did meet, with vigorous, unsophisticated artistic efforts.

The horse is by far the most popular *haniwa* animal. The legs of all the quadrupeds are invariably shapeless cylinders, the elongation compensated for when the legs were pressed into the ground. The horses' legs Fig. 72 tend to establish the nature of the animal as motionless, stolid, shoulders erect. The mane stands high, is tufted over the forehead. The ears are sharp and upright. The faces are usually straight; modelling was only rarely tried and even then added negligibly toward realism. The mouth may be little more than an open tube, cut off at a sharp angle.

Any attempt to render the general notion of the speed of the horse was beyond the ambition of the *haniwa* maker, although some extraordinary sculptor did try this with a wild boar. In this respect the "flying gallop" of common usage in China and known on mirrors carried into Japan, was never employed by Japanese craftsmen whose productions hardly rose above lower conceptual planes.

The illustrated horse from Saitama prefecture is a Fig. 72 male, but it is difficult to determine in old restorations

Plate XI *Haniwa* male figure from Miyake village, Shiki county, Nara prefecture. H. 40 cm. Middle Tomb Period. National Museum, Tokyo

how much is original. Most horses seem to have no special indications of sex, unless the seeming lack is intended to make them female. In numerous instances, large parts of manes, ears, tails, saddles and even legs are restored. The immense horse at Shibayama, associated with a groom, is not less than three-fourths rebuilt.

All horses are caparisoned, apparently ready for action. Hanging high over narrow saddles are small, oval-shaped stirrups, designed for a small rider. Jingle-bells, small suspension bells, a variety of flank and bit ornaments give each horse its own unique personality. The heads are most arresting; the details of the S-shaped, heart-shaped and jingle-bell bridle bits and others are all corroborated by the actual finds in tombs.

The horse among the *haniwa* symbolizes ideally the aspirations of political conquest. Horses were without doubt imported at least until the Middle Tomb period, but the large breeding grounds of the Tsukushi and Kantō plains expanded their business to cope with the demand and were able to supply the needs in subsequent centuries.

Writers of early literature sensed the historic developments in the use of the horse. Emperor Jimmu, for instance, marched into battle. The historians do not make the error of saying that he rode. He was, after all, a local Yayoi tribesman, if anything. Except for Susano-o's unpleasant treatment of the Piebald Colt of Heaven, it took the appearance of the *haniwa* to introduce the horse to Japanese history. The Haji-be were to "take clay and form therewith shapes of men, horses, and various objects" which were presented to Emperor Suinin[37]. Historians might say that this took place during the second half of the third century, at a time before archaeologists would say that human and horse *haniwa* were in production. It does nothing to clarify a confused situation to suggest that Suinin is said to lie in an archaeologically-determined fifth century tomb. But any perusal of the *Nihon Shoki* reveals

a rapid increase in the number of references to horses after the fifth century.

Some of these notations give valuable insights into the status of horse-breeders and the value and use of the horse. The branding of the *be* of grooms was discontinued during the reign of Emperor Richū (ca. 427–32) as directed by the spirit of Izanagi through a medium. Their raw face wounds refused to heal; the odor was intolerable to the deity and he requested that the custom be abandoned. Emperor Yūryaku hunted on horseback. One of his relatives was obligated to pay a fine of eight horses and eight swords after it had been ★Cat. 69 discovered that he had seduced a court attendant. His subsequent poetic comment, purporting to quote ★Cat. 70 others, was that for this particular girl it was a cheap price.

Fighting on horseback took place in Korea as Japanese troops were sent to hold Mimana. Horseback fighting in Japan itself is rarely mentioned by the historians, partly because they did not want to give the effect of that much disunity in the state and partly because by the time the horse was in daily use the major battles were actually over. Except for pockets of obstreperous barbarians, there was little more than incidental skirmishes. The dethronement of Lord Iwai of Tsukushi was one of these, despite the anticipated major battle. Even here no mention is made of cavalry, although Iwai had reached his prominent position through control of the horse-breeding business in north Kyūshū.

That the business was a highly flourishing one, to the point of surplus, is proved by the gifts of horses to foreign rulers. Emperor Keitai sent an envoy to present forty-four Tsukushi horses to the ruler of Paikche in A.D. 512, fifteen years before Iwai obstructed the Korean campaign, and in 545 Emperor Kimmei surpassed even that with a generous gift of seventy-four horses and ten ships to the emissaries of Paikche as they left Japan bound for their home country.

Fig. 90 Heavily attired female *haniwa*, from unknown locality. H. 34.6 cm. Late Tomb Period. National Museum, Tokyo
Fig. 91 *Haniwa* woman with cup on head and child on back, from Kyōizumi, Mōka city, Tochigi prefecture. H. 41.5 cm. Late Tomb Period. National Museum, Tokyo

Any supernatural event concerning a horse stirred the imagination of the early recorders. There was the Piebald Colt of Heaven which was flayed backwards by Susano-o, according to the story; Hyakuson's midnight ride and the magnificent steed turning into a *haniwa* horse; the man from Yamato who bought a phenomenal creature in 546 which raced like a "startled wild goose[38]" and was able to jump sixty meters, yet it could maintain a steady pace and was gentle and obedient; and a horse in a later reference which ran spontaneously around the Main Hall of a temple day and night, pausing only long enough to graze.

Some horses in the other arts of the Tomb period have enlarged, arched tails as if dressed for ceremonial occasions. The horse was a shamanistic vehicle, ridden by the medium as he accompanied the soul of the deceased. Toward the end of the Tomb period special practices emerge in the Yamato and neighboring regions in which small clay horses were used in the cult[39]. More than twenty of these have been found, several at the bottom of wells, deposited there in a water ritual which utilized sympathetic magic to bring rain — or perhaps even to prevent it. Many shrines have a small building housing a life-size model of a horse, offered in substitute for the living animal. The *Ema-e*, the paintings of horses which figure prominently among the votive gifts to shrines, are there because the worshiper has solicited improved health, hopes to overcome barrenness, or is seeking protection for his livestock. In all of these cases, the horse is the intermediary between man and the gods, chosen because of his ability to convey the message at great speed.

Late Jōmon people knew about the horse, and the bones from sites are unmutilated, but it is doubtful if they made much attempt to ride it. Bones preserved from the Yayoi period show that both small and medium horses existed in Japan. Horse bones are almost unknown from the Tomb period, but they have been found of a medium-sized horse at Hiraide, a community site in Nagano prefecture which was occupied from the Jōmon period well into historic centuries. Direct importation of horses was from Korea, but ultimately they were brought from Mongolia or farther west. Horses of the Middle Ages were still chiefly this medium-sized horse.

The sacrifice of horses was common procedure in Central Asia, from where it was introduced to other regions as horses came into wider use. Except for certain tomb paintings which may possibly contain implications of horse sacrifice, the only indication of the custom in Japan is the inclusion of its prohibition in the Taika Reform of 645. The record here may be taken at face value, it seems to me, as an acknowledgment of the fact of the practice and the desirability of putting a stop to it.

Wild boar are still hunted in places where they ravage the crops or threaten domestic animals in snow covered regions in their search for food. Early boar hunts were occasions of great excitement. Emperor Yūryaku scrambled up a tree when a boar turned and charged him. Dogs had been trained for just such hunts in Yayoi times and served to wear down the resistance of the beast, after which it was dispatched with arrows. One *haniwa* boar from Chiba prefecture, with long slender snout and sinister eyes, has an arrow visible on its back as though it were being shot — a genre touch only possible in the Kantō. The animals from the Kansai are of a more mixed breed. At best their shape is never too far from that of a dog, but one from Osaka prefecture is made specifically swine-like by its flattened and slightly upturned nose. A *haniwa* from Nara prefecture is called an *ushi*, a cow, bull or ox, and appears to have once had horns. Local technical features include holes in the shoulders or upper thighs, probably a sign of an early stage of hollow-form modelling. The Kansai people represented their creatures as more gentle; in fact, the crude boar from Osaka is characterized as next to harmless.

Fig. 92   *Haniwa* figure holding offering cup, from Akitsu, Namekata county, Ibaragi prefecture. H. 68.6 cm. Late Tomb Period. Institute of Anthropology, Tokyo University

Fig. 93   *Haniwa* figure making offering (cup missing), from Tokiwa, Higashi-ibaragi county, Ibaragi prefecture. H. 73.5 cm. Late Tomb Period. National Museum, Tokyo

143

Deer hunting was another old sport. The Jōmon people left numerous bones of deer in their sites, while Yayoi artisans frequently illustrated them in their simple art style. With ears outstretched, long tubular nose, rounder eyes than the boar, the many extant heads were fashioned as an animal which bordered on the friendly, if not tame, side. Stumps of horns show that stags may have been infrequently intended; does were certainly preferred.

Deer were fast disappearing by the Tomb period. Any unusual happenings that reached the attention of the historians were inevitably recorded. During the building of Emperor Nintoku's tomb a deer ran into the group of workmen and fell dead. As its death was being investigated, a shrike flew out of its ear. It was soon discovered that the shrike had bitten the inside of the ear down to the bone. All of this was offered by way of explanation for the name of Nintoku's tomb site, Mozu-no-mimi, Ear of a Shrike. The tiny train station nearest the gigantic tomb is called Mozu. Deer were later protected when there arose serious fears for the depletion of the stocks, and under Shinto-Buddhist auspices, Nara's famous Deer Park was enabled to flourish.

Dogs were everywhere and had little prestige value. They were not widely made haniwa and have come almost exclusively from Gumma prefecture. Admiration for faithful dogs is the chief reason for introducing them in the early literature and haniwa makers made them with the same sense of affection as they are written about by the historians. One haniwa dog has its head turned back sharply in a rare attempt to give an extra dimension of interest. The body is a fraction more shapely than the dog illustrated here, although the two come from the same village. With short curled tail, mouth open, tongue hung loosely, and bell on collar, it is a playful creature, to be enjoyed by all around the house.

The haniwa monkey, as the animal does in life, seems almost human. Bewildered and mournful, it was probably a pet. A break on the back gives the impression that it once supported a baby below the shoulders. Other breaks may be seen at the shoulders and ears, and the surface is rough where arms may have been, but how all of these were formed, if at all, is difficult to imagine. A tube below simply widens into shoulders, then into a head turned on the neck. The face has retained its red paint. ★Fig. 74

The Sue libation ware designed for use inside the tombs with its foreign origins naturally contained foreign ideas in its ornamentation. The small human, bird and animal figures which decorate the shoulders on some pieces from the Inland Sea, are derivatives in Japan of Silla pottery decoration and may ultimately owe their debt to Chinese ceramics. These are at least one step removed in quality of workmanship from the Korean examples, and leave much to the imagination. There are boats, water-birds, suspected hunts, apparently wrestlers, deer and an assortment of other animals. It is only in their extreme simplicity that they have anything in common with the little known figurines of this period, and any influence on the gray Sue from the reddish haniwa tradition can be little more than sheer accident. The small figures of the Tomb period relate to the haniwa distantly through a single progenitor, both having their ancestry in Yayoi ceramic work. Fig. 100

HANIWA FIGURES

It may now seem heretical to have arrived at the conclusion that the real meaning of the haniwa is not to be found in the human figures but in other, earlier haniwa forms. The figures are cake icing; they do much to make the cake more attractive, but they also tend to conceal it. Without the icing it is quite edible. The idea of haniwa precedes the human figures; their production was flourishing before human figures were even thought of, and the custom was only enlarged and enriched after most inanimate objects were abandoned in favor of the figures. Changing subjects reflect changing interests, and the meaning of the haniwa does undergo ★Pl. IX

★Pl. VIII

Fig. 94 *Haniwa* figure of seated female shaman with mirror at waist, from Ōkawa, Shiraku county, Gumma prefecture. H. 68.5 cm. Late Tomb Period. National Museum, Tokyo

*Fig. 89
corresponding changes. The artistic evolution is rather slight except for an erratically developing attention to detail and literalism. It is fair to say that the *haniwa* become increasingly decorative, the signs of which include the tendency to bear paint on one side only, to the neglect of the side facing the tomb, and the flattening out of the figures to present a broad surface. This latter results in a shape a fraction closer to the human Fig. 78 body, and is best exemplified by the oval shaped bodies of the old warriors of Shibayama. An arrangement of *haniwa* on a tomb assumes an air of pomp and pageantry, of which visual appeal plays the largest part.

But if I should suggest that the human figures and the earlier *haniwa* result from a two-pronged development, I would not convey my understanding of what transpired. It has been said that the figures did not evolve from the cylinders—that they had an independent evolution[40]. I look on the difference as essentially one of degree, for the fundamental cylindrical form is common to all the figures and I cannot see that the intervening inanimate objects break what is basically an established pattern. All retain a rigid frontality. It is quite true that many of the highly simplified figures which are little more than tubes are rather late in time. They are in no way examples of an early stage in the evolution; they are the consequence of local *Cat. 82, 83
*Fig. 94 working habits, the pressures brought to bear on the craftsmen to get the *haniwa* ready for the tombs, and ever-present tendencies toward mass production.

A cylinder with facial features might be cited. Into its top has been cut a pair of slit eyes, a mouth very little wider, and it has received a vertical strip of clay Fig. 97 for a nose. Slightly more modelled human faces appear on other examples, some of which have remnants of arms that once jutted out. Since almost all are from Ibaragi prefecture in the Kantō, it would hardly be expected that they would be the earliest in time. They are more like one of the many aberrations of the Kantō, coming about through daily manipulation of cylinders. This is what is meant when it is said that *haniwa* figures did not evolve from cylinders.

The well known dancers are little more than tubes rounded and closed at the top. Any further reduction would lead to nothing but incision work to suggest face and limbs, a device that was actually resorted to in one or two fragmentary cases. Structurally and technically the figures were dependent on the cylinders; there was no breaking out of the format once it was established, and the figures seem almost inconceivable without the cylinders.

Adequate articulation of limbs in the human figures was a complicated problem, especially when occupational gestures were called for. More common than arms protruding from shoulderless cylinders was a widening of the upper torso into curved, elbowless tubes. For preservation's sake and particularly for safety in transporting of *haniwa*, the arms were kept relatively close to the body and if possible attached, or were joined to each other while extended in front. They may also clasp or touch weapons or instruments and thus be affixed to a firm surface. Dancers are the sole type which fairly consistently have at least one extended arm, but preference was given to a single arm projected only, and the other was held to the body, doubtless for rhythmical effect.

The difficulty in making legs could legitimately be avoided outright in most cases. When they were attempted in such *haniwa* as the cross-legged, obeisant warrior or the female shaman they were drastically telescoped—far more than even any advanced concept of foreshortening might demand. The difficulty was overcome in one of two ways in standing figures: the cylinder was joined to the lower edge of the tunic around the region of the hips, thus eliminating legs altogether, or using the natural shape of the horse-riding trousers to give strengthened support and by enclosing the leg in armor. The legs of women are almost entirely ignored and, as a normal thing, very few figures of women are even finished off in a full skirt. The attire of the women tends to be quite ceremonial, perhaps because they carried so many of the varied duties in the funeral ceremonies. This general neglect of wo-

Fig. 95 *Haniwa* lady in full dress, from Hachisu, Isezaki city, Gumma prefecture. H. 127 cm. Late Tomb Period. National Museum, Tokyo

men's legs can be construed to reflect some inequality in their status, an inequality which is implied by the occupations themselves.

In an essentially abstract treatment of human features, fine distinctions between sex, age and occupation will have to be culled from the small differences between coiffures, hats, costumes, equipment and gestures. Not even all presumably female figures are breasted. Nippled breasts are commonplace and are often seen over a fairly elaborate costume. Age or social status appears in the treatment of the hair. A young maiden wears hers long to the shoulders; a married woman puts hers up in an arrangement on the head that resembles a mortar board. A comb may hold it in place over the forehead. Age distinctions in men are not so sharp, except for the extraordinary bearded warriors from one of the Shibayama tombs. Men's hair is parted in the middle and allowed to hang to the shoulders. It is often braided, and there is reason to suppose that the fancier the braid, the higher the rank.

The range of suggested occupations is not as great as might at first be supposed. The most conspicuous are the soldiers, but running a close second are those who do the menial tasks. This latter group is dominated by farmers. The military ranks include the very popular heavily-armed soldiers in two classes of uniform, both of whom are the mounted warriors, and the lightly-armed soldiers who might be called the infantrymen. The high number of mounted warriors may be explained as prestige symbols; the fewer number of foot soldiers are merely some note taken of the existence of underlings.

Warriors quite frequently show up as *haniwa* playing a dual role. There is, for instance, the male shaman and the *koto* player. Both are well armed. The Fukushima shaman with his peaked, jingle-bell hat, holds his hands together in a gesture of reverence; he wears hand guards. This seems almost out of place when seen in the *koto* player. But the warrior-actor is nothing more than evidence of the king-priest role, the ruler through his personal relationship to the deities doing the reli-

gious acts on behalf of his followers. These acts are more frequent in times of great stress, and the mood of urgency is heightened by the preparedness of the warrior. The times that the early emperors sacrificed or made offering to the gods were conscientiously recorded in the literature. Emperor Jimmu did the oblations himself before engaging in battle on several occasions when the situation was desperate.

The warriors justifiably draw the widest acclaim. The Kantō excelled in the making of these, but carried their interests to a preoccupation with detail and equipment, and allowed the natural freshness of the *haniwa* to suffer correspondingly. Rather few warriors wear the cuirass. The attire of the highest rank is full slat armor, tied left over right in front, helmet with cheek and neck guards, gauntlets, and leg armor tied with ribbons in the back. Bows, swords, quivers, wrist protectors, pouches and, at Shibayama, a small scabbard that may be for a special type of knife, all help to complete the wardrobe of the well-dressed soldier. Battle dress or for parade, quiver on the side or on the back, these *haniwa* are figures of great eminence, the nobility of the land. *[Cat. 73; *Figs. 78, 79; Fig. 82; Cat. 74]*

The variety of helmets is amazing; some have ornamental wings that rise high on either side of the head and all are heavily riveted, reproducing literally the technical aspects of the actual tomb finds. *[Fig. 83]*

A slightly less formidable group of soldiers is not quite so burdened down with military paraphernalia. No slat marks decorate these costumes. They may be wearing leather armor, or normal riding attire and, while gaily outfitted as though for occasions of show and spectacle, their lack of heavy iron armor may mean they illustrate the next to top rank of the elite.

The headgear resembles hats instead of helmets, sometimes like a bowler or peaked in front, or a skull-cap with a ball on top. An occasional warrior is bare-headed. There are the large circular earrings, the massive braids of hair, a bold flare to the tunic which is overlapped right across left, and the wide, firm stance. The proportions may reach a slightly ludicrous degree; *[*Cat. 83]*

Fig. 96 Female *haniwa* figure with unusual headdress, from Kyōizumi, Mōka city, Tochigi prefecture. H. 39.5 cm. Late Tomb Period. National Museum, Tokyo

Fig. 84 witness the swaggering warrior who wears a pair of jingle-bells just below each knee. Ancient Japan's most ostentatious battle veteran is a member of this group;

Figs. 76, 77 he hails from Gumma prefecture. Bowler hatted, arms shaped like arcs, great girth to his broad skirt and finned trousers, he wears his uniform and weapons like medals and decorations, a proud hero of numerous engagements.

The lightly-armed soldiers have been called in-

*Cat. 83 fantrymen. It might perhaps be better to look on them
Fig. 85 here as bodyguards. They are often hatless and show
*Cat. 84 their hair to have been parted in the middle and simply brought down toward the chest to be double knotted at the end. They must not have been entitled to elaborate braids.

Within the broad warrior class will be found the shield and quiver bearers. The shield bearer swings into action in a defensive manoeuvre when enemy bowmen mass their fire. The Korean wars are graphically described, and tell how deadly this could be. Thus the shield

Fig. 86 bearer is virtually hidden behind the shield, as is his counterpart behind the quiver, permitting only the head to appear above. It would be more than necessary to show a man physically holding his gear, but the result emerges more like a winged man, and the relative size of

*Fig. 88 these objects attests to large shields and quivers in con-
*Cat. 90 trast to the small quiver borne by the mounted warriors.

Hats undoubtedly had some use as indicators of status and occupation, but any governmental formalization of the idea did not come until the seventh century. Empress Suiko was the first to decree it, but it was not for 44 more years, in 647, that Emperor Kōtoku designated thirteen ranks to be distinguished by the color and brocade of each hat. The system was changed to nineteen grades two years after.

Hats known from Central Asia may be found to have some counterparts in the Tomb period in Japan, and similarities exist between Korean and Japanese headgear at this time. But hats have to be used warily for judgment; clearly society has not yet seen to the codification of many of its practices, a point which is all the more apparent in religious ideas. The many farmers from Gumma prefecture, for instance, do not all wear the same type of hat, just as not all the soldiers wear the same type of helmet. We may say, however, that for shaman-like persons there are several possibilities: a crown with a serrated edge, a hat with a high peak at the front marked with triangles, and a high rounded hat also bearing triangles. Another kind is "antlered"; what is left of projections over the temples indicate that some sort of horns existed.

It is often a tight-fitting cap along the order of a skull-cap for the lightly-armed warriors. It may have a wide brim or thick head band. In the case of the band, a strip of clay undulates around the head. The large group of farmers generally wear a small cap, often with brim. If it is brimless, it may be single or double pointed, the two points more or less above the ears. I suspect that many more loose heads wearing rather similar caps are actually those of farmers. The Aikawa Museum has a remarkable number of these tillers of the soil in its collection.

The Shibayama *haniwa* proved the existence of horse grooms. These wear a coolie hat. Some of the stocking-hatted figures turn out to be quiver bearers. Pointed hats of medium height may be tied near the top with a bow. This bow occasionally assumes impressive dimensions, for the "space man" whose antennae give him a true science fiction air, might actually have been bedecked with one of these carried to ridiculous proportions, almost as though satirizing the custom. Included in this high hatted group are several of the faces which are characterized by half-moon shaped eyes and mouth. In the most elementary way, astonishing differences in expression have been shown. Two tall hatted *haniwa* with these humorous expressions are finned as though intended to be quiver bearers. Another is certainly not.

Fig. 97 *Haniwa* cylinder with tilted human face, in Yayoi tradition, from Kamibushi, Sakai-machi, Sawa county, Gumma prefecture. H. 42 cm. Late Tomb Period. Institute of Anthropology, Tokyo University

Fig. 98 Hollow clay figurine with headdress, circular and curved beads, and disc on chest, from Kanoya city, Kagoshima prefecture. L. 18.4 cm. Tomb Period (?). Private Collection, Tokyo

It is possibly an expression used for professional comedians or court jesters, for the foolish looking headgear of the "space man" may perhaps be costuming for such a part. It is known that court jesters were at times employed for imperial services, and it is not entirely impossible that the *haniwa* represent those who may have been cast in a rather similar role for funeral observances.

Just how great an effort the *haniwa* sculptors made to suggest an occupation and mood through facial expression in this essentially primitive and abstract art has come to be judged through subjective evaluation based on evidence provided by isolated examples. Several recognizable dancers of both the male and female sex, including the famous pair, have more than the ordinary slit for a mouth. An attempt has been made to show them singing while they dance, in a simultaneous act that is still seen today in traditional performances.

Our Happy Farmer has been taken as typifying the carefree life of the time, the joy of daily labor and the love of working the land[41]. A quick check with other known farmers shows him to be a light-hearted, likeable freak, blithely going about his way, quite unaware that most husbandmen are glum, grim or figuratively whistling through their teeth. They are not spiritless; they just seem to have accepted their lot with a good deal of wry stoicism. My deduction from this is that it is unsafe to draw conclusions as to the attitude or mood of a class of figures, but that some attempt to increase recognition through occupational expressions or gestures was tried by the sculptors and is logically enough a legitimate basis for identification.

It is not without good reason that one finds so many dancers and offering bearers of both sexes. Although the woman balancing the cup on her head is sometimes said to be performing her daily chores[42], I feel that under the circumstances she is carrying the offering in the manner most familiar to her. The men normally hold the cup in front of them. These people furnished professional services for the graveside obsequies, and the *haniwa* have reached the stage of representing the grand procession and last rites for which hired performers and serving personnel were employed.

Kneeling figures with hands in front have been thought of as official reciters. In the funeral party they may be making the obeisances, as symbolizing the final farewell to the deceased[43]. One of these, a warrior-like figure, is surprisingly well modelled for this complex sculptural form. His hat is horned; small ear-like projections rise above the temples. Another figure from the same Ibaragi prefecture, however, is so feebly fashioned as to be scarcely recognizable. Without better examples for guides, it would be difficult to know what he represents. The shapeless shoulders, arms, body and legs have little normal relationship to each other. The hats of these two also have nothing in common except their location on the top of the head.

Cat. 84

*Fig. 89

The unique *haniwa* claim more notice than might normally be their due. The hawker is one of these. Wearing a banded skull-cap engraved with zigzags and connected arcs, he is attired in the uniform of the lower élite which includes a sword in scabbard and *tomo*, the wrist protector. Shortened arms are covered by guards. On the left wrist sits a large-beaked hawk to whose tail is attached a bell. Like all, it is a frontally disposed figure with characteristic detachment from his surroundings; he neither looks at the hawk nor does the hawk face in his direction. The hawk becomes a simple addition to the stereotyped stance, yet it is hard to question the aristocratic bearing and poise of this figure. He has been classified as a National Treasure.

*Pl. 1

Cat. 81

The *be* of hawk tamers was formed during Emperor Nintoku's reign, if one may accept the *Nihon Shoki* story. One such bird was caught and presented to the emperor who showed it to a Korean prince who was then residing in Japan. The latter's familiarity with these birds in Paikche led to his taming this hawk and proving its value by a demonstration of pheasant hunt-

*Fig. 91

*Cat. 86

*Fig. 92

Fig. 99 Small clay models of horses, legs and rear part of second horse largely restored, from (front) Kamiyoshi, Izushi county, Hyōgo prefecture, and (back) Nagano, Ōeda, Otokuni county, Kyoto prefecture. L. front 20.7 cm., back 24.6 cm. Tomb Period (?). Institute of Archaeology, Kyoto University

ing in the Mozu plain. As the story is told, the Korean prince put a bell on the bird's tail and a leather band around its leg. The bird was trained to come to rest on his forearm. The hawk tamers could proudly point to royal origins — albeit Korean — by tradition, and the distinguished mien of this figure shows they had not forgotten the regal ideal.

Fig. 94   The female shaman is another *haniwa* of rare interest. She is identified as a medium by the jingle-bell mirror dangling from her waist, and her status is further implied by the ornamental throne and a rich array of double necklaces, bracelets and anklets. The coiffure is theatrical. The hands look as though they are en-
★Fig. 87 closed in mittens. Her proportions are reduced progressively from the head to the miniature legs, yet the very fact that she is provided with legs is fair indication of her elevated position in life. The ceremonial nature
★Cat. 96 of the throne is emphasized by the incised triangles which mark the upper half, that part which would have been seen above the ground.

Fig. 91   Children are rare and are to be seen as accouterments on the mother's back. This daily convention is the kind that probably sparked the popular belief that women
★Cat. 97 carrying jars on their heads are simply models of routine activities, not unlike the Ōhara girls of today who descend from the mountainside into Kyoto to sell foodstuffs carried on trays on their heads. If recent Shinto-sponsored dances, such as the fall *obon* festival of returning the spirits to the dead, are any means of judgment, a baby strapped to the back does not prevent participation in a ceremonial event. But Shiba-
Cat. 98 yama has an amorphous creature much like a seal baby, labelled a child at the museum. I do not doubt that Shibayama's range of subjects could include a child, but when one recalls the crudity and ineptness of some of the work there, one is left in a quandary as to what this thing could be. The recent catalogue makes no mention of it as possibly being a child; it speaks of it as a person who looks as though he is swimming[44]. The fin-like hands add substantially to the aquatic

effect, and the merging of body and head, coupled with the almost subhuman face, are contributing features.

    The infrequently illustrated nude figures, two male and one female, pose interesting problems as to meaning. The usual treatment in Japanese literature is to pass them off as representing people of low class without further comment — if they are not ignored entirely. I suspect that several male heads were initially from such figures, because if these two similar faces may be used as a guide (but I have indicated elsewhere that this is risky), some attempt was made to correspond an uncouth expression with the implied occupation. The mouth is warped and twisted; the eyes are tilted at the outer corners. The tight-fitting cap with peaked center and large annular ear ornaments go with the type. But other complete figures will show that the deformed mouth is not the exclusive property of nude figures.

    The male figures, one with phallus still intact, are both from Gumma prefecture, but are such old finds that nothing can be said of where they stood on a tomb or their relative position to other *haniwa*. The female is from another Kantō prefecture — it is doubtful if the home provinces would have found a place for these — and is also an old discovery. She is much restored, perhaps suspiciously so, and I know of no other figure to which she may be compared for verification. There is a conspicuous absence of breasts, yet breasts as bulges or nipples are common enough in numerous female figures. Combed and heavily brushed surfaces may at times be taken as representing exposed flesh, but this is by no means generally applicable and is even more difficult to apply than the idea that cord-marking was used for costumes in the Latest Jōmon (Kamegaoka) figurines in north Japan. Interestingly enough, she obviously had her hair put up in the most lady-like fashion, and this is one reason why I would suggest that she is a woman of pleasure, but her activities were essentially in the line of duty.

    Nude figures are known in the stone statues from Kyūshū, especially from the Iwatoyama Tomb, and

Fig. 100   Animals (dogs with a deer?) on shoulder of Sue libation vessel, from Nishi-miyayama Tomb, Tatsuno city, Hyōgo prefecture. H. of vessel 37.5 cm. Late Tomb Period. National Museum, Kyoto

include both male and female figures. One of the males is ithyphallic. These two regions of Fukuoka and Gumma are poles apart, yet there is no reason why similar practices should not have prevailed. I personally look on these as having to do with the ritual and feel that they cannot be merely glossed over as part of the Kantō genre. They may be a legacy from earlier fertility rites, now much like ritual prostitution, quite likely supervised by the shrines. The complete figure with arched arms affixed to the chest is the habitual stance for laboring people, and certainly there is nothing about these figures which conceals the attempt to connote them with the social level of the working class. It is possible that a professional group had received the assignment to carry out the responsibilities connected with these rites. Fertility symbols have much earlier been described as being closely associated with ideas of death, the afterworld and renewed life; rites along this order would be readily adaptable if thought to be effective. It may be that even the shape of the keyhole tomb was believed to have this meaning.

Face painting of *haniwa* is so frequent, whether it be civilian or soldier, man or woman, that it must reflect a passionate attempt to fulfil a deeply felt need. On the whole one receives the impression that the upper classes indulged in it more often, which includes the shaman or priestly types. But it is no respecter of persons; it does have a strong regional flavor. The red paint may be full face covering, on the forehead, under the eyes, from eyes to ears, down the nose, and even vertical stripes on the chin.

While reminiscent of the face painting on Yayoi human-headed jars—and I do not doubt some connection—I have come to believe that here we are dealing with a practice specifically related to the cult of the dead. A shaman, it is known, felt some uneasiness about escorting the soul of the deceased to the next world for fear that the devilish spirits would prevent his return or perhaps even find a way to earth to destroy him. He often resorted to painting himself as a prophylactic measure to avoid recognition. The *haniwa*,

it has been argued, reproduce certain notions of the afterlife. They show participants in funeral activities—dispatching the dead, so to speak. All who were involved came under the spell of the deceased and were tied to him by invisible spiritual bonds. Face painting may have been indulged in to allay the fears of later identification with the dead. I would suggest that this painting is not for beautification and is entirely without an esthetic motive[45]. Far more cogent reasons demanded it be done. It acted as a deterrent to the malicious spirit of the dead. Quite simply, it protected the living from the dead.

The literary remarks would seem to rule out tattooing here, for it had fallen into disfavor as something practised by barbarians. The Emishi (presumably the Ainu), for instance, were singled out as indulging in this vulgar custom. Tattooing was tantamount to branding and was a stigma at this time for crimes punishable by less than death. The stablemen's *be* were branded on the face for distinctiveness until the reign of Emperor Richū, or so said the historians.

Last as well as least are the genuine figurines of this period and examples which may be a little later but are in the same tradition. Few traditions seem to die in Japan. Many are simply submerged below successive practices. The idea of Jōmon figurines may not even yet be dead.

Cat. 99
*Pl. XII

Small figures of the Tomb period keep coming to light in what seem to be open, ritual sites from regions as distant as Kyūshū and the Kantō. Local, rather personalized rites had not vanished. These figurines are usually as rudimentary as the Yayoi examples from Kofuji village, Fukuoka prefecture, Kyūshū, but by far the most consequential showed up shortly after the last war in the vicinity of Kagoshima city. In light brownish clay, in the native materials and technique in other words, it is a long slender, hollow tube with crudely fashioned headdress, drooping shoulders and much enlarged forearms. The break across the mouth is clumsily repaired. The back is roughly modelled without a trace of ornamental detail. A thick row of

Fig. 98

Plate XII *Haniwa* female dancing figure from Kamishiba tomb, Minosato-machi, Gumma county, Gumma prefecture. H. 88.5 cm. Late Tomb Period. National Museum, Tokyo

156

circular beads surrounds the neck, below which is a pair of large curved beads, the well known *magatama*. Circular beads and another pair of *magatama* were attached below the waist, but one of the latter is now missing. On the chest is what I take to be a mirror, a flat round disc. The significance of all of this can only be conjectured. One does, however, think of the possibility of a simulated burial, as a tradition still preserved from the later Jōmon centuries. It may be a votive figure, but no details are known on the exact context of its discovery. A comparison with small clay figures from Silla in southeast Korea shows a few minor resemblances.

THE HANIWA AND THE CULTS OF THE TIME

The growing stability of Japanese society, commencing with the introductions which created the sedentary life of the Yayoi period, had brought a substantial commitment to anthropomorphic art and alleviated the painful conversion to the more exacting Buddhist artistic requirements in the late sixth century. Work which ultimately went on permanent public exhibition necessitated strict attention to quality, and conversely, at the other extreme, work which was never subject to public scrutiny such as the tomb paintings would also never be exposed to public censure. I would suggest that by and large the *haniwa* represent the highest standard of an almost purely native art, whereas the uneven quality of the tomb paintings and wall carvings may be explained as not having been intended for ordinary human observation.

Two factors came in for almost equal consideration under these circumstances: display and provision for the next world. These tombs far exceeded in grandeur anything ever conceived of for the living. The display was effective, and the physical surroundings for the dead and his possessions were equally as effective as a receptacle for preservation. The mound called attention to the burial and set it apart from the living, with some intention of warning the living of the possibility of disagreeable spirits lurking around. In primitive religious thought dangerous spirits have to

be propitiated, and there can be little question but what a fear of the spirits of the dead was widely held at this time. Offerings to the deceased, especially of food, have been almost universal practice. They placate his spirit, which in a context of rudimentary ancestor worship at this stage could exercise considerable power over the living. It was inevitable that ancestor worship embodied in it certain elements of fertility cults. Early man walked a precarious tightrope between his obligations to the dead ancestor and his need to protect himself from the displeasure or revenge of his predecessor's spirit.

After elaborate construction, the tombs were well cared for. A story is told during Emperor Nintoku's time of a Shiratori Tomb, one of the graves of Prince Yamato-dake, which had always remained empty. Nintoku had every intention of discharging its caretakers and reducing them to the level of common laborers until one was transformed into a white deer and took flight. These guards were the Haji-be, the makers of the *haniwa*, who were therefore unavoidably charged with the preservation of the *haniwa in situ* and presumably were expected to wage a constant war on all flora which might cause their damage or mitigate against their visibility. How well all of this was done will remain a moot question, but the story states in clear terms that Nintoku set no value on merely the appearance of an unoccupied tomb.

Animism is unlikely to foster order or cause a strong codification of religious concepts and practices; Japan was no exception to this. A good example may be cited in the length of time which elapsed between the death of the ruler and his burial. This time span ranges from weeks to years. Buddhism later saw to an orderly arrangement of the funeral ritual and fixed time periods for memorial services and the more general celebrations for the dead. It is this fact which permits the latitude I am taking in suggesting more than one concurrent meaning to the *haniwa*.

Polytheism inspired sacrifices, but not philosophical speculation in the case of Japan. It had, however, encouraged an increasing sense of intimacy with the spirits by the time Buddhism offered these advantages, particularly as ancestor worship was found useful to the Yamato state, aided by persistent inroads of Chinese thought. Much variety was still possible, and regional and local differences in the *haniwa* can be accounted for both in this and other ways. In a high level of generalization, deities were not necessarily specifically expected to serve specialized functions. Virtually any might be approached to provide the basic benefactions of such things as better health, rain, improved crops, and offspring.

Divine kingship in Japan has carried with it an extraordinary degree of autocracy. The practice has helped to solidify the sense of dependence upon higher spirits and has reinforced the position of protohistoric and historic Shinto. Shinto is simply a handy term to describe this loose aggregate of spirits whose manipulation has been historically the monopoly of the state when it deemed it necessary, and has thus merely kept alive a practice dating back to at least Yamato times when religious ideas were forced to serve political ends.

The mediums at this stage—and Shinto tends to evolve from shamanism, for it could at least borrow some cosmic thought and shed the frenzied action—were both male and female shamans, the latter playing a powerful enough part to make a female personification acceptable as the chief deity of the land within the framework of Yamato support. Shamans must have demonstrated some talent or it is unlikely that they could have held the job, yet it is very possible that few were enthusiastic volunteers. This is where politics and religion differ. Shamans were the professional abstainers according to Chinese accounts, who lived comfortably as long as nothing went wrong, but suffered correspondingly at the hands of the people if disaster struck, since disaster was the sign of broken vows. Before Buddhism eventually took over the ceremonies concerned with the dead, the shamans discharged these duties in close association with the world of spirits, and performed the necessary divination to determine the advisability of proceeding with certain projects.

The shaman's unstable, half-world existence placed him in direct contact with the deceased and open to constant need for purification. He devised various precautions against the return of the dead. It may be recalled that the Ainu never go back to the grave. Several east Siberian tribes do not look back once the dead has been buried—a fact that may account for the facing away from the tomb by the *haniwa* figures, and lends greater justification to their invariable and primitive frontality.

Overtones of these ideas of self-protection can be felt in the planting of jars as offerings to the gods, described in the ancient accounts. Emperor Jimmu established the practice early. He was ordered by the Sun Goddess to get clay from Mt. Kagu and from it to make eighty platters and eighty small jars, and sacred jars. These were then used for sacrificial purposes. Using the platters and jars, he received magical signs that his projected conquest of the Yamato region would proceed favorably, and the phenomenal success of this kind of divination in predicting results was just cause for the starting of the custom of setting up sacred jars[46].

At the time of Emperor Sūjin two of his leaders were dispatched to put down revolts. After one successful engagement and prior to another "they took sacred jars and planted them at the top of the acclivity of Takasuki in Wani"[47], as a gesture of offering to the deities for further luck. During the reign of Kōrei, perhaps around the second century, according to the Kojiki a pair of deities planted sacred jars between Harima and Kibi (Okayama prefecture)[48] before conquering the Kibi region. These acts may perhaps have only been recorded when the account could follow through with subsequent military victory; the act and success seem inseparable. A reference in the *Harima Fudoki* which purports to speak of ancient practices, states that when the boundary was marked off between the province of Tamba and Harima, large jars were buried in the ground and in this way the place, Hill of Jars, received its name.

It would be worth adding to the illustrations the early incident in the subjugation story of the Central Land of the Reed Plains as Japan was called, when one of the deities was transformed into a cormorant and swam to the bottom of the sea where he got red clay to make eighty heavenly platters. The success of the rituals which followed allowed him to lay claim to the conquest of the Central Land. A point seems to have been made here of red clay — the usual appearance of early Japanese ceramic products. It was not the foreign, imported gray Sue ware used inside the tombs, but a type which fits into the Yayoi-Haji-*Haniwa* tradition.

If we go back briefly to the Yayoi period's burial of the dead in jars and recall the unbroken line from Yayoi pottery to the earliest cylinders, it may be surmised that magical powers of protection had come to be attributed to all clay containers associated with the dead. An occasional coffin in the Tomb period is little more than a clay cylinder. Jars had ceremonial value; they solicited aid from the deities to safeguard the boundaries from malevolent spirits; they formed a protective fence; they designated sacred spots. If jars took too much time to make at a time when many were needed, the simplest shape of all, a cylinder, might suffice.

We might, therefore, accept the idea that cylinders separate the holy from the profane, and that the psychological complex concerning the dead and compulsion for purification after association with death stemmed from deep-seated fears which led to extreme attempts on the part of the individual to disassociate himself from all of death's aspects and implications. The *haniwa* themselves could have even been thought of as a kind of votive gift, but are doubtless looked on as necessary articles or people for use in the next world. Should one feel that a greater interest in decoration comes with the passage of time, it might be remembered that the most graphic tale of an attempt at self-cleansing after contact with the dead comes at a very early date and was told at that stage to clarify the stand that should be taken toward the dead. It is the account of Izanagi's re-

turn from his experiences in the underworld after his attempt to bring back his wife. If only by omission the literature implies a creeping complacency or slackening fear toward death in later Yamato centuries; if this is true, the decorativeness of the *haniwa* may mirror this modification.

Multiple reasons for the existence of the *haniwa* do not beg a central question regarding their meaning. They got their start in the Kansai; they were less popular in Kyūshū, particularly north Kyūshū, where continental influences were always strong — the *haniwa* are perhaps the most uncontinental of Japanese arts at this time. The Kantō did what the Kansai was unable to do; it carried the development to a rich, engaging climax. The cylinders outlined the sacred precinct and acted as a magical barrier to safeguard the living from the dead. The inanimate objects got their start as simple symbols of the house of the dead, but caught on in the Kantō as symbols of wealth and status. Tomb protection was afforded by arms and armor, and these and other objects served as marks of prestige. Ultimately, from the Middle Tomb period onward, the human figures dominated the scene. Could they have come in about the time human beings were no longer being sacrificed, assuming for the sake of argument that they were? If so, they would be almost literally funerary substitutes, and provided for service in the next world. It is possible. Horse sacrifice was finally banned; the records make a far stronger case for live burials of human beings. But finally, in the rows of human figures and animals in the Kantō there materializes the appearance of a full funeral procession — soldiers, retainers, bodyguards, workers, animals and all. It is theatrical pageantry, a display for the living to gratify the spirit of the dead.

TEXT REFERENCES

[1] N.G. Munro, *Prehistoric Japan*, p. 230.

[2] *Ibid.*, p. 229.

[3] The ancient world is well represented by figurines with magnified eyes. See O.G.S. Crawford, *The Eye Goddess*.

[4] Y. Noguchi in his article entitled "The Development of the So-called 'Goggled Figurines'" presents the ideas that such figurines seem to appear around the beginning of the Latest Jōmon period in rather well developed form. The features degenerate and are fully transformed by the end of this same period. Such figurines were imitated outside the Tōhoku.

[5] R. Torii, "Les Ainou des Iles Kouriles," unnumbered page opposite pl. xv. Neither the modern Ainu of Sakhalin or Hokkaidō made masks at the time of writing. Torii also assumes (p. 204) that wooden masks from the Neolithic period have perished, but the Ainu of the Kuriles may have been responsible for the preservation of ancient practices. Masks are used for mimicking phantoms, whose malevolence was the source of a deep-abiding fear amongst the Ainu.

[6] T. Esaka, *Clay Figurines*.

[7] Y. Noguchi, *Clay Figurines of Japan*.

[8] E. Ōno, "Clay Tablets and Clay Human Figures from the Stone Age Sites in Japan," 1897; also, "Genealogy of Clay Human Images and Clay Tablets made by the Stone Age People of Japan."

[9] Munro, *op.cit.*, p. 226.

[10] R. Torii, "The Religion of the Neolithic Ainu Population of Japan, and in Particular the Cult of the Goddess Cult."

[11] I. Yawata, "The Question of the Religious Beliefs of the Prehistoric Japanese," *Jinruigaku Senshigaku Kōza*; in particular XVIII, 1940, pp. 31–47.

[12] H. Nishioka, *History of Phallicism in Japan*, pp. 11–22, who summarizes successively the theories of Munro, Tsuda, Shibata, Yawata, Torii, Gotō, Kuji, Ōba and Ōyama on religious practices in ancient Japan, especially in regard to figurines.

[13] Esaka, *op.cit.*, pp. 294–99.

[14] Noguchi, *op.cit.*, pp. 130–31.

[15] N. Sakazume in "A Tentative Theory on Primeval Agriculture in Japan" gives a series of cogent reasons why agriculture may have taken place. After offering evidence, his conclusions may be summarized as follows: the discovery of Palaeolithic remains now separates two types of ancient economies more clearly. Remains of communities (groups of pit-dwellings) show the people settled because of the existence of some staple in the area, most likely chestnuts. Walnuts and horse chestnuts are additional possibilities. The female figurines point to a society centered around the maternal principle. Stone tools were used in cultivating the ground, but more popular were wooden and bamboo tools. Probably some vegetables were raised on small plots, and pottery vessels were utilized for the storage of grain.

Esaka reinforces Sakazume's arguments by other means in his article entitled "On the Possibility that Vegetable Cultivation Originated in the Middle Jōmon Period Culture." He sees a sudden development of the Middle Jōmon culture, long habitation in settlements indicated by the mixture of successive pottery types, evidence of people moving out of the highlands toward lower plateaus due to the scarcity of foods and the carrying of horse chestnut seedlings to more spacious areas. Yams (Dioscorea japonica) may have been cultivated, that is, various kinds of potato-like plants (*mizu-imo*, *yama-imo*) and lily bulbs (*yuri*), for which sandstone and shale tools were used. Starch was obtained from horse chestnuts and roots of the taro plants which were leached in the springs.

[16] N. Kawazoe, *Residences of Peoples and Gods*, pp. 97–107, points out that the *Kojiki*, *Nihon Shoki* and *Fudoki*, the eighth century books on myths, history and geography, carry references to a common theme in which the goddesses of the staple foods (*ke*) symbolize this death and ultimate regeneration. Only through death can the life-giving essence be transmitted. As evidence he cites the killing of such female deities as Toyouke, Ukimochi, Ōgetsu, Toyouka, Ukano-mitama, Miketsu, and others, from whose corpses sprang *gokoku* or "five grains."

[17] R.A. Miller, *Haniwa: The Clay Sculpture of Protohistoric Japan*, p. 21.

[18] W.G. Aston, *Nihongi* I, pp. 178–81.

[19] *Ibid.*, I, pp. 357–58.

[20] M. Matsubara, *Haniwa*, p. 27.

[21] These are not limited to Kyūshū, but the availability of a soft stone in Kyūshū encouraged the practice and the proximity to China was the deciding factor.

[22] S. Gotō, *A Study of the Ancient Japanese Culture*, pp. 90–91;

K. Kanaya, *The Birth of Haniwa*, pp. 49–50; J. Buhot, *Histoire des Arts du Japon* I, p. 38, calls them a magical enclosure; Munro, *op.cit.*, p. 545, describes them as a fence without entering into any symbolic intentions.

[23] M. Suenaga, *Report on the Investigations of Historic Sites and Famous Places in Nara Prefecture* 19, pp. 24–28.

[24] T. Katsuya, "A Study of the Rectangular Arrangements of Haniwa," p. 22.

[25] S. Gotō ed., H. Ueda, *Symposium on Japanese Archaeology* 5, pp. 143–45; F. Miki, *Haniwa*, pp. 131–32.

[26] They include the following keyhole tombs: Ebinosu, Kyoto prefecture; Ishiyama, Mie prefecture; Miyayama, Nara prefecture; Kurohimeyama, Osaka prefecture; Kanakurayama, Okayama prefecture; and these round tombs: Shichikan, Osaka prefecture, and Miyasu, Nara prefecture.

[27] The Hachimanzuka appeared in *Archaeology (Kōkogaku)* I/4, 1930, but see Miller, *op.cit.*, fig. 3 for a recent reference.

[28] See Y. Kondō, "Bronze Mirror with Design of Houses Excavated at the Takarazuka Burial Mound, Samida, Yamato Province."

[29] S. Gotō, *op.cit.*, pp. 109–42, where he discusses this entire class of objects.

[30] H. Takiguchi, *Haniwa*, p. 33, pl. 45.

[31] More argument is offered in my *Early Japanese Art*, pp. 143–45.

[32] A fuller analysis is given in my *Early Japanese Art*, pp. 155–66.

[33] Aston, *op.cit.*, I, p. 225, translates it as lute.

[34] F. Miki, *The Beauty of Haniwa*, p. 53, top left.

[35] Y. Kobayashi, *Series of World Art* 2, p. 277, pl. 161.

[36] Kawazoe, *op.cit.*, p. 208.

[37] Aston, *op.cit.*, I, p. 180.

[38] *Ibid.*, II, p. 61.

[39] See M. Doi, "An Investigation of Clay Horses in Yamato".

[40] See Takiguchi, *op.cit.*, English section i, for remarks on this without argumentation, repeating the frequently accepted view.

[41] These ideas of an unoppressed society as reflected in the *haniwa* are rendered into English in Miller's *Haniwa*, pp. 19, 27, 156 (pl. 48), 157 (pl. 51).

[42] *Ibid.*, p. 157 (pl. 55).

[43] Takiguchi, *op.cit.*, p. iii.

[44] *Ibid.*, p. 32.

[45] S. Noma, *The Art of Clay*, pp. 34–35, says that it has often been regarded as tattooing, but that tattooing should be black or blue rather than red, and was used for low class people. He feels that it is probably for beautification and cites the possibility that the pillow word *sanizurau* used before emperor, noble or wife, may mean "pretty – red clay – cheeks".

[46] Aston, *op.cit.*, I, p. 122, note 1, passes on the information that a note in the *Nihon Shoki* says that the jars were set up in the courtyard. This is presumably speaking of a holy spot where the event was marked.

[47] *Ibid.*, I, p. 157.

[48] B.H. Chamberlain, *Kojiki*, pp. 196–97, translates this as "at the front of the River Hi in Harima," a river of unknown location, noting that front may mean a bend.

SELECT BIBLIOGRAPHY

Quantity is a characteristic of Japanese archaeological writing, so that a bibliography of this nature makes no pretense at being exhaustive. I have largely omitted the numerous reports on the recovery of individual figurines and unusual *haniwa*. For the former, however, a reader might be referred to my *Jōmon Pottery of Japan*, 1957, pp. 183–186, for a fuller listing. Only items considered most important prior to the compilation of that bibliography are included here. The Japanese titles have been given directly in English or simply reproduced as they appear on a title page, but notations have been added as to whether western language information accompanies the Japanese text. Where some doubt might arise as to the title, romanization is included.

Abbreviations:

JB	*Jōdai Bunka*	Culture of Antiquity
JGZ	*Jinruigaku Zasshi*	Journal of Anthropology
JRGK	*Jinruigaku Senshigaku Kōza*	Symposium on Anthropology and Prehistory
KGK	*Kodaigaku Kenkyū*	Studies in Antiquity
KGZ	*Kōkogaku Zasshi*	Journal of Archaeology
NKN	*Nihon Kōkogaku Nempō*	Annual Report on Japanese Archaeology
SGZ	*Shizengaku Zasshi*	Journal of Prehistory (Zeitschrift für Praehistorie)
WK	*Wakagi Kōko*	Wakagi Archaeology

GENERAL: JAPANESE LANGUAGE

Higuchi, K., "Body Decorations of Japanese Prehistoric People," *JRGK* XIII, 1939; XIV, 1940.

Ishida, E., Oka, M., Egami, N., and Yawata, I., *Origin of the Japanese People*, Tokyo, 1958.

Kawazoe, N., *Residences of Peoples and Gods*, Tokyo, 1960.

Kodama, K., gen. ed., *An Illustrated Cultural History of Japan* (Nihon Bunka-shi Taikei), I, Tokyo (Shogakkan), 1956.

Koyama, F., Tanaka, S., Mitsuoka, T., and Mizuno, S., editors, *Catalogue of World's Ceramics*, I, Tokyo, 1958. (English summary.)

Mizuno, S., gen. ed., *Illustrated World Culture History Series* (Zusetsu Sekai Bunka-shi Taikei) 20, Japan I, Tokyo (Kadokawa Shōten), 1960.

Mizuno, S., and Kobayashi, Y., *Illustrated Dictionary of Archaeology*, Tokyo, 1959.

Murai, I., *Pottery and Haniwa* (Gendai Kyōyō Bunko Series, No. 235), Tokyo, 1960.

Nishioka, H., *History of Phallicism in Japan*, Tokyo, 1950. (English title.)

Shiratori, K., *A New Study on the Age of the Gods*, Tokyo, 1954.

Takiguchi, S., gen. ed., *World Fine Arts Collection* (Sekai Bijutsu Zenshū) I, Japan (I), Prehistory, Tokyo (Kadokawa Shōten), 1960.

Tōyō Bijutsu: Histoire des Beaux-Arts Japonais, Special Number I, Prehistoric and Protohistoric Period, 1930. (French titles.)

Wakamori, T., *History of Japanese Customs*, I, Tokyo, 1959.

Watanabe, S., *The World After Death*, Tokyo, 1959.

JŌMON PERIOD: JAPANESE LANGUAGE

Commission for the Protection of Cultural Properties, *Stone Remains of Ōyu-machi*, Tokyo, 1953. (English summary.)

Esaka, T., *Prehistoric Period II: Jōmon Culture*, Tokyo, 1957.

Esaka, T., "On the Possibility that Vegetable Cultivation Originated in the Middle Jōmon Period Culture," *KGZ* XLIV/3, 1959. (English summary.)

Esaka, T., *Clay Figurines*, Tokyo, 1960.

Esaka, T., "A Clay Figurine in the Sitting Position," *Yamato Bunka* (Yamato Culture) 34, 1961.

Hasebe, K., "On the So-called Snow Goggles Represented in the Clay Images of the Japanese Stone Age," *KGZ* XIV/10, 1924. (English title.)

Ikegami, K., "Table of Finds of Clay and Stone Plaques," *SGZ* VIII/5, 1936. (German title.)

Imperial Museum, *Postcards of Clay Figurines and Plaques of the Stone Age*, 17 packs of 10 each, Tokyo, no date.

Kambayashi, A., "On the Earthen Idols of Conical Form," *JGZ* LVIII/668, 1943. (English title.)

Kono, I., "Masks in the Stone Age," *Dorumen* (Dolmen) II/1, 1933.

Kono, I., "Notes on the Urns of Human Figures in Prehistoric Japan," *JGZ* LIV/626, 1939. (English title.)

Kono, I., *The Story of Jōmon Pottery*, Tokyo, 1953.

Kusumoto, M., "Horn Articles in the Shape of Human Figures from the Numazu Shell-mound, Miyagi Prefecture," *KGZ* XLIV/3, 1959. (English title.)

Miwa, T., "Stone Age Musical Instruments", *KGZ* XIII/8, 1923. (English title.)

Miyasaka, E., and Yawata, I., *Togariishi*, Kayano-chō, 1957.

Mutō, T., "Clay and Stone Plaques from all Viewpoints," *Dorumen* (Dolmen) IV/5, 1935.

Nagamine, K., "A New Example of a Male Figurine," *JB* XXI, 1951. (English title.)

Nagamine, M., "Earthenware Pieces Found in Komoro, Nagano Prefecture," *KGZ* XLII/2, 1957. (English title.)

Nakajima, T., "On the Breasts and Stomach Protrusions of Stone Age Clay Figurines," *JGZ* LVIII/669, 1943. (German title.)

Nakamura, K., and Teramura, M., "Earthenware in the Shape of Steam-pot in the Jōmon Period with Special Reference to Vessels having Bases with Multiple Pierced Holes, found in Echigo Province," *KGZ* XLII/1, 1956. (English title.)

Nishina, Y., "Stone Age Clay Figures Discovered in Kai Province," *KGZ* XXIII/12, 1933. (English title.)

Noguchi, Y., "Figurines of Moroiso Style Culture," *KGZ* XXXVIII/3, 1952. (English title.)

Noguchi, Y., *Clay Figurines of Japan*, Tokyo, 1959. (On book cover: Life and Form of Japan 1, Jomon Clay Figurines.)

Noguchi, Y., "The Development of the So-called 'Goggled Figurines'," *Museum* 109, 1960. (English title.)

Noguchi, Y., "The Two Prehistoric Figurines from the Yoyama Shell-mound," *Museum* 121, 1961. (English title.)

North Kyūshū Teachers' Association, *Plates of North Kyūshū's Ancient Culture* 1, Kurume, 1950.

Ōba, I., gen. ed., *Hiraide: Synthetic Study on the Remains of Ancient Villages at Sogamura, Nagano Prefecture*, Tokyo, Osaka and Kokura, 1955. (English summary.)

Okonogi, C., "Clay Animal Figures of the Prehistoric Time of Japan," *JGZ* XLII/475, 1927. (English title.)

Ōno, N., "Clay Tablets and Clay Human Figures from the Stone Age Sites in Japan," *JGZ* XII/131, 1897. (English title.)

Ōno, N., "Genealogy of Clay Human Images and Clay Tablets made by the Stone Age People of Japan," *JGZ* XVI/184, 1901. (English title.)

Ōno, N., "Clay Human Figures of the Stone Age with Tattoo-like Markings on their Faces," *JGZ* XXVI/297, 1910. (English title.)

Otagiri, K., "The Distribution of Ainu Prehistoric Remains in Hokkaidō with Clay Figures," *JGZ* XXXII/362, 363, 1917. (English titles.)

Sakai, T., and Esaka, T., "A Clay Figurine Excavated at Sugisawa, Yamagata Prefecture," *KGZ* XXXIX/3, 4, 1954. (English title.)

Sakazume, N., "A Tentative Theory on Primeval Agriculture in Japan," *KGZ* XLII/2, 1957. (English summary.)

Sato, D., "On the Clay Human Figures from the Stone Age Site of Tokomai in Mutsu," *JGZ* XIII/142, 1898. (English title.)

Serizawa, G., *The Stone Age of Japan*, Tokyo, 1960. (English title and list of plates.)

Tanabe, C., "Some Clay Figures with Asphalt Adhered to their Broken Ends," *JGZ* LXI/690, 1949. (English summary.)

Tanikawa (Ōba), I., "On the Totemic Idea in the Japanese Stone Age," *KGZ* XIII/4, 1922; XIII/5, XIII/8, 1923. (English titles.)

Torii, R., "The Religion of the Neolithic Ainu Population of Japan, and in Particular the Cult of the Goddess," *JGZ* XXXVII/427, 1922. (French title.)

Wakabayashi, K., "On Clay Images found among Shell-heaps in Japan," *JGZ* VI/61, 1891. (English title.)

Yamazaki, Y., "A Clay Figurine Excavated at Satohara, Gumma Prefecture," *KGZ* XXXIX/3, 4, 1954. (English title.)

Yawata, I., "The Question of Religious Beliefs of the Prehistoric Japanese," *JRGK* XII, 1939; XIV, XVIII, 1940.

Yawata, I., *The Dawn of the History of Japan*, Tokyo, 1953.

Yawata, I., "Japanese Prehistoric Clay Figurines," *Museum*, 99, 1959. (English title.)

Yawata, I., *Jōmon Pottery and Clay Figurines*, Tokyo, 1963.

Yawata, I., volume editor, *World Archaeology Series* (Sekai Kōkogaku Taikei) 1, Japan I, Tokyo, 1959.

Yoshida, B., "On Some Sorts of Hair Dressings Represented on the Clay Human Figures made by the Stone Age People of Japan," *JGZ* XXI/236, 1905; XXI/238, XXI/239, XXI, 240, 1906. (English titles.)

TOMB PERIOD: JAPANESE LANGUAGE

Akiyama, H., *Shitsudai-bo (Miyayama Tomb): Report on the Investigations of Historic Sites, Famous Places and Spots of Natural Beauty in Nara Prefecture* 18, Nara, 1959.

Asada, Y., "On the Intrinsic Nature of Haniwa," *KGK* 19, 1958.

Ashikaga, G., "Haniwa Cylinders with Engraved Figures," *KGZ* XVIII/1, 1928.

Date, M., "On the Haniwa Cylinder Coffins Excavated at Narayama in Nara City," *KGK* 27, 1961.

Doi, M., "An Investigation of Clay Horses in Yamato," *Kodaigaku* (English title: *Palaeologia*) IV/2, 1955. (English title.)

Gotō, S., *A Study on the Excavation of an Ancient Tomb at Akaborimura*, Tokyo, 1932. (English summary.)

Gotō, S., *Report on the Excavation of the Shōrinzan Tomb, Iwata County, Shizuoka Prefecture*, Shizuoka, 1939.

Gotō, S., *A Study of the Ancient Japanese Culture*, Tokyo, 1942.

Gotō, S., *Haniwa*, Tokyo, 1942.

Gotō, S., ed., H. Ueda, *Symposium on Japanese Archaeology* V, Culture of the Tomb (Period), Tokyo, 1955.

Gotō, S., *The Tombs and their Period*, 2 vols., Tokyo, 1958.

Harada, D., *The Tomb Culture of Japan*, Tokyo, 1954.

Hayashida, S., "Observations on the Ancient Horses of Japan," *JGZ* LXIV/708, 1956. (English summary.)

Higuchi, T., "Recently Excavated Examples of Haniwa in the Shape of Helmets," *KGZ* XLII/1, 1956. (English title.)

Higuchi, T., "Report on the Investigation of Shichikan Tomb of Izumi Province," *KGK* 27, 1961.

Homma, M., "The Treatment of Space in Japanese Primitive Sculpture," *Museum* 133, 1962. (English title.)

Hosaka, S., "Studies on Recent Accessions: Haniwa Figures of Armored Men," *Museum* 111, 1960. (English title.)

Ishibashi, T., "Haniwa Cylinders and Their Problems," *WK* 11, 1955.

Ishibe, M., "Haniwa Cylindrical Coffins," *KGK* 27, 1961.

Kamei, M., "A Personal Opinion on Cylindrical Haniwa," *Kokugakuin Zasshi* LVII/4, 1956.

Kanaseki, H., "Recent Discovered Materials of Archaeological Research: Two Bronze Ring-shaped Pommels from the Tumulus of Tōdaiji-yama, Yamato," *KGZ* XLVII/4, 1962. (English title.)

Kanaya, K., "The Distribution of Haniwa," *WK* 31, 32, 1954.

Kanaya, K., "The Production of Haniwa," *WK* 33, 1954.

Kanaya, K., "Observations on Haniwa," *Kokugakuin Zasshi* LVI/2, 1955.

Kanaya, K., "The Arrangement of Haniwa," *WK* 35, 36, 37, 42, 43, 45, 1955-57.

Kanaya, K., "Haniwa Pots Discovered at Misato village, Kodama county, Musashi," *JB* 27, 1957.

Kanaya, K., *The Birth of Haniwa*, Tokyo, 1959.

Katada, C., "A New Example of a Picture of a Boat on a Haniwa Cylinder," *KGZ* XLV/2, 1959. (English title.)

Katsuya, T., "A Study of Rectangular Arrangement of Haniwa Cylinders," *JB* 24, 1953.

Kimura, M., and Doi, A., "On the Jimbayama Keyhole Tomb in Akaiwa county, Okayama," *Setouchi Kōkogaku* (Setouchi Archaeology), 1, 1957.

Kobayashi, Y., "The Investigation of the Ishiyama Tomb, Second Year," *NKN* 2, 1949; 3, 1950. Tokyo, 1954, 1955.

Kobayashi, Y., section entitled "The Arts of the Japanese Old Tomb Culture," in *Sekai Bijutsu Zenshū* (World Fine Arts Collection) 2, Tokyo (Heibon-Sha), 1956.

Kobayashi, Y., *Discussions on Tombs*, Tokyo, 1959.

Kobayashi, Y., *Haniwa*, Tokyo (Heibon-Sha), 1960.

Kobayashi, Y., volume editor, *World Archaeology Series* (Sekai Kōkogaku Taikei) 3, Japan III, Tokyo, 1959.

Kojima, S., "Cylindrical Coffins from Kuratsuka," *Nara Prefecture Report* (Nara-ken Hōkoku) 12, Nara, 1959.

Kondō, Y., *The Tomb Culture of Japan* (Symposium on Japanese History I), Tokyo, 1956.

Kondō, Y., "Bronze Mirror with Design of Houses Excavated at the Takarazuka Burial Mound, Samida, Yamato Province", *Museum* 114, 1960. (English title.)

Kubo, H., *The Saitobaru Tomb Group*, Miyazaki, 1934.

Masuda, S., "On Types of Horse's Head Harness as Seen on Haniwa," *KGZ* XLV/4, 1960. (English title.)

Matsubara, N., *Haniwa*, Tokyo, 1960.

Mifune, K., "Human-figured Haniwa from Kyono-chō," *Kibi Kōko* (Kibi Archaeology) 91, 1956.

Miki, F., *The Beauty of Haniwa*, Tokyo (Asahi Shashin Buku 28), 1956.

Miki, F., *Haniwa*, Tokyo (Kodan-Sha), 1960.

Miki, F., "Haniwa Shields," *Museum*, 143, 1963. (English title.)

Miyake, Y., and Takahashi, K., *Haniwa in the Collection of the Tokyo Imperial Museum*, 2 vols., Tokyo, 1919. (English list of plates.)

Mori, K., "A Re-examination of the Excavated Condition of Haniwa Figures," *KGK* 29, 1961.

Munakata Shrine, Society for the Restoration of, *The Religious Sites at Okitsugū, Munakata Jinja, Okinoshima* I, 1958; II, 1961. (English summaries.)

Nishikawa, S., "Bird-shaped Haniwa Excavated from Kyōdozuka No. 2, Tabemachi, Kyoto," *KGK* 20, 1959.

Nishitani, S., *Kanakurayama Tomb*, Kurashiki, 1959.

Nishitani, S., "On the Drawings of Boats on Cylindrical Haniwa," *KGK* 25, 1960.

Ōtsuka, S., Suzuki, S., and Sano, I., *Sammaizuka Tomb*, Tokyo, 1960.

Saito, T., *Study of Japanese Tombs*, Tokyo, 1961.

Sano, H., "That Which Resides Within Pots," (Tsubo ni Yoritsuku Mono), *Kokugakuin Zasshi*, LX/11, 1959.

Sano, H., *The Ancient Culture in Japan*, Tokyo, 1960.

Shimizu, J., "Futatsuyama Tomb," *NKN* I, 1948, Tokyo, 1951.

Suenaga, M., *Ancient Weapons of Japan*, Tokyo, 1943.

Suenaga, M., *Haniwa*, Kyoto, 1947.

Suenaga, M., *Study on the Kawachi Kurohimeyama Tomb*, Osaka Cultural Properties Committee Investigation Reports, Section I (Osaka Bunkazai Chōsa Hōkokushō I), Osaka, 1953.

Suenaga, M., *Izumi Koganezuka Tomb*, Kyoto, 1954.

Suenaga, M., *Tombs of Japan*, Tokyo, 1961.

Suenaga, M., *Sakurai Chausuyama Tomb and Kushiyama Tomb*, Report on the Investigations of Historic Sites and Famous Places in Nara Prefecture (Nara-ken Shiseki Meisho Chōsa Hōkoku) 19, 1961.

Suenaga, M., "Haniwa Hawker," *Yamato Bunka* 37, 1963.

Takiguchi, H., and Kuchioka, H., *Haniwa* (Catalogue of Shibayama Haniwa), Tokyo, 1963.

Tanimoto, M., "The Arrangement of Haniwa", *Archaeology* (Kōkogaku) 1/4, 1930.

Umehara, S., "An Inscribed Sword of the Han Chū-hei (period) from Japan," *Yamato Bunka Kenkyū* (Yamato Culture Studies) 7/11, 1962.

Usa, S., and Nishitani, S., "Haniwa Cylinders with Engraved Figures from Nakatsuhime Imperial Mausoleum, Osaka," *KGK* 20, 1958.

Yoshida, S., and Ōtsuka, H., *Primitive Period II, Tomb Culture*, Tokyo, 1957.

WESTERN LANGUAGES

Aston, W.G., *Nihongi*, 2 vols., London, 1896.

Beardsley, R.K., "Japan Before History: A Survey of the Archaeological Record," *The Far Eastern Quarterly*, XIV/3, 1955.

Buhot, J., *Histoire des Arts du Japon*, I, Paris, 1949.

Chamberlain, B.H., *Kojiki*, Tokyo, 1906.

Crawford, O.G.S., *The Eye Goddess*, London, 1958.

Egami, N., "Light on Japanese Cultural Origins from Historical Archaeology and Legend," in *Japanese Culture: Its Development and Characteristics*, Chicago, 1962.

Eliade, M., *La Terre Mère et les Hiérogamies Cosmiques*, Zurich, 1954.

Groot, G.J., *The Prehistory of Japan*, New York, 1951.

Haguenauer, C., *Origines de la Civilisation Japonaise*, I, Paris, 1956.

Inoue, M., "The Dawn of Japanese History," *KBS Bulletin*, 39, 1959.

James, E.O., *Prehistoric Religion*, London, 1957.

James, E.O., *The Cult of the Mother Goddess*, London, 1959.

Kidder, J.E.Jr., *The Jōmon Pottery of Japan*, Ascona, 1957.

Kidder, J.E.Jr., *Japan Before Buddhism*, London, 1959.

Kidder, J.E.Jr., *Early Japanese Art: The Great Tombs and Treasures*, London, 1964.

Maringer, J., *The Gods of Prehistoric Man*, London, 1960.

Miller, R.A., Eng. adaptation of F. Miki, *Haniwa: The Clay Sculpture of Protohistoric Japan*, Tokyo, 1960.

Munro, N.G., *Prehistoric Japan*, Yokohama, 1911.

Nakaya, J., "Contribution à l'étude de la civilisation néolithique du Japon," *Revue des Arts Asiatiques* VI, no. III, 1929–30.

Nakaya, J., "Introduction à l'étude des figurines de l'âge de pierre au Japon," *Jahrbuch für prähist. und ethnogr. Kunst* 1930.

Nakaya, J., "Figurines néolithiques du Japon," *Documents Archéologie Beaux-arts, Ethnographie Variétés*, II:1, 1930.

Neumann, E., *The Great Mother*, New York, 1955.

Noma, S., "Haniwa, Protohistoric Sculpture of Japan," *Oriental Art*, New Series, I, Spring, 1955.

Noma, S., *Haniwa: Catalog of Exhibition of Haniwa from National Museum, Tokyo, being shown in American Museums in 1960*, Tokyo.

Paine, R.T.Jr., "An Ainu Clay Figure," *Bulletin of the Museum of Fine Arts*, XLV, No. 259, 1947.

Przyluski, J., *La Grande Déesse*, Paris, 1950.

Torii, R., "Les Ainou des Iles Kouriles," *Journal of the College of Science, Tokyo Imperial University*, XLII: 1. Tokyo, 1919–21.

Ucko, P.J., "The Interpretation of Prehistoric Anthropomorphic Figurines," *The Journal of the Royal Anthropological Institute*, vol. 92, part I, 1962.

Young, J., *The Location of Yamatai: A Case Study in Japanese Historiography: 720–1945*, Baltimore, 1958.

CATALOGUE

Cat. 1   Simple, undecorated brown colored figurine, from Hanawadai
          shell-mound, Kagane-machi, Kita-sōma county, Ibaragi pre-
          fecture. H. 4.8 cm. Earliest Jōmon Period. Japan Archaeological
          Studies Collection.

Cat. 2   Undecorated, headless, plaque-like object with breasts and navel
          nipple, from Sannai, Aomori city, Aomori prefecture. H. 10.5 cm.
          Early Jōmon Period. Coll. Mr. Hikoei Narita.

Cat. 3   Abdomen and hips of brown colored figurine with hollow base,
          heavily decorated on back, said by the finder to have testicles
          and a missing male member; otherwise termed female by some
          observers, from Sakai, Fujii-machi, Nirasaki city, Yamanashi
          prefecture. H. 10.1 cm. Middle Jōmon Period. Sakai Remains
          Museum.

Head and partial torso of brown to blackish figurine, with raised Cat. 4
spiral on back of head, left eye "weeping", vertical ear holes,
and hole in top of head, from Tonai, Ochiai, Fujimi-machi,
Suwa county, Nagano prefecture. H. 10.5 cm. Middle Jōmon
Period. Idojiri Archaeology Museum.

Head of reddish brown color, grooved decoration on back, hole Cat. 5
in neck to connect with body, and polished areas, from Hiraide,
Sōga ward, Shiojiri city, Nagano prefecture. H. 6.6 cm. Middle
Jōmon Period. Hiraide Archaeology Museum.

Head of gray clay with brownish surface, with hare lip and miss- Cat. 6
ing ears, from Hirobata, Kasuga village, Kita-saku county, Nagano prefecture. H. 7.2 cm. Middle Jōmon Period. Institute of
Anthropology, Tokyo University.

Cat. 7   Head of figurine, found inside Ubayama (Kasori E) type pottery vessel which was standing on a stone slab, at Yosukeone, Togariishi, Toyohirachi ward, Chino city, Nagano prefecture. H. 4.2 cm. Middle Jōmon Period. Togariishi Archaeology Museum.

Cat. 8   Figure 8-shaped object (head and shoulders?) in coarse, brown clay, bearing finely stippled decoration, and "mouth" hole running through to connect with missing part below, from the vicinity of Hiraide, Sōga ward, Shiojiri city, Nagano prefecture. H. 4.6 cm. Middle Jōmon Period. Hiraide Archaeology Museum.

Cat. 9   Headless, flat figurine of light reddish-brown clay, with smooth surfaces, and decoration on back which includes outlined buttocks and incidental incisions, from Niigata prefecture. H. 17 cm. Middle Jōmon Period. National Museum, Tokyo.

Small reddish to black colored vessel of coarse clay, bearing two heads and two spirals on raised discs, and twelve holes at neck, from Sakai, Fujii-machi, Nirasaki city, Yamanashi prefecture. H. 7.4 cm. Middle Jōmon Period. Sakai Remains Museum.   Cat. 10

Rim-head of coarse red, grainy clay, with one loop in the back, from Kogakubo, Kokubunji-machi, Kita-tama county, Tokyo. H. 10.3 cm. Middle Jōmon Period. Institute of Archaeology, Kyoto University.   Cat. 11

Trunk of figurine of light brown clay with strongly protruding abdomen and buttocks, bearing grooves across the shoulder blades and a single broad groove down the back, from Maga-kizawa, Iwae village, Tamura county, Fukushima prefecture. H. 23.5 cm. Middle Jōmon Period. National Museum, Tokyo.   Cat. 12

Cat. 13   Incised figurine with hard surface, from Sannai, Aomori city, Aomori prefecture. H. 9.3 cm. Middle Jōmon Period. Coll. Mr. Tomoyuki Narita.

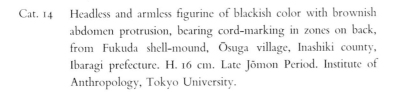

Cat. 14   Headless and armless figurine of blackish color with brownish abdomen protrusion, bearing cord-marking in zones on back, from Fukuda shell-mound, Ōsuga village, Inashiki county, Ibaragi prefecture. H. 16 cm. Late Jōmon Period. Institute of Anthropology, Tokyo University.

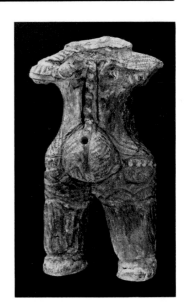

Cat. 15 and 16   Figurine of brown to blackish clay, from Fukuda shell-mound, Ōsuga village, Inashiki county, Ibaragi prefecture. H. 11.5 cm. Late Jōmon Period. Institute of Anthropology, Tokyo University.

Hollow figurine of brown to blackish clay with incised patterns   Cat. 17
on front and back, from Ryūfukuji, Ajiki village, Imba county,
Chiba prefecture. H. 19 cm. Late to Latest Jōmon Period. Coll.
Mr. Etsuzō Tatsuma.

Figurine with rectangular body of light brown color, blackish   Cat. 18
on back, with incised decoration on back, from Yūki city,
Ibaragi prefecture. H. 8.2 cm. Late to Latest Jōmon Period.
Institute of Anthropology, Tokyo University.

Curved figurine of coarse brown clay, missing right stump arm   Cat. 19
and legs, with large loop forming the back of the head, and deep
parallel incisions on back and projected posterior, from Shioya
shell-mound, Okada village, Chikuma county, Nagano prefecture.
H. 11.3 cm. Late Jōmon Period. Institute of Anthropology,
Tokyo University.

Cat. 20   Phallic-shaped figurine of light brown clay, slightly blackened on back, with hole in upper back of head, parallel grooves on back, and breasts attached by insertion into holes, from Tsubo-nouchi, Minami-haibara, Nakayama ward, Matsumoto city, Nagano prefecture. H. 6.8 cm. Late Jōmon Period. Nakayama Archaeology Museum.

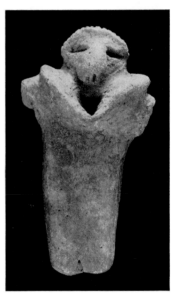

at. 21   Animal-like figurine of brown clay and smooth surface, bearing traces of red paint, missing arms, with deep hole at neck line, simple incised lines on the back, from Location 1, Ikebukuro Ōhana, Fujimi-machi, Suwa county, Nagano prefecture. H. 6.8 cm. Late Jōmon Period. Idojiri Archaeology Museum.

Cat. 22   Figurine bearing extensive cord-marking in zones and stippling on front and back, with strongly projected and tilted face covering a cone-shaped head, from Shinmachi, Tatsuno-chō, Kamiina county, Nagano prefecture. H. 20 cm. Late to Latest Jōmon Period. Coll. Tatsuno-nishi Middle School.

Hollow, bell-shaped figurine with base, dark brown to black   Cat. 23
color, decorated with cord-marking in zones, arm stumps and
ears broken, found without accompanying artifacts, at Sakuōka,
Sakai, Fujii-machi, Nirasaki city, Yamanashi prefecture. H.
25.6 cm. Late to Latest Jōmon Period. Sakai Remains Museum.

Hollow, bell-shaped figurine used as a bone container, of brown   Cat. 24
color and smooth surfaces, from Nakayashiki, Yamada, Ōi-
machi, Ashigarakami county, Kanagawa prefecture. H. 26.7 cm.
Late to Latest Jōmon Period. Coll. Mr. Ryūtarō Komiya.

Crouching figurine of light grayish brown color, with rough   Cat. 25
surfaces and some remaining cord-marking, from Kamegaoka,
Tateoka, Kizukuri-machi, Nishi-tsugaru, county, Aomori prefecture. H. 12.2 cm. Late to Latest Jōmon Period. The Museum
Yamato Bunkakan.

Cat. 26   Figurine of dark brown color, coarse grained clay, flat body but thick head, marked with shoulder blade incisions and curved arcs on the back, from Oyama, Monda village, Kita-aizu county, Fukushima prefecture. H. 15.3 cm. Late Jōmon Period. National Museum, Tokyo.

Cat. 27   Figurine of dark brown color, bearing grooved designs running across shoulders, hips and vertically on the back, with projection from the back of the head with horizontal perforation, from Eto-mo-machi, Muroran city, Hokkaidō. H. 13.7 cm. Late Jōmon Period. National Museum, Tokyo.

Cat. 28   Figurine of reddish black color with traces of red paint, horizontally grooved on the back with a spiral across the shoulders, one peak at the back of the headgear, from Tachigi shell-mound, Tone-machi, Kita-sōma county, Ibaragi prefecture. H. 16.2 cm. Latest Jōmon Period. National Museum, Tokyo.

Trunk of figurine of brown to reddish color, with flat back, protruding abdomen, from Fukuda shell-mound, Ōsuga village, Inashiki county, Ibaragi prefecture. H. 8.5 cm. Latest Jōmon Period. Osaka City Art Museum.

Cat. 29

Human-headed pouring vessel (spout missing), bearing cord-marking in incomplete zones, from Fukuda shell-mound, Ōsuga village, Inashiki county, Ibaragi prefecture. H. 17.4 cm. Latest Jōmon Period. Coll. unknown.

Cat. 30

Hollow figurine of dark brown color, polished surfaces, thin walls, with modern right leg, bearing fine cord-marking within zones, from Kamegaoka, Tateoka, Kizukuri-machi, Nishi-tsugaru county, Aomori prefecture. H. 16.8 cm. Latest Jōmon Period. Institute of Anthropology, Tokyo University.

Cat. 31

Cat. 32   Hollow, thin-walled figurine of dark brown color and smooth surfaces, bearing multi-directional cord-marking, from Kamegaoka, Tateoka, Kizukuri-machi, Nishi-tsugaru county, Aomori prefecture. H. 34.8 cm. Latest Jōmon Period. Kamegaoka Museum.

Cat. 33   Figurine of dark brown clay, smooth surfaces, worn-looking decoration, from Tokomai, Morita village, Nishi-tsugaru county, Aomori prefecture. H. 13 cm. Latest Jōmon Period. Osaka City Art Museum.

Cat. 34   Hollow head of brown to black color, polished surfaces, with small hole in top, and cord-marked eyebrows, from Karumai, Karumai-machi, Kunohe county, Iwate prefecture. H. 8.7 cm. Latest Jōmon Period. Institute of Anthropology, Tokyo University.

Legless, armless, hollow, brittle figure, missing top of head, of gray colored clay, retaining much white and red paint in deep grooves, and bearing fine cord-marking on front and back, from Tōhoku. H 14.1. cm. Latest Jōmon Period. Institute of Anthropology, Tokyo University.

Cat. 35

Simple figurine of light brown to grayish color, typically hard clay, with punctures in headgear, hole in broken section of left leg and deep hole between legs, from Morita village, Nishitsugaru county, Aomori prefecture. H. 8.6 cm. Latest Jōmon Period. Institute of Archaeology, Kyoto University.

Cat. 36

Simplified type of figurine of gray color and dull finish, with both sides rather similar, from Shiojiri city, Nagano prefecture. H. 6.1 cm. Latest Jōmon Period. Institute of Anthropology, Tokyo University.

Cat. 37

Cat. 38   Figurine of brown color bearing wedge-shaped punctates, with tilted, mask-like face and hollow headgear, from Ikarigaseki village, Minami-tsugaru county, Aomori prefecture. H. 23.8 cm. Latest Jōmon Period. Institute of Anthropology, Tokyo University.

Cat. 39   Figurine of light brown color with turban-like headgear, torso incised in parallel lines on front and back, and hips marked with punctates, from Kamabuchi, Mamurogawa-machi, Mogami county, Yamagata prefecture. H. 23 cm. Latest Jōmon Period. Coll. Shōgen-ji.

Cat. 40   Head of figurine of brown color, with mask-like face and turban-like headgear with projecting knobs at back with punctated ends in pits of which are traces of red paint, from Tateishi, Uchikawame village, Hienuki county, Iwate prefecture. H. 5.7 cm. Latest Jōmon Period. Institute of Anthropology, Tokyo University.

Figurine with punctates on forehead, around eyes and mouth, and   Cat. 41
on sex triangle, and deep grooves around neck, rib region and
hips, from Heruke, Taneichi-machi, Kunohe county, Iwate prefecture. H. 17.5 cm. Latest Jōmon Period. Institute of Archaeology, Keio University.

Hollow, open-headed figurine of light brown clay with blackened   Cat. 42 and 43
areas, decorated with interlocked curved incisions, and full perforations for mouth and between legs, from Itakura, Inara village, Ōra county, Gumma prefecture. H. 28.6 cm. Latest Jōmon
Period. Institute of Anthropology, Tokyo University.

Composite figurine of light gray surface, blackish, gritty, hard   Cat. 44
clay, slightly hollowed out vertically on the back, and with
groove running down back of head, from Kashiwara Park,
Kashiwara city, Nara prefecture. H. 15.9 cm. Latest Jōmon
Period. Yamato History Museum.

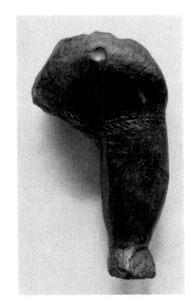

Cat. 45   Abdomen and leg of dark brown color and polished surfaces, with herringbone incisions running down lower abdomen and around legs, and hollowed out buttocks region, from Mimanda Higashi, Nanagi village, Kikuchi county, Kumamoto prefecture. Late to Latest Jōmon Period. Coll. Mr. Keigyō Sakamoto.

Cat. 46   Trunk of undecorated figurine of coarse, gritty clay, with protruding abdomen and slightly projecting posterior, from the grounds of the Nakatsu Minami High School, Nakatsu city, Ōita prefecture. H. 7.6 cm. Latest Jōmon Period. Coll. Nakatsu Minami High School.

Cat. 47   Circular, perforated plaque of light brown clay, undecorated on reverse side, from Kariyahara, Nakagawa village, Kamiina county, Nagano prefecture. D. 6.5 cm. Middle Jōmon Period. Coll. Medical School, Shinshū University.

Hollow, turtle-shaped, light brown object of well polished clay, with two holes, notched outline, and rough grooved decoration some of which runs laterally on the back and is connected by an oval spiral, from Tokoshinai, Susono, Hirosaki city, Aomori prefecture. L. 8.2 cm.; thickness 3.2 cm. Latest Jōmon Period. Institute of Anthropology, Tokyo University.

Cat. 48

Hollow ball, called a rattle, of rough brown clay with blackened areas, decorated on one side only, found with the "male" figure (Cat. 3), at Sakai, Fujii-machi, Nirasaki city, Yamanashi prefecture. D. 4.4 cm. Middle Jōmon Period. Sakai Remains Museum.

Cat. 49

So-called praying mantis-shaped hollow object with thick walls, of brown clay with large blackened areas, complete except for break on one side toward the end, decorated with deep, more or less parallel lines, from Shimonumabe shell-mound, 1 chōme, Denenchōfu, Ōta ward, Tokyo. L. 13.1 cm. Latest Jomōn Period. National Museum, Tokyo.

Cat. 50

Mask with patches of cord-marking and freely handled grooving, the latter also on the slightly concave back, with smooth, brown surface, from Kamegaoka, Tateoka, Kizukuri-machi, Tsugaru county, Aomori prefecture. Maximum D. 9.2 cm. Latest Jōmon Period. Institute of Anthropology, Tokyo University.

Cat. 51

Cat. 52 a and b   Hollow, nose-shaped object with openings for nostrils, bearing perforations along the sides for attachment purposes, of smooth but rather coarse clay, from grounds of Uchikawame Primary School, Tateishi, Uchikawame, Ōhazama-machi, Hienuki county, Iwate prefecture. H. 6 cm. Late to Latest Jōmon Period. Coll. Uchikawame Primary School.

Cat. 53   Cock's-head shaped object of light brown, coarse clay, similar on both sides, with four holes entering at neck, from Kashiwara Park, Kashiwara city, Nara prefecture. H. 6.7 cm. Latest Jōmon Period. Yamato History Museum.

Cat. 54   Wild boar of hard, light brown clay, from Numazu shell-mound, Inai village, Ojika county, Miyagi prefecture. L. 7 cm. Latest Jōmon Period. Institute of Archaeology, Tōhoku University.

Small, brown colored, pointed head, with roughly marked zones   Cat. 55
around eyes and mouth; back of head and lower part mostly
rebuilt, from Megata, Shimodate city, Ibaragi prefecture. H.
8.7 cm. Late Yayoi Period. National Museum, Tokyo.

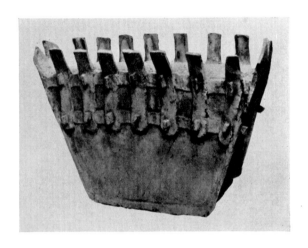

Separate *haniwa* roof with wooden reinforcing planks joined   Cat. 56
with pegs, from Daiko-machi, Seta county, Gumma prefecture.
L. ca. 60 cm. Late Tomb Period. Institute of Anthropology,
Tokyo University.

Haniwa house (sometimes called a storehouse) with two open-   Cat. 57
ings on each side on lower level, a rectangular window on visible
end, and two circular holes, one at each end under roof ridge; red
paint on barge boards and on one side wall, the entire building
much restored, from Yoshii-machi, Ukiha county, Fukuoka
prefecture. H. 53.5 cm. Middle-Late Tomb Period. Coll. Mr.
Hisao Yasumoto.

Cat. 58   Two storied *haniwa* house (sometimes called a storehouse) with two rectangular openings on each side of lower level, one opening only on second level, and simple hipped gable roof, from Inariyama Tomb, Shiraishi, Fujioka city, Gumma prefecture. H. 57.3 cm. Late Tomb Period. National Museum, Tokyo.

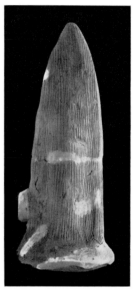

Cat. 59   *Haniwa* spearhead with tang (obscured by stand), spine running down reverse side, heavily combed surfaces, from Higashi-yajima, Nitta county, Gumma prefecture. H. 20.6 cm. Late Tomb Period. Institute of Anthropology, Tokyo University.

Cat. 60   Sheathed *haniwa* sword of so-called fire-extinguisher type, presumably with jewelled handle, sheath fastened by a ribbon, from Denenchofu, Ōta ward, Tokyo. H. 116 cm. Late Tomb Period. National Museum, Tokyo.

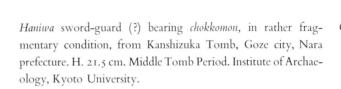

Haniwa sword-guard (?) bearing *chokkomon*, in rather frag-   Cat. 61
mentary condition, from Kanshizuka Tomb, Goze city, Nara
prefecture. H. 21.5 cm. Middle Tomb Period. Institute of Archaeology, Kyoto University.

Haniwa shield rising off original cylinder, bearing striated   Cat. 62
triangles and a shield-shaped pattern in the center, all much restored, from Miyayama Tomb, Muro, Goze city, Nara prefecture.
H. 103.9 cm. Middle Tomb Period. Yamato History Museum.

Haniwa cuirass reproducing riveted bands of iron, of very   Cat. 63
coarse, brown clay, much restored, from a Saitobaru Tomb,
Saitobaru-machi, Koyu county, Miyazaki prefecture. H. 33 cm.
Middle Tomb Period. Institute of Archaeology, Kyoto University.

Cat. 64 Simple *haniwa* boat with strongly tapered bow and stern, combed on interior, from Nigore Tomb, Yasaka-machi, Takeno county, Kyoto prefecture. L. 80 cm. Middle Tomb Period. Institute of Archaeology, Kyoto University.

Cat. 65 *Haniwa* fan with serrated edge and the appearance of riveted reinforcing strips, with incised petal-like patterns in the central field and whirl-like motifs around hole, from Fujioka city (former Akabori village), Sawa county, Gumma prefecture. H. 100 cm. Late Tomb Period. National Museum, Tokyo.

Cat. 66 *Haniwa* ceremonial sunshade with flanged wing-like ornaments bearing decoration in parallel lines, from Anderayama Tomb, Hirono-machi, Uji city, Kyoto prefecture. H. 95.5 cm. Early-Middle Tomb Period. Institute of Archaeology, Kyoto University.

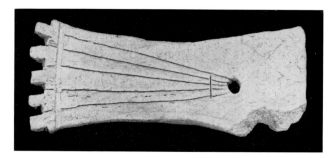

Haniwa five-stringed *koto*, complete except for break in lower corner, from Tsuwa-machi, Niihari county, Ibaragi prefecture. L. 20.5 cm. Late Tomb Period. Coll. Mr. Yōsuke Sera.   Cat. 67

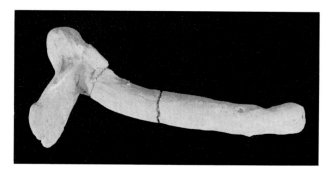

Haniwa hoe blade mounted on curved and shaped handle, from Himezuka Tomb, Shibayama-chō, Sambu county, Chiba prefecture. L. 23.3 cm. Late Tomb Period. Shibayama Haniwa Museum.   Cat. 68

Haniwa head of horse wearing heart-shaped bridle-bit, flesh surfaces finely brushed, much restored on side not shown, from unknown locality in Gumma prefecture. H. 60.5 cm. Late Tomb Period. Coll. Mr. Sango Uno.   Cat. 69

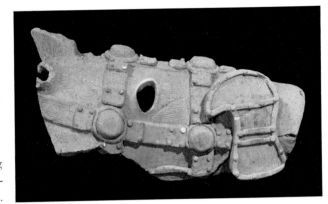

Cat. 70 *Haniwa* head of horse with open mouth, nostril holes, wearing S-shaped bridle-bit, from Gōshi, Sawa county, Gumma prefecture. L. 44 cm. Late Tomb Period. Aikawa Archaeology Museum.

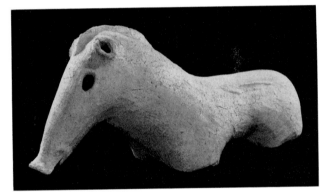

Cat. 71 *Haniwa* wild boar, legs broken off, with unusually sharp nose, ridge over head running toward back, and arrow on its flank, from Abiko-machi, Higashi-katsushika county, Chiba prefecture. L. 63 cm. Late Tomb Period. National Museum, Tokyo.

Cat. 72 *Haniwa* duck sunk into top of tapered cylinder, with hole in its back, from Tonozuka Tomb, Shibayama-chō, Sambu county, Chiba prefecture. L. of bird 23 cm. Late Tomb Period. Shibayama Haniwa Museum.

Haniwa warrior wearing oval-shaped helmet and cuirass, armed with a sheathed sword, from Kamichūjō, Kumagaya city, Saitama prefecture. H. 64.2 cm. Late Tomb Period. Coll. Committee for the Protection of Cultural Properties. — Cat. 73

Detail of pendant or knife case on fragmentary *haniwa* warrior, worn on the left side, all surfaces neatly smoothed, from Tonozuka Tomb, Shibayama-chō, Sambu county, Chiba prefecture. L. of case 14 cm. Late Tomb Period. Shibayama Haniwa Museum. — Cat. 74

Youthful looking *haniwa* warrior in full regalia, very little restoration, from Gōdo, Ōta city, Gumma prefecture. H. 125.7 cm. Late Tomb Period. Aikawa Archaeology Museum. — Cat. 75

Cat. 76　Large *haniwa* warrior with well chiselled, tubular features, wearing short sword and *tomo*, repaired nose, head band, braids of hair and hem of tunic, from Jūjō, Misato, Kodama county, Saitama prefecture. H. of figure 125 cm. Late Tomb Period. National Museum, Tokyo.

Cat. 77　*Haniwa* warrior wearing tight-fitting small tunic with broad belt and sword, with cap bearing forked ornaments, and having holes on either side of body below arms, from Furumi, Ōizumi-machi, Ōra county, Gumma prefecture. H. 122.2 cm. Late Tomb Period. Aikawa Archaeology Museum.

Cat. 78　*Haniwa* warrior with missing braids, wearing necklace doubled down nape of neck, jingle-bells around waist, red paint between parallel lines on cap, below eyes and down front of neck, from Ōsawa, Kodama county, Saitama prefecture. H. 39.5 cm. Late Tomb Period. Institute of Anthropology, Tokyo University.

Helmeted *haniwa* warrior made of two sections (the body and legs are separate, helping to explain the odd proportions), much restored tunic from the waist down; helmet painted in red on back, face painted, armor painted on front and back in alternate rectangles, from Kyōizumi, Mōka city, Tochigi prefecture. H. 131 cm. Late Tomb Period. National Museum, Tokyo.   Cat. 79

Haniwa head of warrior, missing ears, hair braids and short beard, finely smoothed hat completely undecorated, in rich red clay, from Himezuka Tomb, Shibayama-chō, Sambu county, Chiba prefecture. H. 36.9 cm. Late Tomb Period. Shibayama Haniwa Museum.   Cat. 80

Haniwa warrior shown as hawk trainer, with goshawk on left arm, wearing tight cap with head band, necklace, sword and *tomo*, from Fujina, Sakai-machi, Sawa county, Gumma prefecture. H. 74.5 cm. Late Tomb Period. The Museum Yamato Bunkakan.   Cat. 81

Cat. 82   Simply modelled seated *haniwa* figure, with ankles crossed,
wearing conical hat with slightly flared peak, a sheathed sword,
and face painted red on either side of eyes and on chin, from
Kameyama, Mōka city, Tochigi prefecture. H. 73.5 cm. Late
Tomb Period. National Museum, Tokyo.

Cat. 83   *Haniwa* warrior, most likely a shaman, seated cross-legged,
hands together in position of supplication, cap with jingle-bell
tassels, unusual sheathed sword with globular pommel, red
triangles painted on peak of cap, gauntlets, tunic, and face painting around eyes and cheeks, from Tomb 101, Takaku, Taira
city, Fukushima prefecture. H. 91 cm. Late Tomb Period. Iwaki
Senior High School Collection.

Cat. 84   Kneeling male *haniwa* figure, perhaps a reciter or shaman, with
hands on ground in front, sharply outlined face, wearing tall
"horned" cap, plain arm guards and a sheathed sword attached
to the base, from Yamato, Namekata county, Ibaragi prefecture.
H. 55.5 cm. Late Tomb Period. Collection Uncertain.

Haniwa drum beater, probably a male figure, with necklace of large and small beads, holding knobbed drum stick, half of drum absorbed into body, from Sakai-machi, Sawa county, Gumma prefecture. H. 58.5 cm. Late Tomb Period. National Museum, Tokyo.

Cat. 85

Female *haniwa* figure bearing cup on tilted head, cup open at juncture with head, part of broken coiffure visible at back of head, necklace beads mostly missing, from Kōjinzuka Tomb, Takanohe, Takahagi city, Ibaragi prefecture. H. 48.4 cm. Late Tomb Period. Institute of Anthropology, Tokyo University.

Cat. 86

Small female *haniwa* figure holding a cup in her fingers, with trim features, coarse surface, from unknown location. H. 57.6 cm. Late Tomb Period. Coll. Mr. Shō Yoshioka.

Cat. 87

Cat. 88   Male *haniwa* figure wearing a massive pair of trousers decorated with punched polka dots separated by diagonal parallel lines, from Enkōji, Kumayama-machi, Akaiwa county, Okayama prefecture. H. 82.5 cm. Late Tomb Period. Coll. Mr. Haruo Fujiyama.

Cat. 89   Head of "whistling" male *haniwa* figure wearing tight-fitting hat pulled down in the back, with small nose, sharply defined eyes, lightly brushed hat, from unknown locality in Gumma prefecture. H. 16.3 cm. Late Tomb Period. Coll. Mr. Yōsuke Sera.

Cat. 90   Small head of male *haniwa* figure wearing cap with double hollow projections, with annular ears, bead necklace, all without restorations, from unknown location. H. 21.7 cm. Late Tomb Period. Coll. Mr. Ryō Hosomi.

Head of male *haniwa* figure wearing "space man" type hat, Cat. 91
having annular ears, long nose connected to eyebrows, eyes and
mouth in crescent shape, of coarse clay and uneven surface, extremely rough on interior, from Kōjinzuka Tomb, Takanohe,
Takahagi city, Ibaragi prefecture. H. 16.9 cm. Late Tomb
Period. Institute of Anthropology, Tokyo University.

Head of "shouting" male *haniwa* figure, wearing twin peaked Cat. 92
cap which merges with head, replaced nose, slanted eyes,
strongly twisted mouth and coarsely scratched chin, from
Kōjinzuka Tomb, Takanohe, Takahagi city, Ibaragi prefecture.
H. 21 cm. Late Tomb Period. Institute of Anthropology, Tokyo
University.

Simply modelled male *haniwa* figure without extraneous detail, Cat. 93
combed body and cylinder, hole in top of head, holes for ears
and holes under arms, bearing red paint on cheeks and nose,
from Kawataya, Kita-adachi county, Saitama prefecture. H.
65.9 cm. Late Tomb Period. Institute of Anthropology, Tokyo
University.

Cat. 94   Head of *haniwa* male figure with high dome, hole in top, with sharp features, wearing annular earrings, combed on both exterior and interior, from Takigawa, Gumma county, Gumma prefecture. H. 20.4 cm. Late Tomb Period. Institute of Anthropology, Tokyo University.

Cat. 95   Crudely formed head of *haniwa* male figure with sketchily modelled hair, missing the braids, hole in top of head, of rough red clay, from Tonozuka Tomb, Shibayama-chō, Sambu county, Chiba prefecture. H. 21 cm. Late Tomb Period. Shibayama Haniwa Museum.

Cat. 96   Ithyphallic male *haniwa* figure with wide ears, earrings, turned down mouth, and arched arms attached to the chest, from Kami-takeshi, Sakai-machi, Sawa county, Gumma prefecture. H. 53.3 cm. Late Tomb Period. Tenri Reference Museum.

Nude female *haniwa* figure shown as though singing, with orig-   Cat. 97
inal surfaces combed, much restored, from Kyōizumi, Mōka
city, Tochigi prefecture. H. 45.5 cm. Late Tomb Period. National Museum, Tokyo.

Head and torso of amorphous *haniwa* figure with one arm   Cat. 98
intact, a minimum of articulation around neck, shoulders and
arms, said to resemble a swimmer, possibly a child, from Tonozuka, Shibayama-chō, Sambu county, Chiba prefecture. H.
21.5 cm. Late Tomb Period. Shibayama Haniwa Museum.

Figurine of reddish clay with hard finish, broken stump arms   Cat. 99
and legs, head curved forward and thinned toward the top, all
without surface decoration, from Hishikari-machi, Isa county,
Kagoshima prefecture. H. 7.5 cm. Tomb Period (?). Institute of
Archaeology, Kyoto University.

MAPS

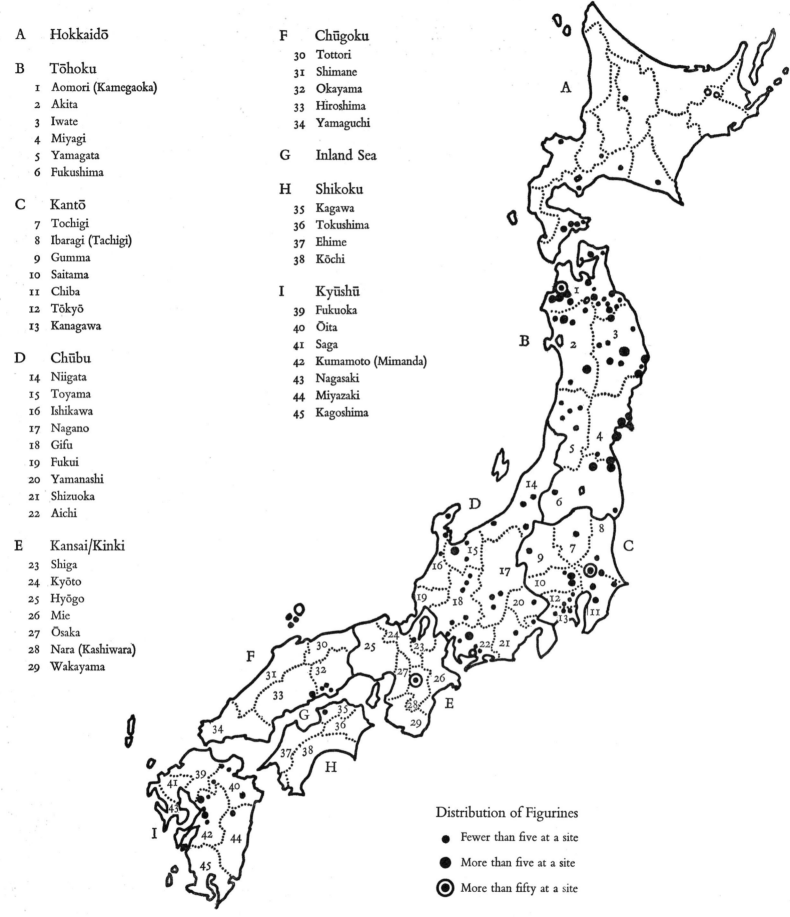

A Hokkaidō

B Tōhoku
  1 Aomori (Kamegaoka)
  2 Akita
  3 Iwate
  4 Miyagi
  5 Yamagata
  6 Fukushima

C Kantō
  7 Tochigi
  8 Ibaragi (Tachigi)
  9 Gumma
  10 Saitama
  11 Chiba
  12 Tōkyō
  13 Kanagawa

D Chūbu
  14 Niigata
  15 Toyama
  16 Ishikawa
  17 Nagano
  18 Gifu
  19 Fukui
  20 Yamanashi
  21 Shizuoka
  22 Aichi

E Kansai/Kinki
  23 Shiga
  24 Kyōto
  25 Hyōgo
  26 Mie
  27 Ōsaka
  28 Nara (Kashiwara)
  29 Wakayama

F Chūgoku
  30 Tottori
  31 Shimane
  32 Okayama
  33 Hiroshima
  34 Yamaguchi

G Inland Sea

H Shikoku
  35 Kagawa
  36 Tokushima
  37 Ehime
  38 Kōchi

I Kyūshū
  39 Fukuoka
  40 Ōita
  41 Saga
  42 Kumamoto (Mimanda)
  43 Nagasaki
  44 Miyazaki
  45 Kagoshima

Distribution of Figurines

• Fewer than five at a site

● More than five at a site

◉ More than fifty at a site

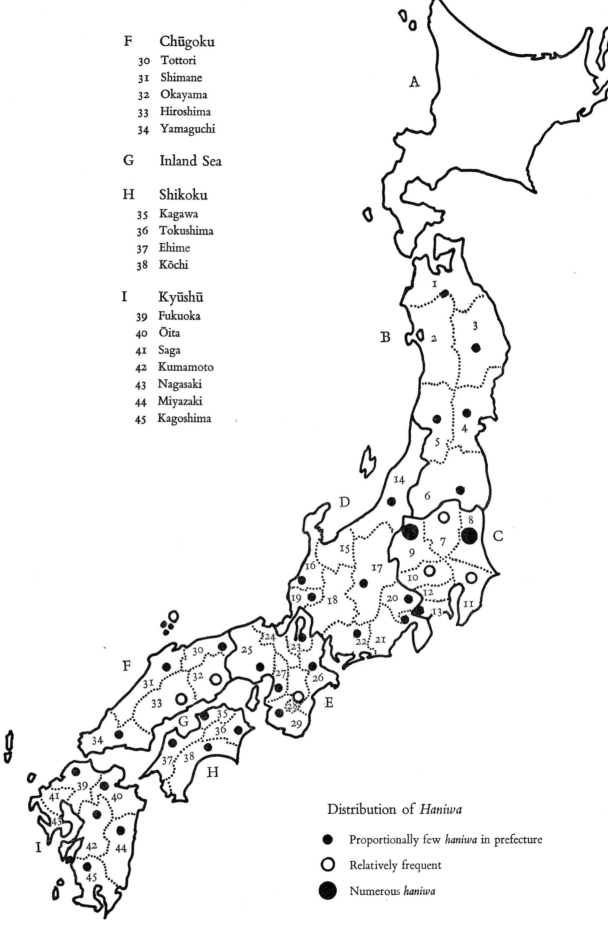

A Hokkaidō

B Tōhoku
  1 Aomori
  2 Akita
  3 Iwate
  4 Miyagi
  5 Yamagata
  6 Fukushima

C Kantō
  7 Tochigi
  8 Ibaragi
  9 Gumma
  10 Saitama
  11 Chiba
  12 Tōkyō
  13 Kanagawa

D Chūbu
  14 Niigata
  15 Toyama
  16 Ishikawa
  17 Nagano
  18 Gifu
  19 Fukui
  20 Yamanashi
  21 Shizuoka
  22 Aichi

E Kansai/Kinki
  23 Shiga
  24 Kyōto
  25 Hyōgo
  26 Mie
  27 Ōsaka
  28 Nara
  29 Wakayama

F Chūgoku
  30 Tottori
  31 Shimane
  32 Okayama
  33 Hiroshima
  34 Yamaguchi

G Inland Sea

H Shikoku
  35 Kagawa
  36 Tokushima
  37 Ehime
  38 Kōchi

I Kyūshū
  39 Fukuoka
  40 Ōita
  41 Saga
  42 Kumamoto
  43 Nagasaki
  44 Miyazaki
  45 Kagoshima

Distribution of *Haniwa*

● Proportionally few *haniwa* in prefecture

○ Relatively frequent

⬤ Numerous *haniwa*

SOURCES OF ILLUSTRATIONS

Photographs not taken by Mr. Kenishi Ozawa are from the following sources: Cat. 1, 39, 41: Noguchi, *Clay Figurines of Japan*, fig. 6, pl. 89, 90; Cat. 2, 13: Mizuno, *Illustrated World Culture History Series*, 175, 176; Cat. 17: Nakaya, "Civilisation Néolithique," XLIV a; Cat. 22, 52: Esaka, *Clay Figurines*, pl. 16, 30 (upper); Cat. 24, 32, 98: Takiguchi, *World Fine Arts Collection*, 38, 35, 89; Cat. 30: Yawata, *Jōmon Pottery and Clay Figurines*, 44; Cat. 38, 51, 83: Koyama, *Catalogue of World's Ceramics*, 113, 109, 124; Cat. 46: North Kyūshū Teachers' Association, *Plates of North Kyūshū's Ancient Culture*, pl. 8, no. 6; Cat. 57, 88, 96: Miller, *Haniwa*, fig. 2, pl. 13, 53; Cat. 58, 65, 84, 85: Kobayashi, *Haniwa*, 56, 59, 25, 21; Cat. 60: Kodama, *An Illustrated Cultural History of Japan*, fig. 424; Fig. 1, 7, 59, 98, Cat. 45: author.

The maps are redrawn from Esaka, *Clay Figurines*, p. 342, and Miller, *Haniwa*, p. 161.

INDEX

Susano-o, 137, 140, 143
Suwa, Lake, 1
swan, 137
swords, 86, 97, 116, 120, 122, 140, 152;
    haniwa, 116, 122, 125, 129, 130, 148,
    187, 188, 192, 193, 194, 195

tablets, 27
Tachigi site, 34, 42, 177
Taika Reform, 143
Taima, 98
T'ai-Tsung, emperor, 104
Taiwan, 5
Takarazuka Tomb, 162
Takasuki, 159
talisman, 55; *see* amulets
tamagaki (magical fence), 108, 160, 162
Tamba province, 159
Taoism, 130
Tateishi site, 52, 181, 185
tatemono, haniwa, 98
tattooing, 34, 42, 74, 156, 162
Temmu, emperor, 125
temples, *see* Buddhism
Terama, 98
textiles, cloth, 98, 129, 133, 137
throne, *haniwa*, 115, 119, 125, 155
tile, roof, 120; tomb tiles, 130, 137
tin, 78
Tochigi prefecture, 93, 112, 125, 134, 137,
    194, 195
Tochikura site, 16
Tochio city, 16
Tōdaijiyama Tomb, 120
Togariishi site, 19, 24, 27, 171
Tōhoku, 1, 7, 8, 11, 12, 16, 23, 33, 38, 41,
    42, 46, 48, 52, 56, 59, 60, 63, 64, 78, 81,
    161, 180, 181, 182, 184, 186; Univer-
    sity, 185
Tōkai, 2, 6, 42, 51

Tokyo, 1, 2, 7, 23, 42, 63, 93, 170, 172,
    173, 174, 179, 187, 189, 191, 193, 195,
    196, 198, 199, 200; University, 48, 63,
    170, 173, 174, 179, 180, 181, 182, 184,
    186, 187, 193, 196, 198, 199
tomo (wrist piece), 130, 148, 152, 193, 194
Tongguk Tonggam, 101
Tonozuka Tomb, 116, 119, 125, 191, 192,
    199, 200
tools, metal, 133; stone, 5, 6, 7, 8, 10, 24,
    161
Torii, R., 63, 66, 161
torii (sacred gate), 120
Tōsan, 2, 27, 33, 41
totemism, 28
Toyohashi city, 42
Toyonaka city, 126
Toyouke, goddess, 137, 161
triangles, painted, 125, 126, 129, 151, 155,
    188, 195
"triangular torso" figurines, 45, 51
Tsuboi, S., 48
Tsugaru Strait, 5
Tsukizaka, 97
Tsukiyomi, god, 137
Tsukushi Plain, 89, 140
T'ung-Kou, 138
turbans, 51, 181
turkey-cock, 133, 134
turtle, 60

Ubayama site, 7; type, 171
Uchiura Bay, 41
Ueda, H., 111
uji (social group), 89; *uji-gami*, 90
Ukemochi (Ukimochi), 137, 161
Unebiyama, 55
Ushikawa, 6
Uwanabe Tomb, 108
Uzuisuzuka Tomb, 115

vegetables, 5; *see* agriculture
volcanic activity, 5, 6

walnuts, 5, 161
Wani, 159
weapons, 84, 97, 147; *haniwa*, 119, 122;
    see spears, swords
Wei Chih, 101
wells, 56, 122, 143
wheat, 137
whistle, 60
"window of the soul", 48
Wo (Japan), 101
wood carving, 46, 52; woodwork, 98
wrestling, 97, 98, 144

Yalu River, 138
yam, 161
Yamagata prefecture, 16, 38, 46, 51, 181
Yamanashi prefecture, 23, 24, 28, 37, 60,
    93, 169, 172, 176, 184
Yamatai, 101
Yamato, clan, 90; Plain, 1, 4, 78, 81, 159,
    162; state, 2, 84, 86, 89, 90, 93, 98, 143,
    159, 160; Yamato-bue, 133; Yamato-
    dake, 125, 134, 158; Yamato-goto, 133;
    Yamato-hiko, 97, 98
Yang-shao, 30
Yatagarasu, *see* crow
Yatsushiro Bay, 1
Yawata, I., 66, 161
Yayoi culture, period, 4, 45, 52, 74, 78,
    81, 84, 90, 120, 122, 130, 137, 138, 140,
    143, 144, 156, 158; pottery, 2, 81, 93,
    98, 156, 160; site, 1
Yokohama, 37
Yoshigo site, 8
Yosukeone site, 12, 19
Yoshii-machi, 138
Yūryaku, emperor, 89, 102, 140, 143

This book was printed and bound in the workshops of Benziger & Co., A.G., Einsiedeln. – The illustrations in four color offset were executed by Imprimeries Réunies, S.A., Lausanne. – The heliogravure reproductions were executed by Braun & Cie S.A., Mulhouse-Dornach. – The halftone blocks were made by Process Engraver Schwitter, Ltd., Basel. – Lay-out by Irmgard Loeb, Basel.
Printed in Switzerland

FREEPORT MEMORIAL LIBRARY